Essays on Social and Political Theory Equality Universality

Essays on Social and Political Theory: Equality Universality

S.K. Desai

CYBER TECH PUBLICATIONS
4264/3, Ansari Road, Daryaganj, New Delhi-110002 (India)
Ph.: 011-23244078, 011-43559448 Fax: 011-23280028
E-Mail: cyberpublicationsdelhi@yahoo.com
Website: www.cybertechpublications.com

ESSAYS ON SOCIAL AND POLITICAL THEORY: EQUALITY AND UNIVERSALITY

S.K. Desai

First Edition 2010

Published by :

G.S. Rawat for **Cyber Tech Publications**
4264/3, Ansari Road, Daryaganj, New Delhi-110002 (India)
Ph.: 011-23244078, 011-43559448 Fax: 011-23280028
E-Mail: cyberpublicationsdelhi@yahoo.com
Website: www.cybertechpublications.com

Printed at: Asian Offset Printers, Delhi-53

Preface

This book brings together and substantially revises Politics and Community. In this book we critically examined both sides of the liberal versus communitarian disputes, finding that, when they are viewed from the perspective of feminism - a political project which seeks to establish a world characterised by sexual equality - both camps are revealed to be unable to provide models of person, society, social institutions and political processes which are adequate to that task.

Laws and Government are to the Political Bodies of Civil Societies, what the Vital Spirits of Life itself are to the Natural Bodies of Animated Creatures; and as those that study the Anatomy of Dead Carkasses may see, that the chief Organs and nicest Springs more immediately required to continue the Motion of our Machine, are not hard Bones, strong Muscles and Nerves, nor the smooth white Skin that so beautifully covers the, but small trifling Films and little Pipes that are either overlook'd, or else seem inconsiderable to Vulgar Eyes; so they that examine into the Nature of Man, abstract from Art and Education, may observe, that what renders him a Sociable Animal, consists not in his desire of Company, good Nature, Pity, Affability, and other Graces of a fair Outside; but that his vilest and most hateful Qualities are the most necessary Accomplishments to fit him for the largest, and according to the World, the happiest and most flourishing Societies.

The papers reworked here continue to elaborate, refine and in some cases amend, our analysis and criticisms of the communitarian side of that divide. In this book I offer a much more detailed study of communitarianism, paying particular attention to what I call 'political communitarianism'. Political communitarianism is the political platform from which would-be political entrepreneurs, political commentators, and some established politicians, attempt to propel communitarian analyses, programmes and projects into practical politics. In particular, I have had the opportunity to study in some detail the relationship between political communitarianism and recent debates about local government, about family policy, and about democracy in general. I have also taken the opportunity to elaborate the methodological arguments and themes - about the role and nature of conceptual analysis, and about interpretivism and social constructionism in political theory.

—Author

CONTENTS

1

INTRODUCTION

Postanarchism is emerging as an important new current in anarchist thought, and it is the source of growing interest and debate amongst anarchist activists and scholars alike, as well as in broader academic circles. Given the number of internet sites, discussion groups, and new books and journal publications appearing on postanarchism, it is time that the challenges it poses to classical anarchist thought and practice are taken more seriously.

Postanarchism refers to a wide body of theory-encompassing political theory, philosophy, aesthetics, literature and film studies-which attempts to explore new directions in anarchist thought and politics. While it includes a number of different perspectives and trajectories, the central contention of postanarchism is that classical anarchist philosophy must take account of new theoretical directions and cultural phenomena, in particular, postmodernity and poststructuralism. While these theoretical categories have had a major impact on different areas of scholarship and thought, as well as politics, anarchism tends to have remained largely resistant to these developments and continues to work within an Enlightenment humanist epistemological framework1 which many see as being in need of updating. At the same time, anarchism-as a form of political theory and practice-is becoming increasingly important to radical struggles and global social movements today, to a large extent supplanting Marxism. Postanarchism seeks to revitalise anarchist theory in light of these new struggles and forms of resistance.

However, rather than dismissing the tradition of classical anarchism, postanarchism on the contrary, seeks to explore its potential and radicalise its possibilities. It remains entirely consistent, I would suggest, with the libertarian and egalitarian horizon of anarchism; yet it seeks to broaden the terms of anti-authoritarian thought to include a critical analysis of language, discourse, culture and new modalities of power. In this sense, postanarchism does not understand post to mean being 'after' anarchism, but post in the sense of working at and extending the limits of anarchist thought by uncovering its heterogeneous and unpredictable possibilities.

This issue explores some of these new approaches to anarchist theory and practice. Benjamin Noys' essay is important in this respect because it seeks to highlight a series of problems and conceptual and practical limitations that these new anarchist approaches often encounter. His essay explores the proximity-as well as critical distance-of contemporary thinker Alain Badiou to anarchism. While Badiou's political thought seems to reflect certain anarchist ideas about a radical politics that is autonomous from the Party and the State, he is also extremely critical of anarchism, and especially of what he sees as the libertarian element of the global anti-capitalist movement. For Badiou, these anti-globalisation 'movementists'-drawing on motifs of flux, flows of desire and deterritorialisation derived from poststructuralists such as Deleuze and Guattari, as well as Hardt and Negri-fetishise and, in a sense, mimic the movement of global capitalism itself, and are unable to gain any critical distance from it. Noys uses this critique to work through questions of strategy, organisation and coherence which are central to the anti-authoritarian radical politics today-for instance, is a contemporary anarchist politics practical and can it achieve anything without some form of organisation; and can the notion of organisation be rethought in ways that avoid the Party form and which do not conflict with anarchism's commitment to decentralised and non-hierarchical forms of activism?

Contrary to what certain anarchist activists and scholars have claimed, postanarchism is not confined to the world of theoretical abstractions; it is concerned with concrete forms of activist politics. In an essay by one of the major theoreticians of poststructuralist anarchism,2 Todd May provides a postanarchist interpretation of a political movement in Canada that fights for the rights of Algerian 'illegal' immigrants, the *sans-statuts* (those without legalised refugee status). The question of 'illegal' immigrants and the rights of those who, as Arendt would say, have not even the right to have rights, is emerging as one of the major points of antagonism in global capitalism-a site for the new biopolitical barbarism of state sovereignty, as well as a site for the emergence of new forms of activism and radical politics.3 May uses the thought of philosopher Jacques Rancière4-which he sees as making a major contribution to anarchism and to radical political theory generally-to explore a political logic based on the presupposition of equality. For Rancière, politics starts with the *fact* of equality, rather than seeing it as a goal to be attained-and it is the assertion of this fact as part of a particular political campaign which has the potential to disrupt the existing political and social order based on relationships of hierarchy, inequality and authority (what Rancière calls the order of *police*). In the same way, as May shows, the Algerian *sans-statuts* in Canada-those absolutely excluded from the dominant order and at the bottom of the social hierarchy-were able to mobilise themselves *as if* they were absolutely equal to the rest of society and as if they had the same rights as everyone else. In my view, this is a genuine example of a 'postanarchist' politics: a concrete, localised, grass-roots struggle engaged in by those directly concerned, but which, importantly, is able at the same time to transcend its position of particularity by inscribing itself on the universal horizon of equality.

The question of universality is important to postanarchism, and it is this question that is considered by Benjamin Franks in relation to the ethics. Franks explores the ethical dimension of anarchist and postanarchist theory, and tries to develop an understanding of ethics which avoids, on the one hand, the universalising Kantian categorical imperative, and on the other, a ethical subjectivism that Franks attributes to Max Stirner and (somewhat unfairly I think) to myself.5 For Franks, both these positions are incompatible with anarchist political practice. As an alternative, he proposes a notion of ethics internal to particular practices and identities, negotiable over time and open to critical dialogue. Franks is correct to show that anarchism is deeply concerned with ethical questions, and his essay makes an important contribution to thinking out a distinctly anarchist form of ethics which, while grounded in particular practices and concrete situations, still offers certain norms and standards that foster non-hierarchical relationships and solidarity with others. I entirely agree with this approach to ethics, and would simply add that it is entirely compatible with postanarchism. Despite what many critics allege-and this is an allegation which is more or less made in Franks' essay-postanarchism does not amount to moral nihilism or ethical subjectivism. Not even Stirner's philosophy of egoism-as I have tried to show elsewhere-precludes ethics, and indeed allows for certain forms of social solidarity, which is implicit in his notion of the 'union of egoists'. Whatever the case, Franks makes an important intervention in exploring the politico-ethical contours of contemporary anti-authoritarian thought.

Along with ethics, one of the other major concerns of postanarchism is the role of images, symbols and language in the construction of political identities and meanings. Unlike the classical anarchists who saw a rational coherence in social relations and a human essence at the base of social identities, a postanarchist analysis privileges the function of language and the symbolic order in creating social and political meaning. However, rather than meanings and identities being fixed within a stable structure, they are inherently unstable and open to different and contingent articulations. It is precisely this point which is emphasised by Lewis Call, who has developed a distinctly postmodern approach to anti-authoritarian practices and discourses through an analysis of popular culture, in particular literature and film.6 In his essay, he explores the graphic novel (1981), and later the film version (2006), V for Vendetta, seeing this as a kind of postanarchist political narrative. Central here is the notion of the 'floating signifier'-derived from Lacanian psychoanalysis-in which a particular word or symbol is not fixed to a particular content, but is mobile and can produce different meanings. The examples Call gives are those of the historical figure Guy Fawkes, and also the character 'V' who directly invokes Fawkes as a symbol of resistance against State authority. 'V' in particular, because he remains masked and thus anonymous, operates as a kind of empty presence through which political authority is destabilised and through which a collective resistance is mobilised. The important lesson to be drawn from Call's analysis is that political domination relies on a certain control and manipulation of symbols, images and discourses-and therefore, any effective resistance must aim at a destabilisation and a resignification of these forms. Struggles against authority take place at the level of symbolic and even visual-indeed there is no separation here between symbolic and 'actual' politics. One only need look at the innovative and politically creative use of symbols and images at anti-global capitalist demonstrations to see examples of this.

One thinker who acknowledges the importance of the visual and aesthetic in radical politics is Jacques Rancière, to whom I have referred above. In some of his recent work, Rancière has reflected on the link between art and politics and has emphasised the political significance of the aesthetic, particularly in the idea that politics disturbs existing 'regimes' of visibility.7 Politics is, in other words, about conflicts over what is visible and what is invisible, and art can therefore contribute to a reconfiguration of space and perception through which new political meanings may emerge. In an interview conducted with Noys, May and myself, Rancière reflects on the position of the artist, as well as the 'anarchist' implications of his own political thinking, and on more general questions about the state of radical politics today. As the reader might have guessed by now, I see Rancière as a thinker whose work has major implications for anarchism: while he departs from classical anarchism in important ways-particularly in his rejection of the conceptual opposition between the 'artificial' State and the 'natural' Society-he also offers new ways of thinking about emancipation, equality, democracy and anti-authoritarian politics. As this issue shows, postanarchism is not a unified doctrine or political practice, and it raises as many questions and problems as it answers. It is best to see it as on ongoing field of enquiry which seeks to explore, unearth, interrogate, rethink and revitalise many aspects of anarchist theory. One thing is for certain though: the contemporary situation demands that anarchism be thought and practiced once again.

Is there a normative deficit in the theory of hegemony?

This discussion might be viewed as the history of a disagreement. In May and June 1990, at the end of my first year's teaching at Essex, Ernesto Laclau and I taught a course together on 'Deconstruction and Politics'. I was trying to formulate the argument that eventually found expression in the concluding chapter of my first book, The Ethics of Deconstruction. My interest in Ernesto's work was less dominated by the way in which the category of hegemony enables a deconstruction of Marxism, of the type executed with such power in Hegemony and Socialist Strategy, and much more preoccupied with how hegemony can be deployed in providing both a logic of the political and a theory of political action that could be related to my understanding of deconstruction. Our disagreement turned on the nature of that understanding. My claim was – and still is – that deconstruction has an overriding ethical motivation provided that ethics is understood in the sense given to it in the work of Emmanuel Levinas. At the time, Ernesto was somewhat perplexed by my talk of ethics, arguably with good reason, and he would only talk of ethics in the Gramscian locution of the 'ethico-political'.

That was ten years ago and since that time I have enjoyed innumerable conversations with Ernesto which have arisen out of a longstanding intellectual collaboration. At the end of this brief history, it might perhaps be concluded that we finally agree, or at least our positions are much closer than they were a decade or so ago. Perhaps, as Wittgenstein speculated, the solution to the problem is the disappearance of the problem. But perhaps not. We shall see.

POLITICS, HEGEMONY AND DEMOCRACY

What is politics? Politics is the realm of the decision, of action in the social world, of what Laclau, following Gramsci, calls 'hegemonization', understood as actions that attempt to fix the meaning of social relations. If we conceive of politics with the category of hegemony – and, in my view, it is best conceived of with that category – then politics is an act of power, force and will that is contingent through and through. Hegemony reveals politics to be the realm of contingent decisions by virtue of which subjects (whether persons, parties or social movements) attempt to articulate and propagate meanings of the social. At its deepest level, the category of hegemony discloses the political logic of the social; that is, civil society is politically constituted through contingent decisions. In my view, the key concept in Laclau's recent work is 'hegemonic universality': political action is action motivated by, or orientated around, a universal term – equality, human rights, justice, individual freedom or whatever – and yet that universality is always already contaminated by particularity, by the specific social context for which the universal term is destined. I shall come back to this below.

With this definition of politics in mind, the first thing to note is that many political decisions, say decisions at the level of the state administration or those wanting to take over the state, attempt to deny their political character. That is, political decisions attempt to erase their traces of power, force, will and contingency by naturalizing or essentializing their contents; for example, 'Kosovo is, was and always will be Serbian', or 'Macedonia is, was, and always will be Greek', or whatever. Much – perhaps most – politics tries to render itself and its operations of power invisible by reference to custom and tradition or, worse, nature and God, or, worse still, custom and tradition grounded in nature and God. Arguably the main strategy of politics is to make itself invisible in order to claim for itself the status of nature or apriori self-evidence. In this way, politics can claim to restore the fullness of society or bring society into harmony with itself – a claim somewhat pathetically exemplified in John Major's wish, after the prolonged torture of the Thatcher years, to govern a country as peace with itself, an England of warm beer, cool drizzle and cricket.

Now, to understand political action as a hegemonic operation is apriori to understand it as a non-naturalizable, non-essentialistic contingent articulation that just temporarily fixes the meaning of social relations. For Laclau, the fullness of society or the harmonization of society with itself is an impossible object of political desire which successive contingent decisions seek to bring about or, to use Lacan's term that Laclau inherits, to suture. So, if a naturalizing or essentializing politics tries to render its contingency invisible by attempting to suture the social into a fantastic wholeness, then hegemony as the disclosure of the political logic of the social reveals the impossibility of any such operation. The moment of final suture never arrives, and the social field is irreducibly open and plural. Society is impossible.

This leads to the significant conclusion that, although the category of hegemony seems at one level to be a simple description of social and political life, a sort of value-neutral Foucauldian power-analytics, it is (and in my view has to be) a normative critique of much that passes for politics insofar as much politics tries to deny or render invisible its contingency and operations of power and force. To anticipate the topic of this paper, the category of hegemony is both descriptive and normative, a characteristic it shares with much social and political theory. As Laclau would acknowledge, Marx's postulate of a society in which the free development of each is the condition for the free development of all is both a descriptive and a normative claim.

To push this a little further, we might say that only those societies that are self-conscious of their political status – their contingency and power operations – are democratic. What I mean is self-conscious at the level of the citizenry, not at the level of the Platonic Guardians, the Prince, or the latter's philosophical adviser. Machiavelli and Hobbes, it seems to me, were perfectly well aware of the contingency and political constitution of the social, but didn't exactly want this news broadcast to the people. Therefore, if all societies are tacitly hegemonic, then the distinguishing feature of democratic society is that it is explicitly hegemonic. Democracy is thus the name for that political form of society that makes explicit the contingency of its foundations. In democracy, political power is secured through operations of competition, persuasion and election based on the hegemonization of the 'empty place' that is the people, to use Claude Lefort's expression. Democracy is distinguished by the self-consciousness of the contingency of its operations of power; in extreme cases, by the self-consciousness of the very mechanisms of power. Personally, and parenthetically, I think this is the positive lesson the U.S. presidential elections in November and December 2000 (this is not to neglect their negative political outcome), where the very meaning of democracy turned on the self-consciousness of the mechanisms of election, from the butterfly ballot in Palm Beach County, to the quasi-theological discussion of the nature of the Floridan 'Chad'. This self-consciousness of the contingent mechanisms of power infected, it seems to me, every layer of the political-legal apparatus, right up to the Supreme Court, and arguably had the beneficial effect of leading voters to raise the Rousseauesque question of the legitimacy of their social contract.

Is the theory of hegemony descriptive, normative, or both at once?

In my view, what Laclau's theory of hegemony can teach us is the ineluctably political logic of the social; the fact that politics is constituted by contingent decisions that can never efface their traces of power in the articulation of the meaning of social relations and the attempt to fix that meaning. But the descriptive gain of Laclau's work also has a normative dimension, a dimension which, until very recently, it has done its best to deny. It is this area upon which I would like to focus in the remainder of this paper, for if I am certainly not writing with the intention of burying Caesar, I do not simply wish to praise him.

Let me go back to the history of our disagreement. In a debate with Rorty, Derrida and Laclau from 1993, I first began to formulate a two-fold critical claim that I sought to sharpen in the following years: on the one hand, in relation to Derrida's introduction of concepts of justice and the messianic apriori, I argued that deconstruction requires the supplement of the theory of hegemony if the ethical moment in Derrida's work is to be more than an empty expression of good conscience. In order for the ethical moment in deconstruction to become effective as both political theory and an account of political action, it is necessary to link it to Laclau's thinking, particularly on the question of the decision. However, on the other hand, I advanced the counter-balancing claim that Laclau's theory of hegemony requires an ethical dimension of infinite responsibility to the other if it is not going to risk collapsing into the arbitrariness of a thoroughgoing decisionism. That is, the emphasis upon the irreducibly political constitution of the social could lead to the accusation of volontarism, where the meanings accorded to social relations depend upon the value-free or value-neutral whims of the subject. Let me now focus on this second claim.

My objection to Laclau can be most succinctly stated in the form of a question: what is the difference between hegemony and democratic hegemony? At the level of what we might call a 'genealogical deconstruction', which is how I would describe the analyses of Hegemony and Socialist Strategy, the theory of hegemony shows the irreducibly political constitution of the social. In the terminology of the late Husserl, that Laclau adopts in the important opening essay – effectively a manifesto – to New Reflections on the Revolution of Our Time, social sedimentation is simply the masking of the operations of power, contingency and antagonism. Social and political life, insofar as it overlooks these operations, is a 'forgetfulness of origins' and the category of hegemony permits the reactivation of sedimented social strata. What the genealogical deconstruction shows is that the fixing of the meaning of social relations is the consequence of a forgotten decision, and every decision is political.

However, Laclau's work – particularly the parts co-authored with Chantal Mouffe – famously and rightly also invokes notions of 'the democratic revolution' and 'radical democracy' as the positive consequence of the genealogical deconstruction of Marxism. That is, the recognition of contingency, antagonism and power does not lead to political pessimism à la Adorno, or the collapse of the public-private distinction à la Rorty, but is rather 'the source for a new militancy and a new optimism'. As such, we do not stand at the end of history, but rather at its beginning.

Yet, if all decisions are political, then in virtue of what is there a difference between democratising and non-democratizing decisions? It seems to me that there are two ways of answering this question, one normative and the other factual, but both of which leave Laclau sitting uncomfortably on the horns of a dilemma. On the one hand, one might say that democratic decisions are more inclusive, participatory, egalitarian, pluralistic or whatever.

But if one grants any such version of this thesis, then one has admitted some straightforwardly normative claim into the theory of hegemony. On the other hand, if one simply states in a quasi-functionalistic manner that 'the democratic revolution' and 'radical democracy' are descriptions of a fact, then in my view one risks collapsing any critical difference between the theory of hegemony and social reality which this theory purports to describe. I think that Laclau risks coming close to this position when he claims that the democratic revolution is simply taking place, or – more problematically – that freedom is the consequence of existing social dislocations.

Laclau writes, 'freedom exists because society does not achieve constitution as a structured objective order'. It is the seemingly causal nature of this 'because' that both interests and worries me. If the theory of hegemony is simply the description of a positively existing state of affairs, then one risks emptying it of any critical function, that is, of leaving open any space between things as they are and things as they might otherwise be. If the theory of hegemony is the description of a factual state of affairs, then it risks identification and complicity with the dislocatory logic of contemporary capitalist societies.

The problem with Laclau's discourse is that he makes noises of both sorts, both descriptive and normative, without sufficiently clarifying what it is that he is doing. This is what I mean by suggesting that there is the risk of a kind of normative deficit in the theory of hegemony.

In my view, the deficit can be made good on the basis of another understanding of the logic of deconstruction. Let me return to the two-fold claim outlined above: if what deconstruction lacks in its thinking of the political is a theory of hegemony, which a reading of Laclau provides, then this needs to be balanced by the second claim that what the theory of hegemony lacks and can indeed learn from deconstruction is the kind of messianic ethical injunction to infinite responsibility described in Derrida's work from the 1990's.

THE ETHICAL AND THE NORMATIVE

In a review of Derrida's Spectres of Marx from 1995, Laclau seemed unconvinced of the ethical sense that I attached to the notion of the messianic apriori, arguing that no ethical injunction of a Levinasian kind follows from the logic undecidability, and furthermore that democratic politics does not need to be anchored in such an ethical injunction.

Needless to say, I do not agree. What is more surprising is that Laclau also does not appear to agree with himself. It would seem to me, on the basis of my reading of Laclau's contributions to a fascinating series of exchanges with Slavoj Zizek and Judith Butler, that his position has changed, and changed significantly.

Firstly, Laclau grants that theory of hegemony cannot be a strictly factual or descriptive affair, both because such a purportedly value-neutral description of the facts is impossible (i.e. all 'facts' are discursive and hence interpretative constructs), and because any apprehension of the facts is governed by normative elements.

Strictly factual description – like sense-data empiricism – is an illusion based on some version of Sellars's 'myth of the given'. So, going back to the horns of the dilemma discussed above, the theory of hegemony is not descriptive but normative.

Well, not quite, because Laclau then wants to introduce a distinction that is novel to his work between the normative and the ethical. He writes,

'I would say that "hegemony" is a theoretical approach which depends on the essentially ethical decision to accept, as the horizon of any possible intelligibility the incommensurability between the ethical and the normative (the latter including the descriptive).'

Let's try and get clear about what is being claimed here. The ethical is the moment of universality or reactivation, when the sedimented and particular normative order of a given society is both invested and placed in question. The emphasis upon both investment and placing in question is important because if the ethical is the moment when the 'the universal speaks by itself', then the specific normative order of a society is always particular. Laclau's claims about the incommensurability of the ethical and the normative entails that there will always be an écart between investment and calling into question. Ethical universality has to be incarnated in a normative order, yet that moment of particular incarnation is incommensurable with universality. In language closer to the work of Alain Badiou, we might say that any normative order of 'ethics' is the sedimented form of an initial ethical event. Hegemony is the expression of a fidelity to an event, an event moreover that is – and has to be – betrayed in any normative incarnation. We can see that the relation between the ethical and the normative is a – perhaps the – privileged expression of the 'hegemonic universality I spoke of in the introduction to this paper. Laclau writes,

'Hegemony is, in this sense, the name for this unstable relation between the ethical and the normative, our way of addressing this infinite process of investments which draws its dignity from its very failure.'

As Levinas is fond of expressing the difficulty of rendering the Saying in the Said, traduire c'est trahir.

A further key aspect of the distinction between the ethical and the normative is that it is echoed in the distinction between form and content. The ethical is the moment of pure formality that has to be filled, in a particular context, with a normative content. The obvious precursor for such an ethical formalism is Kant, where the categorical imperative can be understood as an entirely formal procedure for testing the validity of specific moral norms by seeing whether they can stand the test of universalization-which raises the question as to how Laclau would respond to the charge of ethical formalism, i.e. Hegel's critique of Kantian ethics in the Phenomenology of Spirit and elsewhere. But, I take it, the Lacanian and Heideggerian inflections of this Kantian thought have also been influential on Laclau's understanding of the ethical. In a Lacanian ethics of the Real, the latter is the moment of pure formality, a constitutive lack that is filled with normative content when it has become symbolized in relation to a specific content. Finally, the distinction between the ethical and the normative is thought of in terms of the ontological difference in Heidegger, where the ethical would be ontological and the normative would be ontic.

So, it seems that we are obliged to conclude at this stage in our argument that there is, indeed, no normative deficit in the theory of hegemony. More accurately, at the basis of the latter is an irreducible ethical commitment whose scope is universal. In my view, this is good news, and it is the acknowledgement of some such conception of ethics that I have been trying to urge on Laclau since the beginning of our disagreement.

But that does not entail that I fully agree with the position Laclau has reached and, in conclusion, I would like to launch a final series of questions and queries, all of which touch on the attempted distinction of the ethical from the normative.

1. My initial worry with Laclau's new position is that he deconstructs one distinction – the descriptive/normative – only to insist on another distinction – the ethical/normative. Thus, for him, the question becomes that of the relationship between the ethical and 'descriptive/normative complexes'.

But by virtue of what is this second distinction somehow immune from the kind of deconstruction to which the first distinction was submitted? Logically and methodologically, how can one collapse one distinction only to put in its place another distinction without expecting it also to collapse? I do not see what argument Laclau provides that would protect the second distinction from collapsing like the first one. With this is mind, I would now like to try and deconstruct the ethical/normative distinction a little.

2. Let's look more closely at this distinction between the ethical and the normative and momentarily grant Laclau his premise. Let's imagine that what we have here us an analytic distinction: de jure, one can clearly make the distinction that Laclau is after, between ethical form and normative content, universal and particular. But de facto it would seem to me that the ethical and the normative always come together; that is, in actual moral life the formal moment of universality is always welded to its concrete particularity. Such, it would seem to me, is the ineluctable logic of the concept of hegemony. Thus, to my mind, it would make more sense to speak of de facto moral action in terms of 'ethical/normative complexes', even if one grants de jure that an analytic distinction can be made between the ethical and the normative. But if that is granted, then turning around the question, can one still speak of an equally justified de jure distinction between the normative and the descriptive even if one grants de facto that the two orders are inextricably intertwined? I don't see why not. So, in opposition, to Laclau's distinction between the ethical and 'descriptive/ normative complexes', I think it makes much more sense to speak of a de facto 'ethical/normative/descriptive complex', within which one is entitled to make a series of de jure distinctions.
3. I think my critical question can be made more concrete by probing the language that Laclau uses to make the ethical/

normative distinction and the way in which it runs parallel to the Heidegger's distinction of the ontological from the ontic. Once again, for Heidegger, the distinction between the ontological and the ontic is a de jure distinction that isolates distinct strata in phenomenological analysis. For Heidegger, the ontological is the a priori or transcendentally constitutive features – what Heidegger calls 'existentials' – that can be discerned from socially instituted, ontic or a posteriori life. But de facto, we have to speak – and Heidegger does speak – of Dasein as a unity of the ontological and the ontic. Dasein has precisely an ontico-ontological privilege. I therefore worry about the seeming ease with which Laclau distinguishes the ethico-ontological level from the normative ontic level, as if one could somehow expunge or slough off the ontic from the ontological in ethical. One cannot and, in my view, one should not.

4. There is a separate, but related, problem I have with Laclau's Heideggerian identification of the ethical with the ontological. The assumption behind this identification would seem to be that we can thematize and grasp conceptually the being of the ethical, i.e. that the nature of ethics can be ontologically identified and comprehended. It seems to me that Levinas would have one or two important things to say about this identification ethics and ontology, which for him is the defining gesture by virtue of which philosophers from Aristotle up to Hegel and Heidegger have understood and – on Levinas's account – misunderstood the ethical. For Levinas, the ethical is precisely not a theme of discourse and therefore cannot be ontologized. It is otherwise than being. But if Levinas seems rather opaque – after all, this is not the place to go into an exegesis of how Levinas from his pathbreaking 1951 essay 'Is Ontology Fundamental?' onwards, sought to distinguish ethics from ontology in his attempt to leave the climate of Heidegger's thinking – a similar line of thought can be found in thinkers intellectually

closer to Laclau. In Lacan, the ethical is experienced in relation to the order of the Real insofar as a non-symbolizable Chose – das Ding in Freud – stands in the place of the Real. This Chose is precisely something irreducible to ontological categorization, a permanent excess within discursive symbolization. Also, in Wittgenstein, in his 1929 Cambridge lecture on ethics and elsewhere, the ethical is revealed in running up against the limits of language. The ethical is, strictly speaking, something about which nothing can be said. All propositions in the domain of ethics are nonsensical. Ethics is not something ontologically grasped, but rather apprehended in the silence that falls after reading Proposition 7 of the Tractatus – and it should be recalled that Wittgenstein acknowledged that the entire effort of the Tractatus had an ethical point, a point which could not be expressed in the book itself.

5. Let me stay with the example of Wittgenstein in order to probe further the ethical/normative distinction. In one of his more cryptic remarks on rule following from the Philosophical Investigations, he writes, 'It would almost be more correct to say, not that an intuition was needed at every stage, but that a new decision was needed at every stage (es sei an jedem Punkt eine neue Entscheidung nötig).' This quotation would seem to illustrate well the relation between ethics and normativity, namely that there is a rule, which possesses universality, for example the sequence of prime numbers, and yet each expression of the rule demands a decision, an act of continuing the sequence. In this sense, the rule would be 'ethical' and the particular decision would be normative. But if that is granted, then what is to be gained by attempting to distinguish rigorously between the ethical and the normative? Shouldn't we rather conceive of 'the ethical/normative complex' in similar or analogous ways to the relation between 'a rule' and 'instantiations of following a rule'?

6. Let me come back to a different way of expressing my earlier question as to the difference between hegemony and democratic hegemony. Is the ethical something constitutive of or identifiable within all societies or does it only exist in democratic societies? If it is the former – and I think it is for Laclau – and the ethical exists in all societies, then although this definition would maintain the requirement of strict formality, it might also be accused of banality. If Laclau is making a simple meta-ethical point in his talk of the ethical, then one might well ask, 'well, what is the point of making it?'. However, if it is the latter, and the ethical is part and parcel of democratic societies alone, then it seems to me that one has admitted some specific normative content to the ethical. That is, one has consented to describing the ethical in some way or other and recommending a particular description over another. I would be inclined to say that democratic political forms are simply better than non-democratic ones: more inclusive, more capacious, more just, or whatever. Now, if there is some specific content to the ethical, then the distinction between the ethical and the normative cannot be said to hold; yet, conversely, if there is no content to the ethical at all, then one might be entitled to ask: what's the point? Isn't such a meta-ethical analysis rather banal?
7. I imagine that Laclau's critique of my position would be that insofar as it follows Levinas (although, it must be said, an increasingly heterodox Levinas), it admits some specific content to the ethical. This is indeed true. I accept the criticism unreservedly. My position is that on the basis of a certain meta-ethical picture of what I call 'ethical experience', which I trace back to the debates around the notion of the 'fact of reason' in Kant, I recommend a particular normative conception of ethical experience based on a critical reading of a number of thinkers, Derrida and Levinas included. Be that as it may, my question back to Laclau is that unless one

> wants to engage in a pure diagnostic meta-ethical inquiry divorced from any substantive normative content, I can't see why one should so insistently want to emphasize the content-free character of the ethical. In my view, formal meta-ethics must be linked to normative ethical claims. One of the great virtues of the Laclau's work is that it shows us how to hegemonize a specific normative picture into effective and transformative political action.

Therefore, it would seem that there is still a normative deficit in the theory of hegemony, although it is not at all where I first imagined it to be. So, Ernesto and I still disagree after all, which is perhaps no bad thing as it means that our history can continue.

2

Political Views and Theories of Hegel

SOCIAL AND POLITICAL THOUGHT

Georg Wilhelm Friedrich Hegel is one of the greatest systematic thinkers in the history of Western philosophy. In addition to epitomizing German idealist philosophy, Hegel boldly claimed that his own system of philosophy represented an historical culmination of all previous philosophical thought. Hegel's overall encyclopedic system is divided into the science of Logic, the philosophy of Nature, and the philosophy of Spirit. Of most enduring interest are his views on history, society, and the state, which fall within the realm of Objective Spirit.

Some have considered Hegel to be a nationalistic apologist for the Prussian State of the early 19th century, but his significance has been much broader, and there is no doubt that Hegel himself considered his work to be an expression of the self-consciousness of the World Spirit of his time. At the core of Hegel's social and political thought are the concepts of freedom, reason, self-consciousness, and recognition. There are important connections between the metaphysical or speculative articulation of these ideas and their application to social and political reality, and one could say that the full meaning of these ideas can be grasped only with a comprehension of their social and historical embodiment. The work that explicates this concretizing of ideas, and which has perhaps stimulated as much controversy as interest, is the Philosophy of Right (*Philosophie des Rechts*), which will be a main focus of this essay.

Biography

G.W.F. Hegel was born in Stuttgart in 1770, the son of an official in the government of the Duke of Württemberg. He was educated at the Royal Highschool in Stuttgart from 1777-88 and steeped in both the classics and the literature of the European Enlightenment. In October, 1788 Hegel began studies at a theological seminary in Tübingen, the Tüberger Stift, where he became friends with the poet Hölderlin and philosopher Friedrich Schelling, both of whom would later become famous. In 1790 Hegel received an M.A. degree, one year after the fall of the Bastille in France, an event welcomed by these young idealistic students. Shortly after graduation, Hegel took a post as tutor to a wealthy Swiss family in Berne from 1793-96. In 1797, with the help of his friend Hölderlin, Hegel moved to Frankfurt to take on another tutorship. During this time he wrote unpublished essays on religion which display a certain radical tendency of thought in his critique of orthodox religion.

In January 1801, two years after the death of his father, Hegel finished with tutoring and went to Jena where he took a position as *Privatdozent* (unsalaried lecturer) at the University of Jena, where Hegel's friend Schelling had already held a university professorship for three years. There Hegel collaborated with Schelling on a Critical Journal of Philosophy (*Kritisches Journal der Philosophie*) and he also published a piece on the differences between the philosophies of Fichte and Schelling (*Differenz des Fichte'schen und Schelling'schen Systems der Philosophie*) in which preference was consistently expressed for the latter thinker. After having attained a professorship in 1805, Hegel published his first major work, the Phenomenology of Spirit (*Phänomenologie des Geistes*, 1807) which was delivered to the publisher just at the time of the occupation of Jena by Napoleon's armies. With the closing of the University, due to the victory of the French in Prussia, Hegel had to seek employment elsewhere and so he took a job as editor of a newspaper in Bamberg, Bavaria in 1807 (*Die*

Bamberger Zeitung) followed by a move to Nuremberg in 1808 where Hegel became headmaster of a preparatory school (*Gymnasium*), roughly equivalent to a high school, and also taught philosophy to the students there until 1816. During this time Hegel married, had children, and published his Science of Logic (*Wissenschaft der Logik*) in three volumes.

One year following the defeat of Napoleon at Waterloo (1815), Hegel took the position of Professor of Philosophy at the University of Heidelberg where he published his first edition of the Encyclopedia of the Philosophical Sciences in Outline (*Encyklopädie derphilosophischen Wissenschaften im Grundrisse,* 1817). In 1818 he became Professor of Philosophy at the University of Berlin, through the invitation of the Prussion minister von Altenstein (who had introduced many liberal reforms in Prussia until the fall of Napoleon), and Hegel taught there until he died in 1831. Hegel lectured on various topics in philosophy, most notably on history, art, religion, and the history of philosophy and he became quite famous and influential. He held public positions as a member of the Royal Examination Commission of the Province of Brandenberg and also as a councellor in the Ministry of Education. In 1821 he published the Philosophy of Right (*Philosophie des Rechts*) and in 1830 was given the honor of being elected Rector of the University. On November 14, 1831 Hegel died of cholera in Berlin, four months after having been decorated by Friedrich Wilhelm III of Prussia.

POLITICAL WRITINGS

Apart from his philosophical works on history, society, and the state, Hegel wrote several political tracts most of which were not published in his lifetime but which are significant enough in connection to the theoretical writings to deserve some mention. (These are published in English translation in Hegel's Political Writings and Political Writings, listed in the bibliography of works by Hegel below.)

Hegel's very first political work was on "On the Recent Domestic Affairs of Wurtemberg" (*Über die neuesten innern Verhältnisse*

Württembergs..., 1798) which was neither completed nor published. In it Hegel expresses the view that the constitutional structure of Wurtemberg requires fundamental reform. He condemns the absolutist rule of Duke Ferdinand along with the narrow traditionalism and legal positivism of his officials and welcomes the convening of the Estates Assembly, while disagreeing with the method of election in the Diet. In contrast to the existing system of oligarchic privilege, Hegel argues that the Diet needs to be based on popular election through local town councils, although this should not be done by granting suffrage to an uneducated multitude. The essay ends inconclusively on the appropriate method of political representation.

A quite long piece of about 100 pages, The German Constitution (*Die Verfassung Deutchlands*) was written and revised by Hegel between 1799 and 1802 and was not published until after his death in 1893. This piece provides an analysis and critique of the constitution of the German Empire with the main theme being that the Empire is a thing of the past and that appeals for a unified German state are anachronistic. Hegel finds a certain hypocrisy in German thinking about the Empire and a gap between theory and practice in the German constitution. Germany was no longer a state governed by law but rather a plurality of independent political entities with disparate practices. Hegel stresses the need to recognize that the realities of the modern state necessitate a strong public authority along with a populace that is free and unregimented. The principle of government in the modern world is constitutional monarchy, the potentialities of which can be seen in Austria and Prussia. Hegel ends the essay on an uncertain note with the idea that Germany as a whole could be saved only by some Machiavellian genius.

The essay "Proceedings of the Estates Assembly in the Kingdom of Württemberg, 1815-1816" was published in 1817 in the *Heidelbergische Jahrbücher*. In it Hegel commented on sections of the official report of the Diet of Württemberg, focusing on the opposition by the Estates to the King's request for ratification of a new constitutional charter that recognized recent liberalizing changes and reforms. Hegel sided with King Frederick and criticized the Estates as being reactionary in their appeal to old customary laws and feudal property rights. There has been controversy over whether Hegel here was trying to gain favor with the King in order to attain a government position. However, Hegel's favoring a sovereign kingdom of Wurtemberg over the German Empire and the need for a constitutional charter that is more rational than the previous are quite continuous with the previous essays. A genuine state needs a strong and effective central public authority, and in resisting the Estates are trying to live in the feudal past. Moreover, Hegel is not uncritical of the King's constitutional provisions and finds deficiencies in the exclusion of members of professions from the Estates Assembly as well as in the proposal for direct suffrage in representation, which treats citizens like unintegrated atomic units rather than as members of a political community.

The last of Hegel's political tracts, "The English Reform Bill," was written in installments in 1831 for the ministerial newspaper, the *Preussische Staatszeitung,* but was interrupted due to censure by the Prussian King because of the perception of its being overly critical and anti-English. As a result, the remainder of the work was printed independently and distributed discretely. Hegel's main line of criticism is that the proposed English reforms of suffrage will not make much of a difference in the distribution of political power and may only create a power struggle between the rising group of politicians and the traditional ruling class. Moreover, there are deep problems in English society that cannot be addressed by the proposed electoral reforms, including political corruption in the English burroughs, the selling of seats in parliament, and the general oligarchic nature of social reality including the wide disparities between wealth and poverty, Ecclesiastical patronage, and conditions in Ireland. While Hegel supports the idea of reform with its appeal to rational change as against the "positivity" of customary law, traditionalism and privilege, he thinks that universalizing suffrage with a property qualification without a thorough reform of the system of Common Law and the existing social conditions will only be perceived as token measures leading to greater disenchantment among the newly enfranchised and possibly inclinations to violent revolution. Hegel claims that national pride keeps the English from studying and following the reforms of the European Continent or seriously reflecting upon and grasping the nature of government and legislation.

There are several overall themes that reoccur in these political writings and that connect with some of the main lines of thought in Hegel's theoretical works. First, there is the contrast between the attitude of legal positivism and the appeal to the law of reason. Hegel consistently displays a "political rationalism" which attacks old concepts and attitudes that no longer apply to the modern world. Old constitutions stemming from the Feudal era are a confused mixture of customary laws and special privileges that must give way to the constitutional reforms of the new social and political world that has arrived in the aftermath of the French Revolution. Second, reforms of old constitutions must be thorough and radical, but also cautious and gradual. This might sound somewhat inconsistent, but for Hegel a reform is radical due to a fundamental change in direction, not the speed of such change. Hegel suggests that customary institutions not be abolished too quickly for there must be some congruence and continuity with the existing social conditions. Hegel rejects violent popular action and sees the principal force for reform in governments and the estates assemblies, and he thinks reforms should always stress legal equality and the public welfare. Third, Hegel emphasizes the need for a strong central government, albeit without complete centralized control of public administration and social relations. Hegel here anticipates his later conception of civil society (*bürgerliche Gesellschaft*), the social realm of individual autonomy where there is significant local self-governance. The task of government is not to thoroughly bureaucratize civil society but rather to provide oversight, regulation, and when necessary intervention. Fourth, Hegel claims that representation of the people must be popular but not atomistic. The democratic element in a state is not its sole feature and it must be institutionalized in a rational manner. Hegel rejects universal suffrage as irrational because it provides no means of mediation between the individual and the state as a whole. Hegel believed that the masses lacked the experience and political education to be directly involved in national elections and policy matters and that direct suffrage leads to electoral indifference and apathy. Fifth, while acknowledging the importance of a division of powers in the public authority, Hegel does not appeal to a conception of separation and balance of powers. He views the estates assemblies, which safeguard freedom, as essentially related to the monarch and also stresses the role of civil servants and members of the professions, both in ministerial positions and in the assemblies. The monarchy, however, is the central supporting element in the constitutional structure because the monarch is invested with the sovereignty of the state. However, the power of the monarch is not despotical for he exercises authority through universal laws and statutes and is advised and assisted by a ministry and civil service, all members of which must meet educational requirements.

THE JENA WRITINGS (1802-06)

Hegel wrote several pieces while at the University of Jena that point in the direction of some of the main theses of the Philosophy of Right. The first was entitled "On the Scientific Modes of Treatment of Natural Law–Its Place in Practical Philosophy and Its Relationship to the Positive Science of Law" (*Über die wissenschaftlichen Behandlungsarten des Naturrechts*...), published originally in the *Kritisches Journal der Philosophie* in 1802, edited jointly by Hegel and Schelling. In this piece, usually referred to as the essay on Natural Law, Hegel criticizes both the empirical and formal approaches to natural law, as exemplified in British and Kantian philosophy respectively. Empiricism reaches conclusions that are limited by the particularities of its contexts and materials and thus cannot provide universally valid propositions regarding the concepts of various social and political institutions or of the relation of reflective consciousness to social and political experience. Formalist conclusions, on the other hand, are too insubstantial and abstract in failing to properly link human reason concretely to human experience. Traditional natural law theories are based on an abstract rationalism and the attempts of Rousseau, Kant, and Fichte to remedy this through their various ethical conceptions fail to overcome abstractness. For Hegel, the proper method of philosophical science must link concretely the development of the human mind and its rational powers to actual experience. Moreover, the concept of a social and political community must transcend the instrumentalizing of the state.

Hegel's work entitled "The System of Ethical Life" (*System der Sittlichkeit*) was written in 1802-03 and first published in its entirety by Georg Lasson in 1913 in a volume entitled *Schriften zur Politik und Rechtsphilosophie.* In this work, Hegel develops a philosophical theory of social and political development that correlates with the self-development of essential human powers. Historically, humans begin in an immediate relation to nature and their social existence takes the form of *natürliche Sittlichkeit*, i.e., a non-selfconscious relation to nature and to others. However, the satisfaction of human desires leads to their reproduction and multiplication and leads to the necessity for labor, which induces transformation in the human world and people's connections to it. This process leads to a self-realization that undermines the original naïve unity with nature and others and to the formation of overtly cooperative endeavors, e.g., in the making and use of tools. Another result of labor is the emergence of private property as an embodiment of human personality as well as of sets of legal relationships that institutionalize property ownership, exchange, etc., and deal with crimes against property. Furthermore, disparities in property and power lead to relationships of subordination and the use of the labor of others to satisfy one's increasingly complex and expanded desires. Gradually, a system of mutual dependence, a "system of needs," develops, and along with the increasing division of labor there also develops class differentiations reflecting the types of labor or activity taken up by members of each class, which Hegel classifies into the agricultural, acquisitive, and administerial classes. However, despite relations of interdependence and cooperation the members of society experience social connections as a sort of blind fate without some larger system of control which is provided by the state which regulates the economic life of society. The details of the structure of the state are unclear in this essay, but what is clear is that for Hegel the state provides an increased rationality to social practices, much in the sense that the later German sociologist Max Weber (1864-1920) would articulate how social practices become more rational by being codified and made more predictable.

The manuscripts entitled *Realphilosophie* are based on lectures Hegel delivered at Jena University in 1803-04 (*Realphilosophie I*) and 1805-06 (*Realphilosophie II*), and were originally published by Johannes Hoffmeister in 1932. These writings cover much of the same ground as the *System der Sittlichkeit* in explicating a philosophy of mind and human experience in relation to human social and political development. Some of the noteworthy ideas in these writings are the role and significance of language for social consciousness, for giving expression to a people (*Volk*) and for the comprehending of and mastery of the world, and the necessity and consequences of the fragmentation of primordial social relationships and patterns as part of the process of human development. Also, there is a reiteration of the importance of property relations as crucial to social recognition and how there would be no security of property or recognition of property rights if society were to remain a mere multitude of families.

Such security requires a system of control over the "struggle for recognition" through interpersonal norms, rules, and juridical authority provided by the nation state. Moreover, Hegel repeats the need for strong state regulation of the economy, which if left to its own workings is blind to the needs of the social community. The economy, especially through the division of labor, produces fragmentation and diminishment of human life (compare Marx on alienation) and the state must not only address this phenomenon but also provide the means for the people's political participation to further the development of social self-consciousness. In all of this Hegel appears to be providing a philosophical account of modern developments both in terms of the tensions and conflicts that are new to modernity as well as in the progressive movements of reform found under the influence of Napoleon.

Finally, Hegel also discusses the forms of government, the three main types being tyranny, democracy, and hereditary monarchy. Tyranny is found typically in primitive or undeveloped states, democracy exists in states where there is the realization of individual identity but no split between the public and private person, and hereditary monarchy is the appropriate form of political authority in the modern world in providing strong central government along with a system of indirect representation through Estates. The relation of religion to the state is undeveloped in these writings, but Hegel is clear about the superentinent role of the state that stands above all else in giving expression to the Spirit (*Geist*) of a society in a sort of earthly kingdom of God, the realization of God in the world. True religion complements and supports this realization and thus cannot properly have supremacy over or be opposed to the state.

THE PHENOMENOLOGY OF SPIRIT

The Phenomenology of Spirit (*Die Phänomenologie des Geistes*), published in 1807, is Hegel's first major comprehensive philosophical work. Originally intended to be the first part of his comprehensive system of science (*Wissenschaft*) or philosophy, Hegel eventually considered it to be the introduction to his system. This work provides what can be called a "biography of spirit," i.e., an account of the development of consciousness and self-consciousness in the context of some central epistemological, anthropological and cultural themes of human history. It has continuity with the works discussed above in examining the development of the human mind in relation to human experience but is more wide-ranging in also addressing fundamental questions about the meaning of perceiving, knowing, and other cognitive activities as well as of the nature of reason and reality. Given the focus of this essay, the themes of the Phenomenology to be discussed here are those directly relevant to Hegel's social and political thought. One of the most widely discussed places in the Phenomenology is the chapter on "The Truth of Self-

Certainty" which includes a subsection on "Independence and Dependence of Self-Consciousness: Lordship and Bondage." This section treats of the (somewhat misleadingly named) "master/slave" struggle which is taken by some, especially the Marxian-inspired, as a paradigm of all forms of social conflict, in particular the struggle between social classes. It is clear that Hegel intended the scenario to typify certain features of the struggle for recognition (*Anerkennung*) overall, be it social, personal, etc. The conflict between master and slave (which shall be referred to hereafter as lord and bondsman as more in keeping with Hegel's own terminology and the intended generic meaning) is one in which the historical themes of dominance and obedience, dependence and independence, etc., are philosophically introduced. Although this specific dialectic of struggle occurs only at the earliest stages of self-consciousness, it nonetheless sets up the main problematic for achieving realized self-consciousness–the gaining of self-recognition through the recognition of and by another, through mutual recognition.

According to Hegel, the relationship between self and otherness is the fundamental defining characteristic of human awareness and activity, being rooted as it is in the emotion of desire for objects as well as in the estrangement from those objects, which is part of the primordial human experience of the world. The otherness that consciousness experiences as a barrier to its goal is the external reality of the natural and social world, which prevents individual consciousness from becoming free and independent.

However, that otherness cannot be abolished or destroyed, without destroying oneself, and so ideally there must be reconciliation between self and other such that consciousness can "universalize" itself through the other. In the relation of dominance and subservience between two consciousnesses, say lord and bondsman, the basic problem for consciousness is the overcoming of its otherness, or put positively, the achieving of integration with itself. The relation between lord and bondsman leads to a sort of provisional, incomplete resolution of the struggle for recognition between distinct consciousnesses.

Hegel asks us to consider how a struggle between two distinct consciousnesses, let us say a violent "life-or-death" struggle, would lead to one consciousness surrendering and submitting to the other out of fear of death. Initially, the consciousness that becomes lord or master proves its freedom through willingness to risk its life and not submit to the other out of fear of death, and thus not identify simply with its desire for life and physical being. Moreover, this consciousness is given acknowledgement of its freedom through the submission and dependence of the other, which turns out paradoxically to be a deficient recognition in that the dominant one fails to see a reflection of itself in the subservient one. Adequate recognition requires a mirroring of the self through the other, which means that to be successful it must be mutual. In the ensuing relationship of lordship and bondage, furthermore, the bondsman through work and discipline (motivated by fear of dying at the hands of the master or lord) transforms his subservience into a mastery over his environment, and thus achieves a measure of independence. In objectifying himself in his environment through his labor the bondsman in effect realizes himself, with his transformed environment serving as a reflection of his inherently self-realizing activity.

Thus, the bondsman gains a measure of independence in his subjugation out of fear of death. In a way, the lord represents death as the absolute subjugator, since it is through fear of this master, of the death that he can impose, that the bondsman in his acquiescence and subservience is placed into a social context of work and discipline. Yet despite, or more properly, because of this subjection the bondsman is able to attain a measure of independence by internalizing and overcoming those limitations which must be dealt with if he is to produce efficiently. However, this accomplishment, the self-determination of the bondsman, is limited and incomplete because of the asymmetry that remains in his relation to the lord. Self-consciousness is still fragmented, i.e., the objectification through labor that the bondsman experiences does not coincide with the consciousness of the lord whose sense of self is not through labor but through power over the bondsman and enjoyment of the fruits of the bondsman's labor. Only in a realm of ethical life can self-determination be fully self-conscious to the extent that universal freedom is reflected in the life of each individual member of society.

Thus, in the Phenomenology consciousness must move on through the phases of Stoicism, Skepticism, and the Unhappy Consciousness before engaging in the self-articulation of Reason, and it is not until the section "Objective Spirit: The Ethical Order" that the full universalization of self-consciousness is in principle to be met with. Here we find a shape of human existence where all men work freely, serving the needs of the whole community rather than of masters, and subject only to the "discipline of reason." This mode of ethical life, typified in ancient Greek democracy, also eventually disintegrates, as is expressed in the conflict between human and divine law and the tragic fate that is the outcome of this conflict illustrated in the story of Antigone. However, the ethical life described here is still in its immediacy and is therefore at a level of abstractness that falls short of the mediation of subjectivity and universality which is provided spiritually in revealed Christianity and politically in the modern state, which purportedly provides a solution to human conflict arising from the struggle for recognition. In any case, the rest of the Phenomenology is devoted to examinations of culture (including enlightenment and revolution), morality, religion, and finally, Absolute Knowing.

The dialectic of self-determination is, for Hegel, inherent in the very structure of freedom, and is the defining feature of Spirit (*Geist*). The full actualization of Spirit in the human community requires the progressive development of individuality which effectively begins with the realization in self-consciousness of the "truth of self-certainty" and culminates in the shape of a shared common life in an integrated community of love and Reason, based upon the realization of truths of incarnation, death, resurrection, and forgiveness as grasped in speculative Religion. The articulation Hegel provides in the Phenomenology, however, is very generic and is to be made concrete politically with the working out of a specific conception of the modern nation-state with its particular configuration of social and political institutions. It is to the latter that we must turn in order to see how these fundamental dialectical considerations take shape in the "solution" to the struggle for recognition in self-consciousness. However, before moving directly to Hegel's theory of the state, and history, some discussion of his Logic is in order.

LOGIC AND POLITICAL THEORY

The Logic constitutes the first part of Hegel's philosophical system as presented in his Encyclopedia. It was preceded by his larger work, The Science of Logic (*Wissenschaft der Logik*), published in 1812-16 in two volumes. The "Encyclopedia Logic" is a shorter version intended to function as part of an "outline," but it became longer in the course of the three published versions of 1817, 1827, and 1830. Also, the English translation by William Wallace contains additions from the notes of students who heard Hegel's lectures on this subject. (Reference to the paragraphs of the Encyclopedia will be made with the "¶" character.)

The structure of the Logic is triadic, reflecting the organization of the larger system of philosophy as well as a variety of other motifs, both internal and external to the Logic proper. The Logic has three divisions: the Doctrine of Being, the Doctrine of Essence, and the Doctrine of the Notion (or Concept). There are a number of logical categories in this work that are directly relevant to social and political theorizing.

In the Doctrine of Being, for example, Hegel explains the concept of "being-for-self" as the function of self-relatedness in the resolving of opposition between self and other in the "ideality of the finite". He claims that the task of philosophy is to bring out the ideality of the finite, and as will be seen later Hegel's philosophy of the state is intended to articulate the ideality of the state, i.e., its affirmative and infinite or rational features. In the Doctrine of Essence, Hegel explains the categories of actuality and freedom. He says that actuality is the unity of "essence and existence" and argues that this does not rule out the actuality of ideas for they become actual by being realized in external existence. Hegel will have related points to make about the actuality of the idea of the state in society and history. Also, he defines freedom not in terms of contingency or lack of determination, as is popular, but rather as the "truth of necessity," i.e., freedom presupposes necessity in the sense that reciprocal action and reaction provide a structure for free action, e.g., a necessary relation between crime and punishment.

The Doctrine of the Notion (*Begriff*) is perhaps the most relevant section of the Logic to social and political theory due to its focus on the various dynamics of development. This section is subdivided into three parts: the subjective notion, the objective notion, and the idea which articulates the unity of subjective and objective.

The first part, the subjective notion, contains three "moments" or functional parts: universality, particularity, and individuality. These are particularly important as Hegel will show how the functional parts of the state operate according to a progressive "dialectical" movement from the first to the third moments and how the state as a whole, as a functioning and integrated totality, gives expression to the concept of individuality.

Hegel treats these relationships as logical judgments and syllogisms but they do not merely articulate how the mind must operate (subjectivity) but also explain actual relationships in reality (objectivity). In objective reality we find these logical/dialectical relationships in mechanism, chemism, and teleology. Finally, in the Idea, the correspondence of the notion or concept with objective reality, we have the truth of objects or objects as they ought to be, i.e., as they correspond to their proper concepts. The logical articulation of the Idea is very important to Hegel's explanation of the Idea of the state in modern history, for this provides the principles of rationality that guide the development of Spirit in the world and that become manifested in various ways in social and political life.

THE PHILOSOPHY OF RIGHT

In 1821, Hegel's Philosophy of Right orginally appeared under the double title *Naturrecht und Staatswissenschaften in Grundrisse; Grundlinien der Philosophie des Rechts* (Natural Law and the Science of the State; Elements of the Philosophy of Right). The work was republished by Eduard Gans in 1833 and 1854 as part of *Hegel's Werke*, vol. viii and included additions from notes taken by students at Hegel's lectures. The English language translation of this work by T. M. Knox refers to these later editions as well as to an edition published in 1923 by Georg Lasson, which included corrections from previous editions.

The Philosophy of Right constitutes, along with Hegel's Philosophy of History, the penultimate section of his Encyclopedia, the section on Objective Spirit, which deals with the human world and its array of social rules and institutions, including the moral, legal, religious, economic, and political as well as marriage, the family, social classes, and other forms of human organization. The German word *Recht* is often translated as 'law', however, Hegel clearly intends the term to have a broader meaning that captures what we might call the good or just society, one that is "rightful" in its structure, composition, and practices.

In the Introduction to this work Hegel explains the concept of his philosophical undertaking along with the specific key concepts of will, freedom, and right. At the very beginning, Hegel states that the Idea of right, the concept together with its actualization, is the proper subject of the philosophical science of right. Hegel is emphatic that the study is scientific in that it deals in a systematic way with something essentially rational. He further remarks that the basis of scientific procedure in a philosophy of right is explicated in philosophical logic and presupposed by the former. Furthermore, Hegel is at pains to distinguish the historical or legal approach to "positive law" (*Gesetz*) and the philosophical approach to the Idea of right (*Recht*), the former involving mere description and compilation of laws as legal facts while the latter probes into the inner meaning and necessary determinations of law or right. For Hegel the justification of something, the finding of its inherent rationality, is not a matter of seeking its origins or longstanding features but rather of studying it conceptually.

However, there is one sense in which the origin of right is relevant to philosophical science and this is the free will. The free will is the basis and origin of right in the sense that mind or spirit (*Geist*) generally objectifies itself in a system of right (human social and political institutions) that gives expression to freedom, which Hegel says is both the substance and goal of right. This ethical life in the state consists in the unity of the universal and the subjective will. The universal will is contained in the Idea of freedom as its essence, but when considered apart from the subjective will can be thought of only abstractly or indeterminately. Considered apart from the subjective or particular will, the universal will is "the element of pure indeterminacy or that pure reflection of the ego into itself which involves the dissipation of every restriction and every content either immediately presented by nature, by needs, desires, and impulses, or given and determined by any means whatever".

In other words, the universal will is that moment in the Idea of freedom where willing is thought of as state of absolutely unrestrained volition, unfettered by any particular circumstances or limitations whatsoever–the pure form of willing. This is expressed in the modern libertarian view of completely uncoerced choice, the absence of restraint (or "negative liberty" as understood by Thomas Hobbes). The subjective will, on the other hand, is the principle of activity and realization that involves "differentiation, determination, and positing of a determinacy as a content and object".

This means that the will is not merely unrestrained in acting but that it actually can give expression to the doing or accomplishing of certain things, e.g., through talent or expertise (sometimes called "positive freedom"). The unity of both the moments of abstract universality (the will in-itself) and subjectivity or particularity (the will for-itself) is the concrete universal or true individuality (the will in-and-for-itself). According to Hegel, preservation of the distinction of these two moments in the unity (identity-in-difference) between universal and particular will is what produces rational self-determination of an ego, as well as the self-consciousness of the state as a whole. Hegel's conception of freedom as self-determination is just this unity in difference of the universal and subjective will, be it in the willing by individual persons or in the expressions of will by groups of individuals or collectivities. The "negative self-relation" of this freedom involves the subordination of the natural instincts, impulses, and desires to conscious reflection and to goals and purposes that are consciously chosen and that require commitment to rational principles in order to properly guide action.

The overall structure of the Philosophy of Right is quite remarkable in its "syllogistic" organization. The main division of the work corresponds to what Hegel calls the stages in the development of "the Idea of the absolutely free will," and these are Abstract Right, Morality, and Ethical Life. Each of these divisions is further subdivided triadically: under Abstract Right there is Property, Contract, and Wrong; under Morality falls Purpose and Responsibility, Intention and Welfare, and Good and Conscience; finally, under Ethical Life comes the Family, Civil Society, and the State. These last subdivisions are further subdivided into triads, with fourth level subdivisions occurring under Civil Society and the State. This triadic system of rubrics is no mere description of a static model of social and political life. Hegel claims that it gives expression to the conceptual development of Spirit in human society based upon the purely logical development of rationality provided in his Logic. Thus, it is speculatively based and not derivable from empirical survey, although the particularities of the system do indeed correspond to our experience and what we know about ourselves anthropologically, culturally, etc.

The transition in the Logic from universality to particularity to individuality (or concrete universality) is expressed in the social and political context in the conceptual transition from Abstract Right to Morality to Ethical Life. In the realm of Abstract Right, the will remains in its immediacy as an abstract universal that is expressed in personality and in the universal right to possession of external things in property. In the realm of Morality, the will is no longer merely "in-itself," or restricted to the specific characteristics of legal personality, but becomes free "for-itself," i.e., it is will reflected into itself so as to produce a self-consciousness of the will's infinity. The will is expressed, initially, in inner conviction and subsequently in purpose, intention, and conviction.

As opposed to the merely juridical person, the moral agent places primary value on subjective recognition of principles or ideals that stand higher than positive law. At this stage, universality of a higher moral law is viewed as something inherently different from subjectivity, from the will's inward convictions and actions, and so in its isolation from a system of objectively recognized legal rules the willing subject remains "abstract, restricted, and formal". Because the subject is intrinsically a social being who needs association with others in order to institutionalize the universal maxims of morality, maxims that cover all people, it is only in the realm of Ethical Life that the universal and the subjective will come into a unity through the objectification of the will in the institutions of the Family, Civil Society, and the State.

In what follows, we trace through Hegel's systematic development of the "stages of the will," highlighting only the most important points as necessary to get an overall view of this work.

Abstract Right

The subject of Abstract Right (*Recht*) is the person as the bearer or holder of individual rights. Hegel claims that this focus on the right of personality, while significant in distinguishing persons from mere things, is abstract and without content, a simple relation of the will to itself. The imperative of right is: "Be a person and respect others as persons". In this formal conception of right, there is no question of particular interests, advantages, motives or intentions, but only the mere idea of the possibility of choosing based on the having of permission, as long as one does not infringe on the right of other persons. Because of the possibilities of infringement, the positive form of commands in this sphere are prohibitions.

Property (the universality of will as embodied in things)

A person must translate his or her freedom into the external world "in order to exist as Idea", thus abstract right manifests itself in the absolute right of appropriation over all things. Property is the category through which one becomes an object to oneself in that one actualizes the will through possession of something external. Property is the embodiment of personality and of freedom. Not only can a person put his or her will into something external through the taking possession of it and of using it, but one can also alienate property or yield it to the will of another, including the ability to labor for a restricted period of time. One's personality is inalienable and one's right to personality imprescriptible. This means one cannot alienate all of one's labor time without becoming the property of another.

Contract (the positing of explicit universality of will)

In this sphere, we have a relation of will to will, i.e., one holds property not merely by means of the subjective will externalized in a thing, but by means of another's person's will, and implicitly by virtue of one's participation in a common will. The status of being an independent owner of something from which one excludes the will of another is thus mediated in the identification of one's will with the other in the contractual relation, which presupposes that the contracting parties "recognize each other as persons and property owners". Moreover, when contract involves the alienation or giving up of property, the external thing is now an explicit embodiment of the unity of wills. In contractual relations of exchange, what remains identical as the property of the individuals is its value, in respect to which the parties to the contract are on an equal footing, regardless of the qualitative external differences between the things exchanged. "Value is the universal in which the subjects of the contract participate".

Wrong (the particular will opposing itself to the universal)

In immediate relations of persons to one another it is possible for a particular will to be at variance with the universal through arbitrariness of decision and contingency of circumstance, and so the appearance (*Erscheinung*) of right takes on the character of a show (*Schein*), which is the inessential, arbitrary, posing as the essential. If the "show" is only implicit and not explicit also, i.e., if the wrong passes in the doer's eyes as right, the wrong is non-malicious. In fraud a show is made to deceive the other party and so in the doer's eyes the right asserted is only a show. Crime is wrong both in itself and from the doer's point of view, such that wrong is willed without even the pretense or show of right. Here the form of acting does not imply a recognition of right but rather is an act of coercion through exercise of force. It is a "negatively infinite judgement" in that it asserts a denial of rights to the victim, which is not only incompatible with the fact of the matter but also self-negating in denying its own capacity for rights in principle.

The penalty that falls on the criminal is not merely just but is "a right *established* within the criminal himself, i.e., in his objectively embodied will, in his action," because the crime as the action of a rational being implies appeal to a universal standard recognized by the criminal. The annulling of crime in this sphere of immediate right occurs first as revenge, which as retributive is just in its content, but in its form it is an act of a subjective will and does not correspond with its universal content and hence as a new transgression is defective and contradictory. All crimes are comparable in their universal property of being injuries, thus, in a sense it is not something personal but the concept itself which carries out retribution.

Crime, as the will which is implicitly null, contains its negation in itself, which is its punishment.

The nullity of crime is that it has set aside right as such, but since right is absolute it cannot be set aside. Thus, the act of crime is not something positive, not a first thing, but is something negative, and punishment is the negation of crime's negation.

Morality

The demand for justice as punishment rather than as revenge, with regard to wrong, implies the demand for a will which, though particular and subjective, also wills the universal as such. In wrong the will has become aware of itself as particular and has opposed itself to and contradicted the universal embodied in rights. At this stage the universally right is abstract and one-sided and thus requires a move to a higher level of self-consciousness where the universally right is mediated by the particular convictions of the willing subject. We go beyond the criminal's defiance of the universal by substituting for the abstract conception of personality the more concrete conception of subjectivity. The criminal is now viewed as breaking his own law, and his crime is a self-contradiction and not only a contradiction of a right outside him. This recognition brings us to the level of morality (*Moralität*) where the will is free both in itself and for itself, i.e., the will is self-conscious of its subjective freedom.

At the level of morality the right of the subjective will is embodied in immediate wills (as opposed to immediate things like property). The defect of this level, however, is that the subject is only for itself, i.e., one is conscious of one's subjectivity and independence but is conscious of universality only as something different from this subjectivity. Therefore, the identity of the particular will and the universal will is only implicit and the moral point of view is that of a relation of "ought-to-be," or the demand for what is right. While the moral will externalizes itself in action, its self-determination is a pure "restlessness" of activity that never arrives at actualization.

The right of the moral will has three aspects. First, there is the right of the will to act in its external environment, to recognize as its actions only those that it has consciously willed in light of an aim or purpose (purpose and responsibility). Second, in my intention I ought to be aware not simply of my particular action but also of the universal which is conjoined with it. The universal is what I have willed and is my intention. The right of intention is that the universal quality of the action is not merely implied but is known by the agent, and so it lies from the start in one's subjective will. Moreover, the content of such a will is not only the right of the particular subject to be satisfied but is elevated to a universal end, the end of welfare or happiness (intention and welfare). The welfare of many unspecified persons is thus also an essential end and right of subjectivity. However, right as an abstract universal and welfare as abstract particularity, may collide, since both are contingent on circumstances for their satisfaction, e.g., in cases where claims of right or welfare by someone may endanger the life of another there can be a counter-claim to a right of distress. "This distress reveals the finitude and therefore the contingency of both right and welfare". This "contradiction" between right and welfare is overcome in the third aspect of the moral will, the good which is "the Idea as the unity of the concept of the will with the particular will".

In addition to the right of the subjective will that whatever it recognizes as valid shall be seen by it as good, and that an action shall be imputed to it as good or evil in accordance with its knowledge of the worth which the action has in its external objectivity, which together constitute a "right of insight," the will also must recognize the good as its duty, which is, to begin with, duty for duty's sake, or duty formally and without content (e.g., as expressed in the Kantian "categorical imperative"). Because of this lack of content, the subjective will in its abstract reflection into itself is "absolute inward certainty (*Gewißheit*) of self," or conscience (*Gewissen*). While true or authentic conscience is the disposition to will what is absolutely good, and thus correspond with what is objectively right, purely formal conscience lacks an objective system of principles and duties. Although conscience is ideally supposed to mean the identity of subjective knowing and willing with the truly good, when it remains the subjective inner reflection of self-consciousness into itself its claim to this identity is deficient and one-sided. Moreover, when the determinate character of right and duty reduces to subjectivity, the mere inwardness of the will, there is the potentiality of elevating the self-will of particular individuals above the universal itself, i.e., of "slipping into evil". What makes a person evil is the choosing of natural desires in opposition to the good, i.e., to the concept of the will. When an individual attempts to pass off his or her action as good, and thus imposing it on others, while being aware of the discrepancy between its negative character and the objective universal good, the person falls into hypocrisy. This is one of several forms of perverse moral subjectivity that Hegel discusses at length in his remarks.

Ethical Life

Hegel's analysis of the moral implications of "good and conscience" leads to the conclusion that a concrete unity of the objective good with the subjectivity of the will cannot be achieved at the level of personal morality since all attempts at this are problematic. The concrete identity of the good with the subjective will occurs only in moving to the level of ethical life (*Sittlichkeit*), which Hegel says is "the Idea of freedom...the concept of freedom developed into the existing world and the nature of self-consciousness". Thus, ethical life is permeated with both objectivity and subjectivity: regarded objectively it is the state and its institutions, whose force (unlike abstract right) depends entirely on the self-consciousness of citizens, on their subjective freedom; regarded subjectively it is the ethical will of the individual which (unlike the moral will) is aware of objective duties that express one's inner sense of universality. The rationality of the ethical order of society is thus constituted in the synthesis of the concept of the will, both as universal and as particular, with its embodiment in institutional life.

The synthesis of ethical life means that individuals not only act in conformity with the ethical good but that they recognize the authority of ethical laws. This authority is not something alien to individuals since they are linked to the ethical order through a strong identification which Hegel says "is more like an identity than even the relation of faith or trust". The knowledge of how the laws and institutions of society are binding on the will of individuals entails a "doctrine of duties." In duty the individual finds liberation both from dependence on mere natural impulse, which may or may not motivate ethical actions, and from indeterminate subjectivity which cannot produce a clear view of proper action. "In duty the individual acquires his substantive freedom".

In the performance of duty the individual exhibits virtue when the ethical order is reflected in his or her character, and when this is done by simple conformity with one's duties it is rectitude. When individuals are simply identified with the actual ethical order such that their ethical practices are habitual and second nature, ethical life appears in their general mode of conduct as custom (*Sitten*). Thus, the ethical order manifests its right and validity vis-à-vis individuals. In duty "the self-will of the individual vanishes together with his private conscience which had claimed independence and opposed itself to the ethical substance. For when his character is ethical, he recognizes as the end which moves him to act the universal which is itself unmoved but is disclosed in its specific determinations as rationality actualized. He knows that his own dignity and the whole stability of his particular ends are grounded in this same universal, and it is therein that he actually attains these".

However, this does not deny the right of subjectivity, i.e., the right of individuals to be satisfied in their particular pursuits and free activity; but this right is realized only in belonging to an objective ethical order. The "bond of duty" will be seen as a restriction on the particular individual only if the self-will of subjective freedom is considered in the abstract, apart from an ethical order (as is the case for both Abstract Right and Morality). "Hence, in this identity of the universal will with the particular will, right and duty coalesce, and by being in the ethical order a man has rights in so far as he has duties, and duties in so far as he has rights".

In the realm of ethical life the logical syllogism of self-determination of the Idea is most clearly applied. The moments of universality, particularity, and individuality initially are represented respectively in the institutions of the family, civil society, and the state. The family is "ethical mind in its natural or immediate phase" and is characterized by love or the feeling of unity in which one is not conscious of oneself as an independent person but only as a member of the family unit to which one is bound. Civil society, on the other hand, comprises an association of individuals considered as self-subsistent and who have no conscious sense of unity of membership but only pursue self-interest, e.g., in satisfying needs, acquiring and protecting property, and in joining organizations for mutual advantage. Finally, the constitution of the political state brings together in a unity the sense of the importance of the whole or universal good along with the freedom of particularity of individual pursuits and thus is "the end and actuality of both the substantial order and the public life devoted thereto".

The Family

The family is characterized by love which is "mind's feeling of its own unity," where one's sense of individuality is within this unity, not as an independent individual but as a member essentially related to the other family members. Thus, familial love implies a contradiction between, on the one hand, not wanting to be a self-subsistent and independent person if that means feeling incomplete and, on the other hand, wanting to be recognized in another person. Familial love is truly an ethical unity, but because it is nonetheless a subjective feeling it is limited in sustaining unity.

Marriage

The union of man and woman in marriage is both natural and spiritual, i.e., is a physical relationship and one that is also self-conscious, and it is entered into on the basis of the free consent of the persons. Since this consent involves bringing two persons into a union, there is the mutual surrender of their natural individuality for the sake of union, which is both a self-restriction and also a liberation because in this way individuals attain a higher self-consciousness.

Family Capital

The family as a unit has its external existence in property, specifically capital (*Vermögen*) which constitutes permanent and secured possessions that allow for endurance of the family as "person". This capital is the common property of all the family members, none of whom possess property of their own, but it is administered by the head of the family, the husband.

Education of Children & Dissolution of the Family

Children provide the external and objective basis for the unity of marriage. The love of the parents for their children is the explicit expression of their love for each other, while their immediate feelings of love for each other are only subjective. Children have the right to maintenance and education, and in this regard a claim upon the family capital, but parents have the right to provide this service to the children and to instill discipline over the wishes of their children. The education of children has a twofold purpose: the positive aim of instilling ethical principles in them in the form of immediate feeling and the negative one of raising them out of the instinctive physical level. Marriage can be dissolved not by whim but by duly constituted authority when there is total estrangement of husband and wife. The ethical dissolution of the family results when the children have been educated to be free and responsible persons and they are of mature age under the law. The natural dissolution of the family occurs with the death of the parents, the result of which is the passing of inheritance of property to the surviving family members. The disintegration of the family exhibits its immediacy and contingency as an expression of the ethical Idea.

Civil Society

With civil society (*bürgerliche Gesellschaft*) we move from the family or "the ethical idea still in its concept," where consciousness of the whole or totality is focal, to the "determination of particularity," where the satisfaction of subjective needs and desires is given free reign. However, despite the pursuit of private or selfish ends in relatively unrestricted social and economic activity, universality is implicit in the differentiation of particular needs insofar as the welfare of an individual in society is intrinsically bound up with that of others, since each requires another in some way to effectively engage in reciprocal activities like commerce, trade, etc. Because this system of interdependence is not self-conscious but exists only in abstraction from the individual pursuit of need satisfaction, here particularity and universality are only externally related. Hegel says that "this system may be prima facie regarded as the external state, the state based on need, the state as the Understanding (*Verstand*) envisages it". However, civil society is also a realm of mediation of particular wills through social interaction and a means whereby individuals are educated (*Bildung*) through their efforts and struggles toward a higher universal consciousness.

The System of Needs

This dimension of civil society involves the pursuit of need satisfaction. Humans are different from animals in their ability to multiply needs and differentiate them in various ways, which leads to their refinement and luxury. Political economy discovers the necessary interconnections in the social and universalistic side of need. Work is the mode of acquisition and transformation of the means for satisfying needs as well as a mode of practical education in abilities and understanding. Work also reveals the way in which people are dependent upon one another in their self-seeking and how each individual contributes to the need satisfaction of all others. Society generates a "universal permanent capital" that everyone in principle can draw upon, but the natural inequalities between individuals will translate into social inequalities.

Furthermore, labor undergoes a division according to the complexities of the system of production, which is reflected in social class divisions: the agricultural (substantial or immediate); the business (reflecting or formal); and the civil servants (universal). Membership in a class is important for gaining status and recognition in a civil society. Hegel says that "A man actualizes himself only in becoming something definite, i.e., something specifically particularized; this means restricting himself exclusively to one of the particular spheres of need. In this class-system, the ethical frame of mind therefore is rectitude and *esprit de corps*, i.e., the disposition to make oneself a member of one of the moments of civil society by one's own act ... in this way gaining recognition both in one's own eyes and in the eyes of others".

The "substantial" agricultural class is based upon family relationships whose capital is in the products of nature, such as the land, and tends to be patriarchial, unreflective, and oriented toward dependence rather than free activity. In contrast to this focus on "immediacy," the business class is oriented toward work and reflection, e.g., in transforming raw materials for use and exchange, which is a form of mediation of humans to one another. The main activities of the business class are craftsmanship, manufacture, and trade. The third class is the class of civil servants, which Hegel calls the "universal class" because it has the universal interests of society as its concern. Members of this class are relieved from having to labor to support themselves and maintain their livelihood either from private resources such as inheritance or are paid a salary by the state as members of the bureaucracy. These individuals tend to be highly educated and must qualify for appointment to government positions on the basis of merit.

Administration of Justice

The principle of rightness becomes civil law (*Gesetz*) when it is posited, and in order to have binding force it must be given determinate objective existence. To be determinately existent, laws must be made universally known through a public legal code. Through a rational legal system, private property and personality are given legal recognition and validity in civil society, and wrongdoing now becomes an infringement, not merely of the subjective right of individuals but also of the larger universal will that exists in ethical life. The court of justice is the means whereby righ is vindicated as something universal by addressing particular cases of violation or conflict without mere subjective feeling or private bias. "Instead of the injured party, the injured *universal* now comes on the scene, and ... this pursuit consequently ceases to be the subjective and contingent retribution of revenge and is transformed into the genuine reconciliation of right with itself, i.e, into punishment". Moreover, court proceedings and legal processes must take place according to rights and rules of evidence; judicial proceedings as well as the laws themselves must be made public; trial should be by jury; and punishment should fit the crime. Finally, in the administration of justice, "civil society returns to its concept, to the unity of the implicit universal with the subjective particular, although here the latter is only that present in single cases and the universality in question is that of *abstract* right".

The Police and the Corporation

The Police (*Polizei*) for Hegel is understood broadly as the public authorities in civil society. In addition to crime fighting organizations, it includes agencies that provide oversight over public utilities as well as regulation of and, when necessary, intervention into activities related to the production, distribution, and sale of goods and services, or with any of the contingencies that can affect the rights and welfare of individuals and society generally (e.g., defense of the public's right not to be defrauded, and also the management of goods inspection). Also, the public authority superintends education and organizes the relief of poverty. Poverty must be addressed both through private charity and public assistance since in civil society it constitutes a social wrong when poverty results in the creation of a class of "penurious rabble". Society looks to colonization to increase its wealth but poverty remains a problem with no apparent solution.

The corporation (*Korporation*) applies especially to the business class, since this class is concentrated on the particularities of social existence and the corporation has the function of bringing implicit similarities between various private interests into explicit existence in forms of association. This is not the same as our contemporary business corporation but rather is a voluntary association of persons based on occupational or various social interests (such as professional and trade guilds, educational clubs, religious societies, townships, etc.) Because of the integrating function of the corporation, especially in regard to the social and economic division of labor, what appear as selfish purposes in civil society are shown to be at the same time universal through the formation of concretely recognized commonalities. Hegel says that "a Corporation has the right, under the surveillance of the public authority, (a) to look after its own interests within its own sphere, (b) to co-opt members, qualified objectively by requisite skill and rectitude, to a number fixed by the general structure of society, (c) to protect its members against particular contingencies, (d) to provide the education requisite to fit other to become members. In short, the right is to come on the scene like a second family for its members ...".

Furthermore, the family is assured greater stability of livelihood insofar as its providers are corporation members who command the respect due to them in their social positions. "Unless he is a member of an authorized Corporation (and it is only by being authorized that an association becomes a Corporation), an individual is without rank or dignity, his isolation reduces his business to mere self-seeking, and his livelihood and satisfaction become insecure". Because individual self-seeking is raised to a higher level of common pursuits, albeit restricted to the interest of a sectional group, individual self-consciousness is raised to relative universality. Hence, "As the family was the first, so the Corporation is the second ethical root of the state, the one planted in civil society".

The State

The political State, as the third moment of Ethical Life, provides a synthesis between the principles governing the Family and those governing Civil Society. The rationality of the state is located in the realization of the universal substantial will in the self-consciousness of particular individuals elevated to consciousness of universality. Freedom becomes explicit and objective in this sphere. "Since the state is mind objectified, it is only as one of its members that the individual has objectivity, genuine individuality, and an ethical life ... and the individual's destiny is the living of a universal life". Rationality is concrete in the state in so far as its content is comprised in the unity of objective freedom (freedom of the universal or substantial will) and subjective freedom (freedom of everyone in knowing and willing of particular ends); and in its form rationality is in self-determining action or laws and principles which are logical universal thoughts (as in the logical syllogism).

The Idea of the State is itself divided into three moments: (a) the immediate actuality of the state as a self-dependent organism, or Constitutional Law; (b) the relation of states to other states in International Law; (c) the universal Idea as Mind or Spirit which gives itself actuality in the process of World-History.

Constitutional Law

The Constitution (internally)

Only through the political constitution of the State can universality and particularity be welded together into a real unity. The self-consciousness of this unity is expressed in the recognition on the part of each citizen that the full meaning of one's actual freedom is found in the objective laws and institutions provided by the State. The aspect of identity comes to the fore in the recognition that individual citizens give to the ethical laws such that they "do not live as private persons for their own ends alone, but in the very act of willing these they will the universal in the light of the universal, and their activity is consciously aimed at none but the universal end". The aspect of differentiation, on the other hand, is found in "the right of individuals to their particular satisfaction," the right of subjective freedom which is maintained in Civil Society. Thus, according to Hegel, "the universal must be furthered, but subjectivity on the other hand must attain its full and living development. It is only when both these moments subsist in their strength that the state can be regarded as articulated and genuinely organized".

As was indicated in the introduction to the concept of Ethical Life above, the higher authority of the laws and institutions of society requires a doctrine of duties. From the vantage point of the political State, this means that there must be a correlation between rights and duties. "In the state, as something ethical, as the interpenetration of the substantive and the particular, my obligation to what is substantive is at the same time the embodiment of my particular freedom. This means that in the state duty and right are united in one and the same relation". In fulfilling one's duties one is also satisfying particular interests, and the conviction that this is so Hegel calls "political sentiment" (*politische Gesinnung*) or patriotism. "This sentiment is, in general, trust (which may pass over into a greater or lesser degree of educated insight), or the consciousness that my interest, both substantive and particular, is contained and preserved in another's (i.e., the state's) interest and end, i.e., in the other's relation to me as an individual".

Thus, the "bond of duty" cannot involve being coerced into obeying the laws of the State. "Commonplace thinking often has the impression that force holds the state together, but in fact its only bond is the sense of order which everybody possesses".

According to Hegel, the political state is rational in so far as it inwardly differentiates itself according to the nature of the Concept (*Begriff*). The principle of the division of powers expresses inner differentiation, but while these powers are distinguished they must also be built into an organic whole such that each contains in itself the other moments so that the political constitution is a concrete unity in difference. Constitutional Law is accordingly divided into three moments:

(a) the Legislature which establishes the universal through lawmaking;

(b) the Executive which subsumes the particular under the universal through administering the laws;

(c) the Crown which is the power of subjectivity of the state in the providing of the act of "ultimate decision" and thus forming into unity the other two powers.

Despite the syllogistic sequence of universality, particularity, and individuality in these three constitutional powers, Hegel discusses the Crown first followed by the Executive and the Legislature respectively. Hegel understands the concept of the Crown in terms of constitutional monarchy.

The Crown

"The power of the crown contains in itself the three moments of the whole, viz., (a) the *universality* of the constitution and the laws; (b) counsel, which refers the *particular* to the universal; and (g) the moment of ultimate decision, as the *self-determination* to which everything else reverts and from which everything else derives the beginning of its actuality". The third moment is what gives expression to the sovereignty of the state, i.e., that the various activities, agencies, functions and powers of the state are not self-subsistent but rather have their basis ultimately in the unity of the state as a single self or self-organized organic whole. The monarch is the bearer of the individuality of the state and its sovereignty is the ideality in unity in which the particular functions and powers of the state subsist. "It is only as a person, the monarch, that the personality of the state is actual. Personality expresses the concept as such; but the person enshrines the actuality of the concept, and only when the concept is determined as a person is it the Idea or truth".

The monarch is not a despot but rather a constitutional monarch, and he does not act in a capricious manner but is bound by a decision-making process, in particular to the recommendations and decisions of his cabinet (supreme advisory council). The monarch functions solely to give agency to the state, and so his personal traits are irrelevant and his ascending to the throne is based on hereditary succession, and thus on the accident of birth. "In a completely organized state, it is only a question of the culminating point of formal decision ... he has only to say 'yes' and dot the 'i' .... In a well organized monarchy, the objective aspect belongs to law alone, and the monarch's part is merely to set to the law the subjective 'I will'". The "majesty of the monarch" lies in the free asserting of 'I will' as an expression of the unity of the state and the final step in establishing law.

The Executive

The executive has the task of executing and applying the decisions formally made by the monarch. "This task of merely subsuming the particular under the universal is comprised in the executive power, which also includes the powers of the judiciary and the police". Also, the executive is the higher authority that oversees the filling of positions of responsibilities in corporations. The executive is comprised of the civil servants proper and the higher advisory officials organized into committees, both of which are connected to the monarch through their supreme departmental heads. Overall, government has its division of labor into various centers of administration managed by special officials. Individuals are appointed to executive functions on the basis of their knowledgibility and proof of ability and tenure is conditional on the fulfillment of duties, with the offices in the civil service being open to all citizens.

The executive is not an unchecked bureaucratic authority. "The security of the state and its subjects against the misuse of power by ministers and their officials lies directly in their hierarchical organization and their answerability; but it lies too in the authority given to societies and corporations ...". However, civil servants will tend to be dispassionate, upright, and polite in part as "a result of direct education in thought and ethical conduct". Civil servants and the members of the executive make up the largest section of the middle class, the class with a highly developed intelligence and consciousness of right. Moreover, "The sovereign working on the middle class at the top, and Corporation-rights working on it at the bottom, are the institutions which effectively prevent it from acquiring the isolated position of an aristocracy and using its education and skill as a means to an arbitrary tyranny".

The Legislature

For Hegel, "The legislature is concerned (a) with the laws as such in so far as they require fresh and extended determination; and (b) with the content of home affairs affecting the entire state".

Legislative activity focuses on both providing well-being and happiness for citizens as well as exacting services from them (largely in the form of monetary taxes). The proper function of legislation is distinguished from the function of administration and state regulation in that the content of the former are determinate laws that are wholly universal whereas in administration it is application of the law to particulars, along with enforcing the law. Hegel also says that the other two moments of the political constitution, the monarchy and the executive, are the first two moments of the legislature, i.e., are reflected in the legislature respectively through the ultimate decision regarding proposed laws and an advising function in their formation.

Hegel rejects the idea of independence or separation of powers for the sake of checks and balances, which he holds destroys the unity of the state. The third moment in the legislature is the estates (*Stände*), which are the classes of society given political recognition in the legislature.

In the legislature, the estates "have the function of bringing public affairs into existence not only implicitly, but also actually, i.e., of bringing into existence the moment of subjective formal freedom, the public consciousness as an empirical universal, of which the thoughts and opinions of the Many are particulars". Not only do the estates guarantee the general welfare and public freedom, but they are also the means by which the state as a whole enters the subjective consciousness of the people through their participation in the state. Thus, the estates incorporate the private judgment and will of individuals in civil society and give it political significance.

The estates have an important integrating function in the state overall. "Regarded as a mediating organ, the Estates stand between the government in general on the one hand, and the nation broken up into particulars (people and associations) on the other. ... [I]n common with the organized executive, they are a middle term preventing both the extreme isolation of the power of the crown ... and also the isolation of the particular interests of persons, societies and Corporations". Also, the organizing function of the estates prevents groups in society from becoming formless masses that could form anti-government feelings and rise up in blocs in opposition to the state.

The three classes of civil society, the agricultural, the business, and the universal class of civil servants, are each given political voice in the Estates Assembly in accordance with their distinctiveness in the lower spheres of civil life. The legislature is divided into two houses, an upper and lower. The upper house comprises the agricultural estate (including the peasant farmers and landed aristocracy), a class "whose ethical life is natural, whose basis is family life, and, so far as its livelihood is concerned, the possession of land. Its particular members attain their position by birth, just as the monarch does, and, in common with him, they possess a will which rests on itself alone". Landed gentry inherit their estates and so owe their position to birth (primogeniture) and thus are free from the exigencies and uncertainties of the life of business and state interference. The relative independence of this class makes it particularly suited for public office as well as a mediating element between the crown and civil society.

The second section of the estates, the business class, comprises the "fluctuating and changeable element in civil society" which can enter politics only through its deputies or representatives (unlike the agricultural estate from which members can present themselves to the Estates Assembly in person). The appointment of deputies is "made by society as a society" both because of the multiplicity of members but also because representation must reflect the organization of civil society into associations, communities, and corporations. It is only as a member of such groups that an individual is a member of the state, and hence rational representation implies that consent to legislation is to be given not directly by all but only by "plenipotentiaries" who are chosen on the basis of their understanding of public affairs as well as managerial and political acumen, character, insight, etc. Moreover, their charge is to further the general interest of society and not the interest of a particular association or corporation instead.

The deputies of civil society are selected by the various corporations, not on the basis of universal direct suffrage which Hegel believed inevitably leads to electoral indifference, and they adopt the point of view of society. "Deputies are sometimes regarded as 'representatives'; but they are representatives in an organic, rational sense only if they are representatives not of individuals or a conglomeration of them, but of one of the essential spheres of society and its large-scale interests. Hence, representation cannot now be taken to mean simply the substitution of one man for another; the point is that the interest itself is actually present in its representative, while he himself is there to represent the objective element of his own being".

The debates that take place in the Estates Assembly are to be open to the public, whereby citizens can become politically educated both about national affairs and the true character of their own interests. "The formal subjective freedom of individuals consists in their having and expressing their own private judgements, opinions, and recommendations as affairs of state. This freedom is collectively manifested as what is called 'public opinion', in which what is absolutely universal, the substantive and the true, is linked with its opposite, the purely particular and private opinions of the Many".

Public opinion is a "standing self-contradiction" because, on the one hand, it gives expression to genuine needs and proper tendencies of common life along with common sense views about important matters and, on the other, is infected with accidental opinion, ignorance, and faulty judgment. "Public opinion therefore deserves to be as much respected as despised — despised for its concrete expression and for the concrete consciousness it expresses, respected for its essential basis, a basis which only glimmers more or less dimly in that concrete expression". Moreover, while there is freedom of public communication, freedom of the press is not totally unrestricted as freedom does not mean absence of all restriction, either in word or deed.

Hegel calls the class of civil servants the "universal class" not only because as members of the executive their function is to "subsume the particular under the universal" in the administration of law, but also because they reflect a disposition of mind (due perhaps largely from their education) that transcends concerns with selfish ends in the devotion to the discharge of public functions and to the public universal good. As one of the classes of the estates, civil servants also participate in the legislature as an "unofficial class," which seems to mean that as members of the executive they will attend legislative assemblies in an advisory capacity, but this is not entirely clear from Hegel's text. Also, given that the monarch and the classes of civil society when conceived in abstraction are opposed to each other as "the one and the many," they must become "fused into a unity" or mediated together through the civil servant class. From the point of view of the crown the executive is such a middle term, because it carries out the final decisions of the crown and makes it "particularized" in civil society. On the other hand, in order for the classes of civil society to actually sense this unity with the crown a mediation must occur from the other direction, so to speak, where the upper house of the estates, in virtue of certain likenesses to the Crown (e.g., role of birth for one's position) is able to mediate between the Crown and civil society as a whole.

Sovereignty vis-à-vis foreign States

The interpenetration of the universal with the particular will through a complex system of social and political mediations is what produces the self-consciousness of the nation-state considered as an organic (internally differentiated and interrelated) totality or concrete individual. In this system, particular individuals consciously pursue the universal ends of the State, not out of external or mechanical conformity to law, but in the free development of personal individuality and the expression of the unique subjectivity of each. However, individuality is not something possessed by particular persons alone, or even primarily by such persons. The state as a whole, i.e., the nation-state as distinct from the political state as one of its moments, constitutes a higher form of individuality. In principle, Mind or Spirit possesses a singleness in its "negative self-relation," i.e., in the sense that unity in a being is a function of setting itself off from other beings.

"Individuality is awareness of one's existence as a unit in sharp distinction from others. It manifests itself here in the state as a relation to other states, each of which is autonomous vis-à-vis the others. This autonomy embodies mind's actual awareness of itself as a unit and hence it is the most fundamental freedom which a people possesses as well as its highest dignity". For any being to have self-conscious independence requires distinguishing the self from any of its contingent characteristics (inner self-negation), which externally is a distinction from another being. This consciousness of what one is not is for the nation-state its negative relation to itself embodied externally in the world as the relation of one state to another. However, this is not a mere externality, "But in fact this negative relation is that moment in the state which is most supremely its own, the state's actual infinity as the ideality of everything finite within it".

According to Hegel, war is an "ethical moment" in the life of a nation-state and hence is neither purely accidental nor an inherent evil. Because there is no higher earthly power ruling over nation-states, and because these entities are oriented to preserving their existence and sovereignty, conflicts leading to war are inevitable. Also, defense of one's nation is an ethical duty and the ultimate test of one's patriotism is war. "Sacrifice on behalf of the individuality of the state is the substantial tie between the state and all its members and so is a universal duty". In making a sacrifice for the sake of the state individuals prove their courage, which involves a transcendence of concern with egoistic interests and mere material existence. "The intrinsic worth of courage as a disposition of mind is to be found in the genuine absolute, final end, the sovereignty of the state. The work of courage is to actualize this final end, and the means to this end is the sacrifice of personal actuality". Moreover, war, along with catastrophy, disease, etc, highlights the finitude, insecurity, and ultimate transitoriness of human existence and puts the health of a state to a test. Hegel does not consider the ideal of "perpetual peace," as advocated by Kant, a realistic goal towards which humanity can strive. Not only is the sovereignty of each state imprescriptible, but any alliance or league of states will be established in opposition to others.

International Law

"International law springs from the relations between autonomous states. It is for this reason that what is absolute in it retains the form of an ought-to-be, since its actuality depends on different wills each of which is sovereign".

States are not private persons in civil society who pursue their self-interest in the context of universal interdependence but rather are completely autonomous entities with no relations of private right or morality. However, since a state cannot escape having relations with other states, there must be at least some sort of recognition of each by the other. International law prescribes that treaties between states ought to be kept, but this universal proviso remains abstract because the sovereignty of a state is its guiding principle, hence states are to that extent in a state of nature in relation to each other (in the Hobbesian sense of there being natural rights to one's survival with no natural duties to others). "Their rights are actualized only in their particular wills and not in a universal will with constitutional powers over them. This universal proviso of international law therefore does not go beyond an ought-to-be, and what really happens is that international relations in accordance with treaty alternate with the severance of these relations". Obviously, if states come to disagree about the nature of their treaties, etc., and there is no acceptable compromise for each party, then matters will ultimately be settled by war.

States recognize their own welfare as the highest law governing their relations to one another, however, the claim by a state to recognition of this welfare is quite different from claims to welfare by individual person in civil society. "The ethical substance, the state, has its determinate being, i.e., its right, directly embodied in something existent … and the principle of its conduct and behavior can only be this concrete existent and not one of many universal thoughts supposed to be moral commands". States recognize each other as states, and even in war there is awareness of the possibility that peace can be restored and that therefore war ought to come to an end, as well as understandings about the proper limitations on the waging of war. However, at most this translates into the *jus gentium*, the law of nations understood as customary relationships, which remains a "maelstrom of external contingency." The principles of the mind or spirit (*Volksgeist*) of a nation-state are wholly restricted because its particularity is already that of realized individuality, possessing objective actuality and self-consciousness. Hence, the reciprocal relations of states to one another partake of a "dialectic of finitude" out of which arises the universal mind, "the mind of the world, free from all restriction, producing itself as that which exercises its right– and its right is the highest right of all–over these finite minds in the 'history of the world which is the world's court of judgment'".

World History

To say that history is the world's court of judgment is to say that over and above the nation-states, or national "spirits," there is the mind or Spirit of the world (*Weltgeist*) which pronounces its verdict through the development of history itself. The verdicts of world history, however, are not expressions of mere might, which in itself is abstract and non-rational. Rather than blind destiny, "world history is the necessary development, out of the concepts of mind's freedom alone, of the moments of reason and so of the self-consciousness and freedom of mind". The history of Spirit is the development through time of its own self-consciousness through the actions of peoples, states, and world historical actors who, while absorbed in their own interests, are nonetheless the unconscious instruments of the work of Spirit. "All actions, including world-historical actions, culminate with individuals as subjects giving actuality to the substantial. They are the living instruments of what is in substance the deed of the world mind and they are therefore directly at one with that deed though it is concealed from them and is not their aim and object". The actions of great men are produced through their subjective willing and their passion, but the substance of these deeds is actually the accomplishment not of the individual agent but of the World Spirit (e.g., the founding of states by world-historical heroes).

Hegel says that in the history of the world we can distinguish several important formations of the self-consciousness of Spirit in the course of its free self-development, each corresponding to a significant principle. More specifically, there are four world-historical epochs, each manifesting a principle of Spirit as expressed through a dominant culture. In the Philosophy of Right, Hegel discusses these in a very abbreviated way in paragraphs 253-260, which brings this work to an end. Here we will draw from the more elaborated treatment in the appendix to the introduction to Hegel's lectures on the Philosophy of World History.

The Oriental Realm (mind in its immediate substance)

Here Spirit exists in its substantiality (objectivity) without inward differentiation. Individuals have no self-consciousness of personality or of rights–they are still immersed in external nature (and their divinities are naturalistic as well). Hegel characterizes this stage as one of consciousness in its immediacy, where subjectivity and substantiality are unmediated. In his Philosophy of History Hegel discusses China, India, and Persia specifically and suggests that these cultures do not actually have a history but rather are subject to natural cyclical processes. The typical governments of these cultures are theocratic and more particularly despotism, aristocracy, and monarchy respectively. Persia and Egypt are seen as transitional from these "unhistorical" and "non-political" states. Hegel calls this period the "childhood" of Spirit.

The Greek Realm (mind in the simple unity of subjective and objective)

In this realm, we have the mixing of subjective freedom and substantiality in the ethical life of the Greek *polis*, because the ancient

Greek city-states give expression to personal individuality for those who are free and have status. However, the relation of individual to the state is not self-conscious but is unreflective and based on obedience to custom and tradition. Hence, the immediate union of subjectivity with the substantial mind is unstable and leads to fragmentation. This is the period of the "adolescence" of Spirit.

The Roman Realm (mind in its abstract universality)

At this stage, individual personality is recognized in formal rights, thus including a level of reflection absent in the Greek realm of "beautiful freedom."

Here freedom is difficult because the universal subjugates individuals, i.e., the state becomes an abstraction over above its citizens who must be sacrificed to the severe demands of a state in which individuals form a homogeneous mass. A tension between the two principles of individuality and universality ensues, manifesting itself in the formation of political despotism and insurgency against it. This realm gives expression to the "manhood" of Spirit.

The Germanic Realm (reconciled unity of subjective and objective mind)

This realm comprises along with Germany and the Nordic peoples the major European nations (France, Italy, Spain) along with England. The principle of subjective freedom comes to the fore in such a way as to be made explicit in the life of Spirit and also mediated with substantiality.

This involves a gradual development that begins with the rise of Christianity and its spiritual reconciliation of inner and outer life and culminates in the appearance of the modern nation-state, the rational Idea of which is articulated in the Philosophy of Right. (Along the way there are several milestones Hegel discusses in his Philosophy of History that are especially important in the developing of the self-consciousness of freedom, in particular the Reformation, the Enlightenment, and the French Revolution.) One of the significant features of the modern world is the overcoming of the antithesis of church and state that developed in the Medieval period. This final stage of Spirit is mature "old age."

In sum, for Hegel the modern nation-state can be said to manifest a "personality" and a self-consciousness of its inherent nature and goals, indeed a self-awareness of everything which is implicit in its concept, and is able to act rationally and in accordance with its self-awareness.

The modern nation-state is a "spiritual individual," the true historical individual, precisely because of the level of realization of self-consciousness that it actualizes. The development of the perfected nation-state is the end or goal of history because it provides an optimal level of realization of self-consciousness, a more comprehensive level of realization of freedom than mere natural individuals, or other forms of human organization, can produce.

CLOSING REMARKS

In closing this account of Hegel's theory of the state, a few words on a "theory and practice" problem of the modern state. In the preface to the Philosophy of Right Hegel is quite clear that his science of the state articulates the nature of the state, not as it ought to be, but as it really is, as something inherently rational.

Hegel's famous quote in this regard is "What is rational is actual and what is actual is rational," where by the 'actual' (*Wirklich*) Hegel means not the merely existent, i.e., a state that can be simply identified empirically, but the actualized or realized state, i.e., one that corresponds to its rational concept and thus in some sense must be perfected. Later in the introduction of the Idea of the state in paragraph 258, Hegel is at pains to distinguish the Idea of the state from a state understood in terms of its historical origins and says that while the state is the way of God in the world we must not focus on particular states or on particular institutions of the state, but only on the Idea itself.

Furthermore he says, "The state is no ideal work of art; it stands on earth and so in the sphere of caprice, chance, and error, and bad behavior may disfigure it in many respects. But the ugliest of men, or a criminal, or an invalid, or a cripple, is still always a living man.

The affirmative, life, subsists despite his defects, and it is this affirmative factor which is our theme here". The issue, then, is whether the actual state — the subject of philosophical science — is only a theoretical possibility and whether from a practical point of view all existing states are in some way disfigured or deficient. Our ability to rationally distill from existing states their ideal characteristics does not entail that a fully actualized state does, or will, exist. Hence, there is perhaps some ambiguity in Hegel's claim about the modern state as an actualization of freedom.

3

Decolonizing Political Theory

This article discusses a political theory course design, "Humanity" and the Atlantic Slave Trade", that contextualizes political theory within its colonial presumptions about race, humanity and the good political community. I argue that political theory needs to be "raced", that is, unpacked and contextualized in ways which make visible the racialized interests present within concepts of the "good life" or "good community", concepts that are reflective and productive of "whiteness". Such an approach highlights the subjectivity of political theory and potentially demonstrates the ways that subjectivity is central to situating political theory in its moral and intellectual context. In tandem with feminist critiques and multicultural approaches that might include authors as critics of Enlightenment ideals or which expand the actors involved in the making of political theory, the approach I suggest considers what we already know (the canon) in relation to things we do not normally consider; that is, the race of political theory.

The Problem with Political Theory

This article discusses a pedagogical approach and course design that aims to contextualize political theory, and in particular, liberalism, within its colonial presumptions about race, humanity and the good political community. As it is, the study of political theory in English-speaking universities is almost entirely confined to the Euro-American intellectual tradition, one that has not incorporated a colonial reading of political theory in significant ways. The field of political theory privileges the Occidental development of concepts such as democracy, rights, individualism, freedom and humanity and the authors from the trajectory that runs between Plato and Rawls. There is some sense to this focus given that the idea of political theory itself is derived through European philosophical preoccupations and is the prevailing set of ideas that shapes our sensibilities about politics in Western locations. However, the problem arises when concepts of political theory are presented as objective and universal, or as Donna Haraway (1991) states, as simultaneously "views from nowhere" and "views from everywhere".1 Absent of social location, historical and cultural specificity, Eurocentric political theory is presented through the turn of what Haraway (1991) calls the "god-trick", the omnipotent view of enlightened agents in a world of primitive and backwards preoccupations. As such, our comprehension of the extent to which colonial preoccupations infuse the concepts we grapple with today is limited.

In response to the omissions and exclusions of western political theory, political theory scholars and critics have aimed to expand the field. Perhaps some of the most thorough critiques have been made from feminist perspectives that argue that the masculinist biases of political theory exclude the experiences of women. In excluding their experiences, feminists argue that in practice, women are denied access to the freedoms and equalities that are granted to men.2< Several implications derive from these critiques. One is that political theory is forced to reconcile its claims about universality and objectivity by either including the experiences of women or offering caveats to the omissions of political theory, thus limiting claims to universality and objectivity. Another implication is that because the omissions and exclusions of political theory are systemic and integral in many cases, political theorists are compelled to note that the field depends upon certain exclusions to make claims about the conditions of belonging to political communities. This has been an exceedingly valuable insight of feminist critiques in that it becomes possible to interrogate further exclusions of political theory and to arrive at critiques which are "intersectional" (Crenshaw 1991), not only noting the sexism but also the classism, racism and other prejudices embedded in such concepts as "freedom", "progress" or "autonomy". This is, most often, toward reconceptualizing cherished ideas so that they might become more inclusive and thereby more democratic. There are great explanatory potentials that have been productively mined from the openings made by feminist critiques, and many of the foundational concepts of the course discussed here draw on these ideas.3

There are other movements to revise and recast the field of political theory. For instance, relatively new fields of comparative political thought adopt global perspectives about both the history of political ideas and contemporary political philosophy. Within this, we see trends to develop areas called "non-western political thought", which aim to account for the ideas and questions of traditions other than European and American liberalism. Comparative or non-western political theory might include studies of Confucianism, Buddhism, Afrocentricism, Islam or Hinduism, or the generalized category of "Asian values", which appears not only under the category of political thought but also in the study of international relations. Further, there are a number of US Political Science programs that offer courses on African American Political Thought, or Comparative Global Political Thought, including ones at CUNY and Princeton. A recent job posting for a political theorist at University of California Riverside asks for an expert in Comparative Political Thought to potentially teach Confucius in relation to Plato, Gandhi compared with Thoreau or Oakeshott compared with Maruyama. There are well-considered and thoughtful reasons for stretching traditionally Eurocentric fields of study in these ways, and there are also pitfalls to be negotiated while doing so. For instance, Arif Dirlik (1997), notes the problematic ways that concepts such as "Asian values" and other claims about non-western knowledge are approached, suggesting that including non-western theory in curricula has to be accompanied by revised epistemologies, if the aim is field transformation.

These areas of study appear on curricula as "alternative" or "multicultural" political theory, and along with feminist, Marxist and other critiques of liberalism, are meant to address the omissions of western political theory. They also intend, in part, to make the concepts of political theory more inclusive of and relevant to the experiences of previously marginalized populations. These developments suggest that political theory as a discipline is expanding and that any claim of universality is necessarily deferred until the strategic omissions of political theory are addressed.

These are welcome developments in political theory and serve important purposes of democratizing the idea of political theory and expanding our concepts of what it means to be human, what it means to live in communities and what we mean by "the good life". However, there are some institutional limitations to the kinds of disciplinary transformations we might anticipate with the inclusion of feminist, multicultural or global approaches to political theory teaching. That is, including alternative approaches does not necessarily disrupt canonical curricula. Feminist, non-western or global political thought is often presented as alternative or additional to the core of political theory, meant to add on the concerns of the marginalized perhaps, or to bring new perspectives on core ideas. This is problematic because conventional authors and concepts are left as the canon, undisturbed in many ways, and all non-canonical theory occupies a secondary place in the imaginations of both students and instructors. This is especially the case in those instances where the majority of political theory teaching is not engaged in feminist or decolonizing pedagogical practices. In these instances, there may only be one or two courses in a program that provide feminist and anti-colonial perspectives on the subject of political theory.

The question arises: how might we teach political theory in ways that are attentive to core concepts and authors while also expanding the relevance of political theory to understanding the larger social and political world from whence it came? Further, how might those who wish to teach political theory 'against the grain' make productive interventions with limited opportunities to do so and limited intellectual support from the institutions and departments? One way to approach the problem is to teach the 'race' of political theory, that is, to unpack and contextualize theory in ways which make visible the racialized interests present within concepts of the "good life" or "good community", concepts reflective and productive of "whiteness". Such an approach highlights the subjectivity of political theory and potentially demonstrates the ways that subjectivity is central to situating political theory in its moral and intellectual context.

That is, political theory reflects the embodied subjectivity of the authors and constructs the subjectivities of the Euro-American subject in tandem with the production of racialized and/or colonized subjectivities, all within the European imagination of a hierarchy of humanity. In concert with multicultural approaches that might include authors as critics of Enlightenment ideals or which expand the actors involved in the making of political theory, the approach I suggest considers what we already know (the canon) in relation to things we do not normally consider; that is, the race of political theory. The production of whiteness, ultimately, is inseparable from the production of a notion of humanity and its related concepts of freedom, autonomy, equality, progress, rationality and individuality. This approach offers students ways to critically analyze claims to objectivity and universality, the power of making such claims and overall, recasts political theory and in particular, liberalism, in a context that offers them tools to continuously raise questions of material they might encounter in other venues.

Why teach the canon?

Some might argue that if traditional knowledges are so infused with exclusions and biases and prejudices, perhaps we are better to stop studying "dead white men" and replace them with more progressive thinkers. At the same time, however, there are sound arguments to support the continued teaching of traditional canons. One reason is that political theory exists as the central core of political thinking in Western traditions. Individual instructors, students or even programs might choose to not engage the field in all of its traditions, yet for the most part, the traditional field remains definitional of what counts as political theory.

Another reason to teach the traditional core of political theory is that students ought to comprehend the ideas that shape their subjectivities and political locations to understand their sense worlds through relevant explanatory language. It is also the case that without comprehending the ideas that shape us in our political locations, we are without the necessary language to challenge and disrupt the continued institutionalization of traditional concepts and ideals.

For instance, it can be argued that the production of "whiteness" is inseparable from the production of a notion of humanity and related concepts of democracy, freedom, autonomy, rationality and individuality. Without a foundation in core political theory authors and concepts, it would be quite impossible to understand the ways that racial identity matters. Further, the racialized hierarchies of political theory have ideological and material effects in determining the lines between those who are excluded (from humanity) and those who are included and/or representative of humanity. Thus, the debate is not only academic but resonates throughout political communities that adhere to liberalism's central concepts. Edward Said argues similar points in relation to Orientalist literature and the production of the Oriental subject:

...there is no avoiding the fact that even if we disregard the Orientalist distinctions between "them" and "us", a powerful series of political and ultimately ideological realities inform scholarship today. No one can escape dealing with, if not the East/West division, then the North/South one, the have/have not one, the imperialist/ anti-imperialist one, the white/coloured one. We cannot get around them all by pretending they do not exist; on the contrary, contemporary Orientalism teaches us a great deal about the intellectual dishonesty of dissembling on that score, the result of which is to intensify the divisions and make them both vicious and permanent (Said, 1979, pg 327).

Further, when considering the roots of intellectual developments such as feminism or critical race studies, they are located within hegemonic traditions of knowledge, situated both as oppositional to and simultaneously drawing from hegemonic traditions for their points of opposition. Critiques of knowledge that are not familiar with traditional disciplines would be too abstract and removed from the object of criticism. Further, their claims would likely be utopic and fantasy-based, as though prevailing knowledges did not wield power or establish parameters of legitimacy or authorize some to speak and others to be silent. Most oppositional knowledges – feminism, critical race theory, class analysis and others – derive their basic sets of concepts from dominant disciplines and frameworks, including very often the methodological and epistemological frameworks of prevailing knowledge. For these reasons, it is crucial that alternative knowledge or critical analysis are developed from knowing very well what is, to develop new ways of thinking what ought to be. As such, having students understand the concept of humanity as it figures in political theory is one part of the puzzle to understanding the ways that political theory is raced, toward decolonizing the political theory classroom altogether.

CONTEMPORARY THEMES IN POLITICAL THEORY: "HUMANITY" AND THE ATLANTIC SLAVE TRADE

As a temporary lecturer in the Department of Political Science, University of Victoria, Canada, I was offered the opportunity to teach a senior "contemporary themes in political theory" seminar. Since I had been teaching courses on colonial and postcolonial theory in global politics to fairly receptive students, it was an ideal opportunity to develop a course that placed political theory in its racial and colonial context. Further, because it was a senior seminar, students had enough preparation to be able to consider the field they already knew and to interrogate the 'race' of the field. This was the first course in the department to approach political theory from a 'decolonizing' perspective and the only course at the time to do so. As such, I designed the course to take advantage of the location and the population, which I discuss later in the paper. I was also aware that as a singular opportunity to offer this material, it would be most effective if connected with the material students were learning in other classes. The class had about fifteen senior political theory students, many of whom were familiar with my classroom approach and political commitments. The course put Enlightenment authors such as Friedrich Hegel, Immanuel Kant, Johann Blumenbach, and later thinkers like John Stuart Mill, in conversation with slave narratives from Olaudah Equiano and Frederick Douglass, anti-colonial texts by Frantz Fanon and C.L.R. James, Toni Morrison's literary representation of Margaret Garner in *Beloved,* and claims from both historical and contemporary reparations (for slavery) movements. "Humanity" is the key concept of the course, and throughout the material was the question of how subjectivity, a central presumption of what it means to be human, was denied to the colonized and the enslaved by dominant knowledges. At the same time, we noted that those who were colonized and enslaved were continuously possessed with and expressive of self-knowledge and selfhood. The course material showed that contrary to common assumptions, the enslaved and the colonized were active resistors who could and did speak and write on their own behalf.

A key question that frames the course is: under what conditions could philosophers formulate ideas about universality, liberty, equality and justice while in the same moment justifying the enslavement of Africans? Since the concept of "humanity" is at the center of contemporary reparations debates about the Atlantic Slave Trade, that is, groups seek to have the Atlantic Slave Trade declared a "crime against humanity", another question is: how is it that populations can be restored to a sense of humanity after suffering inhumane violence when at the inception of a notion of humanity, Africans were deliberately excluded?4 Further, if the Western notion of humanity is formulated with deliberate exclusions, what does that say about our membership or the means to formulating a more inclusive notion of membership? Finally, in terms of pedagogy, the guiding inquiry was: what might students gain in their understanding of political theory as a result of racing political theory and decolonizing the classroom?

The next section discusses the context and demographics of the University of Victoria, British Columbia Canada, where the course was taught in the Department of Political Science. The following sections discuss the theoretical frameworks of the course, several of the course texts and the rationale for their use. The article concludes with some reflections on the value of an embodied pedagogy as a means of decolonising the classroom.

TEACHING ABOUT RACE ON AN ISLAND IN MULTICULTURAL CANADA

Canadian nationalism is infused with many commitments, as all nationalisms are, thus making the topic quite complicated to engage in this short space. However, there are three prongs of Canadian nationalism that are relevant to a discussion of decolonizing knowledge. The first prong that is encountered is the enduring core commitment to be distinct and unique from Americans. The task for a "middle power" to carve out a unique identity and global presence when so proximate to the imperial US is an enormous one, and one that consumes much of Canadian cultural and political debates.

The second and related prong of Canadian nationalism is "official multiculturalism", instituted during the government of Prime Minister Pierre Elliot Trudeau in the late 1970s. Complex and multiple ideological functions were imagined for the new policies, all toward specific nation-building impulses. In some aspects, official multiculturalism was designed to quell Quebec separatist and "distinct society" desires through promoting the idea of Canada as an inclusive yet difference-respecting nation that promises unity without homogenization. In other aspects, it was a plan to help lubricate local populations already accustomed to Euro-derived immigration to accept increasing numbers of non-European immigrants in the workforce. This came as European immigration declined while Canadian economic projections demanded continued high levels of immigrant labour. Further, multiculturalism policies promote Canada as an inclusive, tolerant and thereby sophisticated nation primed for participation in the global marketplace. Finally, official multiculturalism suggests that because Canada is inclusive, tolerant and capable of 'unity through diversity', racism and related bigotries are minimized.5

The third aspect of Canadian nationalism at stake is the fact that Canada is not an imperial nation. This means that the state has more investments in peacekeeping versions of militarism, humanitarian missions, development projects, and the promotion of human rights than it does in high-stakes militarism. Canadian nationalism, then, revolves around the self-image of being peaceful, cooperative and rights-respecting in conjunction with the idea of multicultural maturity. 6

Further complications and opportunities derive from the small West Coast city of Victoria that is on Vancouver Island, a two-hour ferry ride from the Canadian mainland as well as the US mainland. Victoria was founded by British settlers who felt that Britain was losing its charm by the presence of too many people from the colonies, including British colonists returning from outposts, indentured labourers and freed persons after the slave trade. The fantasy of Victoria was to be more British than Britain had ever been, "a little piece of England", and the founding ideas resonate to mark Victoria as a safe haven for whiteness. 7

Victoria began as a place of escape and it continues to be that as people move to the area to escape the hardships of other cities, including harsh winters and large migrant/racialized populations. Further, even though there are and have been many racialized people in the area, from indigenous peoples to waves of non-European immigrants from India, China and Japan, there is a way that their presence is effectively disappeared by the hegemony of British fantasy culture. Not surprisingly then, the student population at the University of Victoria, a small research and teaching institution with a student population of about 16,000 students, is disproportionately white, fairly affluent and relatively parochial. The Department of Political Science has a reputation for its commitment to teaching social, cultural and political theory, and for the most part, a relatively progressive view of domestic and global politics.8

The first problem of teaching about race in Canada is the problem of moving students past the mental barrier to thinking that racism is something the US invented and perfected and thus, not something endemic to Canadian life. The nationalist effort to distance Canadians from the US means that to talk about race, we are compelled to first bring to consciousness students' own nationalist subjectivities and investments in Canadian mythology and Eurocentric concepts. Following from this, the task is to unravel the ideologies that mystify the very real relations of power, racial hierarchies and related bigotries that infuse Canadian society. Certainly, there are profound differences between the US and Canada in terms of political culture. However, as in any 'white settler' state, race matters a great deal to the organization of belonging and community in Canada, beginning with the displacement of Aboriginal peoples and extending those violent exclusions to all "non-white" peoples over the history of the nation (Dua, 1999). Sherene Razack describes the way that the mythology of the origins of Canada mystifies relations of racialized power, exactly the mythologies that have to be disrupted for students to understand their own racialized subjectivities:

When we think of mythology, or stories that are told about a nation's origins and history, we first need to consider the cast of characters in the story. A snowy, Northern land that is empty has few Aboriginal peoples. We can easily see the characters that make the story come to life: the first fur traders, explorers, and so on. In fact, the first Europeans. Europeans who are at home in snow and wilderness are nearly always men. If we see anybody at all in this snowy landscape it would have to be an intrepid man paddling a canoe, surrounded by decaying totem poles (Emily Carr), big trees and magnificent lakes (the entire group of Seven), or wide expanses of snow (Lauren Harris) ...The original inhabitants, a Nordic race able to vanquish the cold, have the first claim on the land. When the Others come, they pollute the pristine landscape; they flood it and make it "foreign." This story is the one we see repeated over and over again in racist immigration laws, in the courts when the claims for justice of Aboriginal peoples and people of colour are considered. It effectively shuts them out of the national story, and thus out of any claims for equal citizenship (Razack, "In Conversation").

Given the national and local context, there is much classroom work to be done to first bring to consciousness the ways that race, nation and culture shape perspectives and knowledge, and to then show how it is that the unique situation of the University of Victoria in the country of Canada creates particular kinds of subjectivities as well. Victoria is an excellent place to highlight the European and imperial influences that impact Canadians because of the city's history and culture. The traces are not too difficult to find. Thus, the national and municipal locales serve as very useful pedagogical supplements to the course material itself.

POLITICAL THEORY AS COLONIAL KNOWLEDGE

Colonial knowledge refers to the philosophical thought that accompanied the period of modern European colonialism and the European experience of colonial administration, imperial rivalries and nation-building, abroad and at home. Most of liberalism, modernist philosophy and Enlightenment thought were developed in tandem with the European experience of modern European colonialism. As such, much of the preoccupation of European philosophers of the time was with determining what it was that constituted " Europe" and the "European", particularly in relationship with non-Europeans. Edward Said's key point in *Orientalism* — that knowledge of the superiority of a European Self was derived through the construction of a lesser non-European Other — highlights the relationship between Self and Other that resonates throughout European philosophy (Said, 1979).

In the framework of colonial knowledge, when Man is invoked as the highest achievement of human life, Man refers to European Man. Further, European Man is propertied, heterosexual, of appropriate lineage, well mannered and in control of his emotions and passions. In this way, "whiteness" is defined. Not merely descriptive of skin colour, the concept of "whiteness" captures an overall sensibility about moderation, self-control and reason that makes the bearer of the sensibility "white". Part of the liberal argument suggests that it is a struggle for humans to achieve whiteness, that is, for humans to achieve mastery of reason over emotion, and thus, it is a lifelong project to keep aspiring to liberal moderation and control. We see this kind of argument in John Stuart Mill's (1859) discussion of utilitarianism and the good society. A good society is one that facilitates the possibility of citizens to evolve so that they choose "higher pleasures" which include moderation, reason and sedate endeavors, over "base" pleasures, which include excesses of all kinds and immediate bodily desires. Similarly, Sigmund Freud's (1930; 1923) divided self is a clash of superego and id as the internal rationality of the superego struggles to gain supremacy over the primal instinct-driven emotional id. The superego must continuously control the id; otherwise, it would not be possible to live in societies that approximate "civilization.

In these formulations of the good citizen, of course, women are excluded, as are non-Europeans, non-propertied peoples, working classes, non-heterosexuals, those who express their emotions publicly, those who admit or act upon their lust or desire or appetites and those whose gender, class, race and demeanor confound their ability to achieve whiteness in their public status. These are shifting designations that are reworked and re-invoked to suit different political purposes. In western philosophical traditions especially of the modern European colonial period, whiteness, inclusive of masculinity, is in part defined as the capacity to hide or control ones' emotions, desires and the more primitive impulses in favour of the exercise of reason and rationality. Several feminist authors on the subject of western knowledge and the place of the feminine (usually understood as juvenile or primitive), including Elizabeth Grosz 1993; Sandra Harding 1993; Sara Ruddick, 1995; Susan Bordo 1995; make these points. Their analyses demonstrates that certain and quite common aspects of human existence are coded as gendered, classed, and racialized. To be a Man, and thus to be fully human, is to be white.

David Theo Goldberg's book *Racist Culture: Philosophy and the Politics of Meaning* is part of the inspiration for the course. Goldberg argues that liberalism plays a foundational part in the process of normalizing racial dynamics and racist exclusions. He states that "(r)ace is one of the central conceptual inventions of modernity" (the period emerging between the 16th century and the formulation of the 'West' as a self-conscious entity) and that the invention of race is tied to the universalistic claims of Man and related concepts (Goldberg, pg. 6, 1993). His argument traces the work of canonical political theorists such as Hobbes, Locke, Rousseau, Kant, Bentham, the Mills, Von Hayek, Nozick and Rawls among others, and shows that the commitment to a core set of ideas about individualism, universality, progress, equality and human nature was accompanied by two key claims. One claim is that race is a morally irrelevant category. This is the familiar idea of neutrality that infuses liberal societies, the idea that structures and institutions and particularly the market are neutral mechanisms, and that individuals are successful through their gifts and talents and efforts to achieve.

The other simultaneous and contradictory claim these authors and others share is in their assumptions about racial hierarchies. Goldberg offers a few examples:

Kant, citing with approval David Hume's likening of learning by 'negroes' to that of parrots, insisted upon the natural stupidity of blacks. John Stuart Mill, like his father, presupposed nonwhite nations to be uncivilized and so historically incapable of self-government. Benjamin Disraeli captured the sensibility of the mid-nineteenth century by declaring the only truth to be that 'all is race'. The basic human condition – and so economic, political, scientific, and cultural positions – was taken to be race determined. By the turn of the century, Cromer and Balfour, the most important –some would say greatest – British colonial administrators, took it as a matter of course that Europeans (and the British in particular) were the master race, all others were 'subject races'. More recently we have come to witness the expression of racism by other means… (sociobiology, socioscience, genetic dispositions for crime, intelligence; or overt concerns about immigration, welfare, unemployment, work habits) (Goldberg, 1993, pg.6).

Given that the authors associated with Enlightenment and liberal ideas stated their racial ideas overtiy and since they wrote during the time of widespread slavery and colonialism, surely race matters to how they think about politics. However, philosophical commitments to universality and equality mean that liberalism regularly denies its own racist exclusions and therefore gives the appearance of being structurally neutral. This serves to individualize the lack of (market) success in social institutions that many might face, and since the highest rates of poverty in Western industrialized nations is amongst the racialized (and most often female), the appearance is that there are racial inferiorities at work rather than systemic exclusions. As Goldberg states:

The irony of modernity, the liberal paradox comes down to this: As modernity commits itself progressively to idealized principles of liberty, equality, and fraternity, as it increasingly insists upon the moral irrelevance of race, there is a multiplication of racial identities and the sets of exclusions they prompt and rationalize, enable and sustain. Race is irrelevant, but all is race. The more abstract modernity's universal identity, the more it has to be insisted upon, the more it needs to be imposed (Goldberg, 1993, pg. 6).

Racist Culture is an excellent foundation for a course that aims to 'race' political theory because of the thoroughness of Goldberg's analysis, the in-depth readings of authors familiar to political theory and the contextualizing of concepts such as equality, democracy and freedom within the landscape of racial culture. The point is made carefully and thoroughly-that political theory depends upon certain racial exclusions to be able to claim universal applicability. As such, students are encouraged to think about racial thinking in Hegel's 'master-slave' dialectic, or JS Mill's ideas about progress, or Marx's ideas about 'barbarous nations', or Kant's arguments about the physical geography of moral worth, at the same time that they gain some insight into the formulation of political theory as a discipline of study. Goldberg's text is paired with *Race and the Enlightenment: The Reader*, edited by Emmanuel Chukwudi Eze. In this text, there are a number of useful excerpts that illuminate and expand on Goldberg's analysis, including Carl von Linné on "*The God-given Order of Nature*"; David Hume, "*Negroes...naturally inferior to the whites*"; Johann Freidrich Blumenbach, "*The Degeneration of Races*", and Hegel, "*Colonialism in the Internal Logic of Capitalist Modernity*" (Eze, 1997). These texts illustrate very clearly that political theorists had strong commitments to racial distinctions as the basis of defining the nature of the European and thus, the nature of the highest form of humanity. As such, key concepts of political theory are shown to be raced.

THE SUBJECTIVITY OF THE COLONIZED

It is an easy assumption to make that because we do not read or hear the voices of the enslaved or the colonized in traditional political theory courses, that they are not capable or able to speak on their own behalf or to resist or reflect on their status. As such, material such as slave narratives and anti-colonial writings both demonstrate the active intellect and subjectivities of enslaved peoples. It also expresses the violence of being denied the claim over one's own subjectivity. Subjectivity is a crucial aspect of what political theorists understand to be human – the ability to contemplate a self with an interior existence and interpretive capacity, to know oneself as a thinking being with a sense of past and future, a sense of self as a mortal being – these are, in part, attributes that distinguish humans from animals. Alerting students to the fact of subjectivity contributes to a multifaceted decolonization process in that they are encouraged to think about their own interior selves and interpretive frameworks while contemplating the role that subjectivity plays in colonization and decolonization. Several of the course texts spoke to these claims, including Frantz Fanon's text *Black Skin, White Masks*

(1967); Toni Morrison's *Beloved* (1994), alongside some journalistic narratives about Margaret Garner, slave woman; and slave narratives such as: *Olaudah Equiano, an 11-year old Ibo from Nigeria remembers his kidnapping into slavery, the Middle Passage and arrival in the New World (West Indies) (1789); Frederick Douglass resists a slave breaker (1845) and Margaret Garner kills her daughter rather than see her returned to slavery (1876).* 10

Frantz Fanon relates in *Black Skin White Masks* the subjectivity of a man, a human, which is confronted by the failure of the French to recognize him as a man.

Black Skin, White Masks is a text that embodies the pain of being read as non-human and against the grain of his own subjectivity. The text is brutal and visceral. The basis of the problem outlined by Fanon is that he has been excised from the category of humanity and thus torn from his own humanity, by being interpellated into the social world as a black man, one who could only be known in contrast to the superior white man. He states: "For not only must the black man be black; he must be black in relation to the white man" (Fanon, 1967: 110). He asks: "What else could it be for me but an amputation, an excision, a hemorrhage that spattered my whole body with black blood?" (Fanon, 1967: 112). He concludes: "At the risk of arousing the resentment of my colored brothers, I will say that the black is not a man" (Fanon, 1967: 8).

There are a number of issues raised by Fanon's text that are useful to unpacking some political theory concepts. For instance, Fanon is describing the clash of his subjectivity with the external world and the shock and pain of knowing himself to be human and being categorized as non-human or merely Negro. He recounts the experience of being interpellated as a black man:

"Dirty nigger!" Or simply, "Look, A Negro!"

I came into the world imbued with the will to find a meaning in things, my spirit filled with the desire to attain to the source of the world, and then I found that I was an object in the midst of other objects" (Fanon, 1967: 109).

Fanon's risky statement – "the black is not a man" (Fanon, 1967: 8), is an observation of the way that humanity, defined by Europeans in their own self-image, was not inclusive of the black man, a fact that Fanon challenges throughout the text. Interesting, however, is that Fanon does not challenge the concept of humanity to expand its definition and include him. Rather, Fanon offers contrary characterizations of what it means to be human, based on aspects of human existence that are seen to be a problem for the good political community – emotions, the body and poetry. He states:

Yes, we are – we Negroes – backward, simple, free in our behaviour. That is because for us the body is not something opposed to what you call the mind. We are in the world. Besides, our men of letters helped me to convince you; your white civilization overlooks subtle riches and sensitivity. (quoting Léopold Senghor) "Listen: Emotive sensitivity. Emotion is completely Negro as reason is Greek" (Fanon,127).

Instead of claiming to be every bit as rational as Man and thus worthy of inclusion within humanity in this passage, Fanon turns the formulation on its head to suggest that it is the fact of emotions themselves that makes humans human. Fanon continues:

I made myself the poet of the world. The white man had found a poetry in which there was nothing poetic. The soul of the white man was corrupted, and, as I was told by a friend who was a teaching in the US, (Léopold Senghor) 'the presence of the Negroes beside the whites is in a way an insurance policy on humanness. When the whites feel that they have become too mechanized, they turn to the men of color and ask them for a little human sustenance.' At last I had been recognized, I was no longer a zero (Fanon, 129).

Here too, Fanon takes issue with the rationality/emotion dualism of European philosophy. Rather than demand that he be seen as a human in the tradition of European philosophy, Fanon instead suggests that there are in fact other ways of being human and that to be emotional, poetic and embodied is to be the sustenance of a human existence, qualities that are necessary even to the white man.

Fanon's formulations are useful in classroom discussions as they highlight some of the narrowness and lack of variation of our prevailing concepts of humanity. They also offer contrary explanations and perhaps open the conversation to more imaginative ways of thinking. Finally, they offer some openings for thinking about decolonization projects in political theory, and the practice of decolonizing subjectivity altogether. These are some of the outcomes of reading *Black Skin White Masks* in the context of the course.

While Fanon's text is in a passionate voice, it is also a work of theoretical and interpretive psychoanalysis and philosophy and thus, a highly intellectualized set of emotions. Other kinds of texts communicate similar emotions but leave more of them to be interpreted by the readers themselves. For this reason, the course included *Beloved* as a text that expresses the subjectivity of the colonized, specifically the subjectivity of Sethe, a slave woman who kills her infant daughter to spare her from being enslaved. Some students questioned the inclusion of *Beloved* as a core text of the course since it is literature and not political theory.

Literature, however, communicates precisely what political theory does not communicate, that is, the depth and complexity of affect and emotion, the interior consciousness of knowing and acting subjects. Many political theory concepts are relevant when reading *Beloved*, including the nature of reason and rationality, choice, freedom and most significantly, human agency.

The central character, Beloved, is the ghost of the infant that Sethe kills. She returns to be with her mother and in many literary interpretations, is the embodiment of the history of slavery that is described as haunting descendants of slaves today. In part, the story of Sethe is Toni Morrison's version of the Margaret Garner story, one that is known mainly through journalistic accounts and court transcripts (Coffin, 1876). Margaret Garner was held for trial and a large element of her defense was on the grounds of her mental stability. The argument that derived sympathy for her was that she was not in her right mind and thus, could not be held responsible for the killing of her infant. However, the court ruled that in the case of escaped slaves, the question was not one of feeling as much as it was about property. Garner was returned to slavery and eventually drowned when the slave ship she was on capsized.

The novel and narrative accounts of the trial of Margaret Garner are useful ways of raising questions of agency and choice, as well as resistance and subjectivity. For instance, if we consider that Garner/Sethe are reasonable and rational in that they are capable of calculating their interests and seeking the means to achieve them, then killing one's infant in a slavery context seems to imply sanity and a rational response to an irrational circumstance. Or, as Elliot (2000) argues, developing "black subjectivity" or a non-commodified sense of self is something that becomes possible for Sethe once she is no longer enslaved and in a communal context, hence she is able to resist surrender of her daughter to slave-holders.

Similarly, the texts offer a way to discuss Western political theory ideas of rationality and sanity and peoples' relationship to their context. Slave narratives offer similar avenues for discussing agency, choice, resistance and subjectivity in that those who are enslaved are well aware of the differences between being a slave in Africa and being a slave in Europe (Equiano,1789) or of the indignities of being treated less than the children of a household (Douglass, 1845) and of the injustice itself of being enslaved and denied subjectivity or autonomy.

In conjunction with the other texts of the course, literary and first-person accounts of the experience of being denied subjectivity and thus, being denied humanity allows students to further explore the race of political theory. Further, simply reading first-person narratives of those imagined to be unable to express themselves is a itself a decolonizing move in that it challenges the singular and authorial claims of political theory about what it means to be human.

MULTICULTURAL CLASSROOMS AND SHARED SUBJECTIVITIES

The content of political theory needs to be reconsidered to "race" political theory. It is also relevant to revise the pedagogical methods of delivering political theory to students. There are a number of trends to recognize the diversity of experience that students bring to a class and to adjust pedagogical methods to compensate.

For instance, multicultural approaches to pedagogy suggest that teaching methods have to be revised in light of the diversity of student populations. The "multicultural classroom", more often than not, is posed as a problem for educators and students alike, mainly as it poses barriers to teaching material that purports to be universally applicable and valid. The problem is usually framed as the need to reconcile differences between students while acknowledging the veracity of their differences as a means to overcoming the barriers to speaking in universal terms.

At the same time, particularly when discussing how we might teach political theory, it is fair to suggest that there is a subjectivity that is shared to some extent amongst students in Euro-derived states and at the meta-theoretical level of ideas about race, humanity, gender, sexuality, nation, freedom, democracy and autonomy.

In this regard, the pedagogical approach being suggested is one that takes as central the production of the liberal self as raced, the production of students and instructors as raced and both as the micro-embodiments of liberalism itself. In doing so, the shared subjectivities are highlighted not as expressions of universally valid concepts and ideals, but as the results of being both subjects of and subject to liberal democratic relations of power. In this way, the universality of political theory is questioned and subjectivity becomes the site of students' engagement with the material and their own ways of knowing.

The course "Humanity and the Atlantic Slave Trade" offered ways to see the investments of political theory in the creation of hierarchies, justified through the concept of humanity. Further, the course offered conceptual tools to understand the continuing relevance of these concepts as reflective of the vested interests to maintain the hierarchies derivative of colonial relationships in the contemporary world.

Rather than leave concepts as timeless, universally valid or objectively true about the human condition, the aim of the course was to show how historically situated ideas reflect structural hierarchies and political investments of their authors. While there may be several potential consequences of this approach to teaching political theory, one that is pedagogically noteworthy is that casting political theory in relation to its historical context highlighted for students that political theory emanates from material lived realities and as such, is dynamic, alive and relevant to contemporary political life.

Throughout the course, students were actively engaged, moved, disturbed and inspired, and several took seriously the task of 'decolonizing the mind' as a key element of decolonizing political theory.

As both intellectual support and opportunities are limited, offering students critical concepts, recasting non-traditional material as political theory and contextualizing the 'race' of political theory are entry points that offer students a wider set of questions and a deeper sense of the often silent racial commitments of the field

This article is written with the intent to share a pedagogical experiment that aimed to productively mine the possibilities of a particular location, drawing on what could be seen as limitations (homogenous student population, strong nationalist commitments, limited intellectual and field support, temporary lecturer status) to make use of as strengths in the classroom. It would be too ambitious to suggest that a singular attempt to decolonize the political theory classroom such as this should change the lives of students or the trajectory of deeply entrenched intellectual disciplines, and too limiting to suggest that these are the only ways to evaluate the worth of a course. The process of rethinking the field and creatively recasting key concepts has intrinsic value, and there is value in the attempt when and where those of us with a pedagogical commitment to decolonizing political theory find opportunities.

For me, designing, teaching and reflecting on this course has deepened and strengthened my commitment and strategies for communicating the 'race' of political theory in subsequent teaching and scholarship. The effects of introducing such questions to a field of study are yet to be known; the process however, is deeply rewarding.

4

Kant's Social and Political Philosophy

Kant wrote his social and political philosophy in order to champion the Enlightenment in general and the idea of freedom in particular. His work came within both the natural law and the social contract traditions. Kant held that every rational being had both a innate right to freedom and a duty to enter into a civil condition governed by a social contract in order to realize and preserve that freedom.

His writings on political philosophy consist of one book and several shorter works. The "Doctrine of Right", Part One of his two-part *Metaphysics of Morals* and first published as a stand-alone book in February 1797, contains virtually every directly political topic he treats.

Other shorter works include a useful short summary of his discussion of the basis and role of the state in the second section of the essay "Theory and Practice", an extended discussion of international relations in the essay "Toward Perpetual Peace", and the essay "An Answer to the Question: What is Enlightenment?." Other published material relevant to the topics include material on history, on practical philosophy in general, and, for his social philosophy, his work on religion and anthropology. Kant also offered a biannual lecture course on "Natural Right", a student's (Feyerabend) transcript of which is forthcoming in English translation.

THE PLACE OF POLITICAL PHILOSOPHY WITHIN KANT'S PHILOSOPHICAL SYSTEM

Kant's political philosophy is a branch of practical philosophy, one-half of one of the broadest divisions in Kant's thought between practical and theoretical philosophy. This division between practical and theoretical strictly speaking holds only for the system of pure philosophical cognitions, the whole of which is distinct from the preparatory philosophical project of critique that investigates pure human faculties, in particular, reason (A841 / B869). Kant's three critiques, according to this description, are neither practical nor theoretical but are all collectively critical. Only the systematic metaphysical works, such as the *Metaphysics of Morals*, would properly speaking be considered practical.

While political philosophy is part of that practical element, it is also to be distinguished within practical philosophy from both empirical elements and from virtue proper. The separation from virtue is treated in the next paragraph. But here it is worth mentioning that practical philosophy, as the rules governing free behavior of rational beings, covers all human action in both its pure and applied (empirical, or "impure") aspects. Pure practical philosophy, alleged to be the rational elements of practical philosophy in abstraction from anything empirical, is called by Kant "metaphysics of morals" (4:388). Kant so emphasized the priority of the pure aspect of political philosophy that he wrote part of his essay "On the Common Saying: That May be Correct in Theory, but it is of No Use in Practice" in opposition to the view he associates with Hobbes that the politician need not be concerned with abstract right but only with pragmatic governance (8:289-306).

Yet Kant also included the more pragmatic, impure, empirical study of human behavior as part of practical philosophy. For ethics in general, Kant called the empirical study of human beings as agents within particular cultures and with particular natural capacities "anthropology". Some of Kant's social philosophy fits into this rubric. Is there a corresponding applied political philosophy for

Kant? The advice he gives rulers regarding perpetual peace and some of the related work on history is as close as Kant gets to an anthropology of political right.

Kant's practical philosophy and the categorical imperative that governs it were intended to form the basis not only of what is thought today to be ethics proper but also with everything that broadly speaking had to do with the deliberative human behavior. He defined practical philosophy as that concerned with "rules of behavior in regard to free choice", as opposed to theoretical philosophy that concerned "the rule of knowledge" (Kant 27: 243). Practical philosophy provided rules to govern human deliberative action. The *Groundwork for the Metaphysics of Morals* provided Kant's main arguments that the categorical imperative is the supreme rule for human deliberative action. In its Preface, he notes that the *Groundwork* is to be a preparatory book for a future *Metaphysics of Morals*. Twelve years later he published that *Metaphysics of Morals* in two parts, the "Doctrine of Right" and the "Doctrine of Virtue". Both are equally parts of Kant's practical philosophy, and both thus have the categorical imperative as their highest principle, although there is some scholarly disagreement about this relationship.

The book *Metaphysics of Morals* had two distinct parts: the "Doctrine of Right" and the "Doctrine of Virtue". Kant sought to separate political rights and duties from what we might call morals in the narrow sense. He limits right by stating three conditions (6:230) that have to be met for something to be enforceable as right: first, right concerns only actions that have influence on other persons, meaning duties to the self are excluded, second right does not concern the wish but only the choice of others, meaning that not mere desires but only decisions which bring about actions are at stake, and third right does not concern the matter of the other's act but only the form, meaning no particular desires or ends are assumed on the part of the agents. As an example of the latter he considers trade, which for right must have the form of being freely agreed by both parties but can have any matter or purpose the agents want.

These criteria appear to be less rigid than Kant ultimately intends, for they would include under Right actions even those imperfect duties that "influence" others by improving their lot, such as benificent acts of charity. John Stuart Mill's "harm principle" does not face this problem since it specifies that the influence to be subject to law is always negative. In addition to these three conditions for right, Kant also offers direct contrasts between right and virtue. He thinks both relate to freedom but in different ways: right concerns outer freedom and virtue concerns inner freedom (being master of one's own passions) (6:406-07).

Right concerns acts themselves independent of the motive an agent may have for performing them, virtue concerns the proper motive for dutiful actions (6:218-221). In another formulation (6:380-81) he says that right concerns universality as a formal condition of freedom while virtue concerns a necessary end beyond the mere formality of universality, thus appearing to tie the distinction to the first two formulas of the categorical imperative in the *Groundwork*. In yet another he says that right concerns narrow duties and virtue wide duties (6:390). In the Feyerabend lectures, Kant notes that right is the subset of morally correct actions that are also coercible (27:1327). These various alternative formulations of the distinction would exclude imperfect duties not because imperfect duties do not "influence" others (they do) but because, as imperfect, they cannot be coerced in particular instances, since imperfect duties always allow for the moderating role of an individual's inclinations. While these various formulations of the distinction appear to be quite different, they can in general be summarized by saying that right concerns outer action corresponding to perfect duty that affects others regardless of the individual's internal motivations or goals.

FREEDOM AS THE BASIS OF THE STATE

"There is only one innate right," says Kant, "Freedom (independence from being constrained by another's choice), insofar as it can coexist with the freedom of every other in accordance with a universal law" (6:237). Kant rejects any other basis for the state, in particular arguing that the welfare of citizens cannot be the basis of state power. He argues that a state cannot legitimately impose any particular conception of happiness upon its citizens (8:290-91). To do so would be for the ruler to treat citizens as children, assuming that they are unable to understand what is truly useful or harmful to themselves.

This claim must be understood in light of Kant's more general claim that moral law cannot be based upon happiness or any other given empirical good. In the *Groundwork* Kant contrasts an ethics of autonomy, in which the will (*Wille*, or practical reason itself) is the basis of its own law, from the ethics of heteronomy, in which something independent of the will such as happiness is the basis of moral law (4:440-41). In the *Critique of Practical Reason* he argues that happiness (the agreeableness of life when things go in accordance with one's wishes and desires), although universally sought by human beings, is not specific enough to entail any universal desires in human beings. Further, even were there any universal desires among human beings, those desires would, as empirical, be merely contingent and thus unworthy of being the basis of any pure moral law (5:25-26). No particular conception of happiness can be the basis of the pure principle of the state, and the general conception of happiness is too vague to serve as the basis of a law. Hence, a "universal principle of right" cannot be based upon happiness but only on something truly universal, such as freedom. The "universal principle of right" Kant offers is thus "Any action is right if it can coexist with everyone's freedom in accordance with a universal law, or if on its maxim the freedom of choice of each can coexist with everyone's freedom in accordance with a universal law" (6:230).

This explains why happiness is not universal, but not why freedom is universal. By "freedom" in political philosophy, Kant is not referring to the transcendental conception of freedom usually associated with the problem of the freedom of the will amid determinism in accordance with laws of nature, a solution to which is provided in the Third Antinomy of the *Critique of Pure Reason*. Rather, freedom in political philosophy is defined, as in the claim above about the only innate right, as "independence from being constrained by another's choice". His concern in political philosophy is not with *laws of nature* determining a human being's choice but by *other human beings* determining a human being's choice, hence the kind of freedom Kant is concerned with in political philosophy is individual freedom of action. Still, the universality of political freedom is linked to transcendental freedom. Kant assumes that a human being's use of choice is (at least when properly guided by reason) free in the transcendental sense. Since every human being does enjoy transcendental freedom by virtue of being rational, freedom of choice is a universal human attribute. And this freedom of choice is to be respected and promoted, even when this choice is not exercised in rational or virtuous activity.

Presumably respecting freedom of choice involves allowing it to be effective in determining actions; this is why Kant calls political freedom, or "independence from being constrained by another's choice", the only innate right. One might still object that this freedom of choice is incapable of being the basis of a pure principle of right for the same reason that happiness was incapable of being its basis, namely, that it is too vague in itself and that when specified by the particular decisions individuals make with their free choice, it loses its universality. Kant holds that this problem does not arise for freedom, since freedom of choice can be understood both in terms of its content (the particular decisions individuals make) and its form (the free, unconstrained nature of choice of any possible particular end) (6:230). Freedom is universal in the proper sense because, unlike happiness, it can be understood in such a way that it is susceptible to specification without losing its universality. Right will be based on the form of free choice.

The very existence of a state might seem to some as a limitation of freedom, since a state possesses power to control the external freedom of individual citizens through force. This is the basic claim of anarchism. Kant holds in contrast that the state is not an impediment to freedom but is the means for freedom. State action that is a hindrance to freedom can, when properly directed, support and maintain freedom if the state action is aimed at hindering actions that themselves would hinder the freedom of others. Given a subject's action that would limit the freedom of another subject, the state may hinder the first subject to defend the second by "hindering a hindrance to freedom". Such state coercion is compatible with the maximal freedom demanded in the principle of right because it does not reduce freedom but instead provides the necessary background conditions needed to secure freedom. The amount of freedom lost by the first subject through direct state coercion is equal to the amount gained by the second subject through lifting the hindrance to his actions. State action sustains the maximal amount of freedom consistent with identical freedom for all without reducing it.

Freedom is not the only basis for principles underlying the state. In "Theory and Practice" Kant makes freedom the first of three principles (8:290):

1. The freedom of every member of the state as a human being.
2. His equality with every other as a subject.
3. The independence of every member of a commonwealth as a citizen.

Equality is not substantive but formal. Each member of the state is equal to every other member of the state before the law. Each has equal coercive right, that is, the right to invoke the power of the state to enforce the laws on her behalf. (Kant exempts the head of state from this equality, since the head of state cannot be coerced by anyone else). This formal equality is perfectly compatible with the inequality of members of the state in income, physical power, mental ability, possessions, etc. Further, this equality supports an equality of opportunity: every office or rank in the political structure must be open to all subjects without regard for any hereditary or similar restrictions.

Independence concerns a citizen being subject to laws he gives himself, i.e. as co-legislator of the laws. While this principle appears to require universal democratic decision making for particular laws, Kant instead understands this principle on two levels, one of which is not universal and the other of which is not for particular laws. All members of the state, as subjects of the law, must be able to will the basic law that governs them. This basic law is the "original contract" and will be discussed in the next section. The basic law is willed by each subject in the sense that the "will of all" or a "public will", or "general will" (Kant uses Rousseau's term) determines the basic law. Particular laws, in contrast, are to be determined by a majority of the citizens with voting rights.

SOCIAL CONTRACT

Kant provides two distinct discussions of social contract. One concerns property and will be treated in more detail in section 5 below. The second discussion of social contract comes in the essay "Theory and Practice" in the context of an a priori restriction on the legitimate policies the sovereign may pursue. The sovereign must recognize the "original contract" as an idea of reason that forces the sovereign to "give his laws in such a way that they could have arisen from the united will of a whole people and to regard each subject, insofar as he wants to be a citizen, as if he has joined in voting for such a will" (8:297). This original contract, Kant stresses, is only an idea of reason and not a historical event. Any rights and duties stemming from an original contract do so not because of any particular historical provenance, but because of the rightful relations embodied in the original contract.

No empirical act, as a historical act would be, could be the foundation of any rightful duties or rights. The idea of an original contract limits the sovereign as legislator. No law may be promulgated that "a whole people could not possibly give its consent to" (8:297). The consent at issue, however, is also not an empirical consent based upon any actual act. The set of actual particular desires of citizens is not the basis of determining whether they could possibly consent to a law. Rather, the kind of possibility at issue is one of rational possible unanimity based upon fair distributions of burdens and rights in abstraction from empirical facts or desires. Kant's examples both exemplify this consideration of possible rational unanimity. His first example is a law that would provide hereditary privileges to members of a certain class of subjects.

This law would be unjust because it would be irrational for those who would not be members of this class to agree to accept fewer privileges than members of the class. One might say that empirical information could not possibly cause all individuals to agree to this law. Kant's second example concerns a war tax. If the tax is administered fairly, it would not be unjust. Kant adds that even if the actual citizens opposed the war, the war tax would be just because it is possible that the war is being waged for legitimate reasons that the state but not the citizens know about. Here empirical information might cause all citizens to approve the law. In both these examples, the conception of "possibly consent" abstracts from actual desires individual citizens have. The possible consent is not based upon a hypothetical vote given actual preferences but is based on a rational conception of agreement given any possible empirical information.

Kant's is similar to the social contract theory of Hobbes in a few important characteristics. The social contract is not a historical document and does not involve a historical act. In fact it can be dangerous to the stability of the state to even search history for such empirical justification of state power (6:318). The current state must be understood, regardless of its origin, to embody the social contact. The social contract is a rational justification for state power, not a result of actual deal-making among individuals or between them and a government. Another link to Hobbes is that the social contract is not voluntary. Individuals may be forced into the civil condition against their consent (6:256).

Social contract is not based on any actual consent, one might say the voluntary choice to join a society. Since the social contract reflects reason, each human being as a rational being already contains the basis for rational agreement to the state. Are individuals then coerced to recognize their subjection to state power against their will? Since Kant defines "will" as "practical reason itself" (*Groundwork*, 4:412), the answer for him is "no." If one defines "will" as arbitrary choice, then the answer is "yes." This is the same dichotomy that arises with regard to Kant's theory of punishment (section 7). A substantial difference between Kant and Hobbes is that Hobbes bases his argument on the individual benefit for each party to the contract, whereas Kant bases his argument on Right itself, understood as freedom for all persons in general, not even just for the individual benefit that each party to the contract obtains in his or her own freedom. To this extent Kant is influenced more by Rousseau's idea of the General Will.

REPUBLICS, ENLIGHTENMENT, AND DEMOCRACY

Kant was a central figure in the philosophy of the Enlightenment. One of his popular essays, "An Answer to the Question: What is Enlightenment?" discusses Enlightenment in terms of the use of an individual's own reason (8:35f). To be Enlightened is to emerge from one's self-incurred minority (juvenile) status to a mature ability to think for oneself. In another essay, "What Does it Mean to Orient Oneself in Thought?" Kant defines Enlightenment as "the maxim of always thinking for oneself" (8:146). "What is Enlightenment" distinguishes between the public and private uses of reason. The private use of reason is, for government officials, the use of reason they must utilize in their official positions. For example, a member of the clergy (who in Kant's Prussia were employees of the state) is required to espouse the official doctrine in his sermons and teachings.

The public use of reason is the use an individual makes of his reason as a scholar reaching the public world of readers. For example, the same member of the clergy could, as a scholar, explain what he takes to be shortcomings in that very same doctrine. Similarly, a military officer can, using public reason, question the methods and goals of his own military orders, but in his function as an officer, using private reason, is obliged to obey them. Since the sovereign might err, and individual citizens have the right to attempt to correct the error under the assumption that the sovereign does not intend to err, "a citizen must have, with the approval of the ruler himself, the authorization to make known publicly his opinions about what it is in the ruler's arrangements that seems to him to be a wrong against the commonwealth," writes Kant in "Theory and Practice" (8:304).

One would expect from this emphasis that Kant would insist that the proper political system is one that not only allows individuals to think for themselves about political issues, but also contains a mechanism such as voting to translate those well reasoned opinions into government policy. One would be wrong. Kant does not stress self-government. In his discussion in "Perpetual Peace" of the traditional division of the types of government Kant classifies governments in two dimensions (8:352). The first is the "form of sovereignty", concerning who rules, and here Kant identifies the traditional three forms: either rule by one person, rule by a small group of people, or rule by all people. The second is the "form of government" concerning how those people rule, and here Kant offers a variation on the traditional good/bad dichotomy: either republican or despotic. By "republican," Kant means "separation of the executive power (the government) from the legislative power".

Despotism is their unity such that the regent has given laws to himself and in essence made his private will into the public will. Republics require representation in order to ensure that the executive power only enforces the public will by insisting that the executive enforce only laws that representatives of the people, not the executive itself, make. But a republic is compatible with a single individual acting as legislator provided that others act as executives; for example, a king would issue laws in the name of the people's will but the king's ministers would enforce those laws. Kant's claim that such a government is republican (see also 27:1384) showcases his view that a republican government need not require actual participation of the people in making the laws, even through elected representatives, as long as the laws are promulgated with the whole united will of the people in mind. Kant does, nonetheless, think that an elected representative legislator is the best form of a republic (8:353). Whether elected or unelected, the moral person who holds legislative power is representative of the people united as a whole, and is thus sovereign. The people themselves are sovereign only when they are electing a new set of representatives. When Kant discusses voting for representatives, he adheres to many prevailing prejudices (8:295). The right to vote requires "being one's own master" and hence having property or some skill that can support one independently. The reason given for this, that if someone must acquire something from another to make a living he alienates what belongs to him, is so vague that Kant himself admits in a footnote "It is, I admit, somewhat difficult to determine what is required in order to be able to claim the rank of a human being who is his own master." Kant also leaves women out of the voting populations for what he calls "natural" reasons but does not specify. Kant's state, then, does not require that actual decisions are made by the people at large, even through elected representatives. He holds that a single individual or small group can themselves adequately represent the people at large simply by adopting the point of view of the people. Insistence on a representative system (8:353) is not insistence on an *elected* representative system. Nonetheless it is clear that Kant holds that such an elective representative system is ideal. Republican constitutions, he claims, are prone to avoid war because, when the consent of the people is needed, they will consider the costs they must endure in a war (fighting, taxes, destruction of property, etc), whereas a non-republican ruler has no such concerns. In the "Doctrine of Right" he also notes that a republican system not only represents the people but does so "by all the citizens united and acting through their delegates" (6:342). These indications are not definitive but do point toward Kant favoring elected representatives.

PROPERTY AND CONTRACT RIGHT

The book "Doctrine of Right" begins with a discussion of property, showing the importance of this right for the implementation of the innate right to freedom. Property is defined as that "with which I am so connected that another's use of it without my consent would wrong me" (6:245). In one sense, if I am holding an object such as an apple, and another snatches it out of my hands, I have been wronged because in taking the object from my physical possession, the other harms me (Kant does not specify whether this harm is because one's current use of the apple is terminated or because one's body is affected, but the latter fits the argument better). Kant calls this "physical" or "sensible" possession. It is not a sufficient sense of possession to count as rightful possession of an object. Rightful possession must be possession of an object without holding it so that another's use of the object without my consent harms me even when I am not physically affected and not currently using the object. Kant calls this "intelligible possession".

His proof that there must be this intelligible possession and not merely physical possession turns on the application of human choice (6:246). An object of choice is one that some human has the capacity to use for his purposes. Rightful possession would be the right to make use of such an object. Suppose that for some particular object, no one has rightful possession. This would mean that a usable object would be beyond possible use. Kant grants that such a condition does not contradict the principle of right because it is compatible with everyone's freedom in accordance with universal law. But putting an object beyond rightful use when humans have the capacity to use it would "annihilate" the object in a practical respect, treat it as nothing. Kant claims that this is problematic because in a practical respect an object is considered merely as an object of possible choice. This consideration of the mere form alone, the object simply as an object of choice, cannot contain any prohibition of use for an object, for any such prohibition would be freedom limiting itself for no reason. Thus in a practical respect an object cannot be treated as nothing, and so the object must be considered as at least potentially in rightful possession of some human being or other. So all objects within human capacity for use must be subject to rightful or intelligible possession.

Intelligible possession, then, is required by right in order for free beings to be able to realize their freedom by using objects for their freely chosen purposes. This conclusion entails the existence of private property but not any particular distribution of private property. All objects must be considered as potential property of some human being or other. Now if one human being is to have intelligible possession of a particular object, all other human beings must refrain from using that object. Such a one-sided relation would violate the universality of external right. Kant further worries that any unilateral declaration by one person that an object belongs to him alone would infringe on the freedom of others. The only way that intelligible possession is possible without violating the principle of right is when each person agrees to obligate mutually all others to recognize each individual's intelligible possessions. Each person must acknowledge that he is obligated to refrain from using objects that belong to another. Since no individual will can rightfully make and enforce such a law obligating everyone to respect others' property, this mutual obligation is possible only in accordance with a "collective general (common) and powerful will", in other words, only in a civil condition. The state itself obligates all citizens to respect the property of other citizens. Without a state to enforce these property rights, they are impossible.

This creation of a civil condition is Kant's first manner of discussing a social contract mentioned in section 3. Prior to a social contract the only manner in which human beings can control things is through empirical possession, actual occupation and use of land and objects. In order to gain full property rights to land and objects, individuals must all agree to respect the property rights of others in a social contract. They are in fact required, as a duty, to enter into a social condition in order to defend their own and everyone's property rights. Only in such a society can persons exercise their freedom, that is their pursuit of ends, by legitimately using objects for their own purposes without regard for others. Hence a social contract is the rational justification of the state because state power is necessary for each individual to be guaranteed access to some property in order to realize their freedom. While the discussion in "Theory and Practice" of a social contract as an idea of reason constrains the sovereign in promulgating laws, it does not explain why the state is necessary in the first place. The discussion in "Doctrine of Right" of property as the basis of a social contract explains why individuals are in fact rationally required to enter into a social contract.

A puzzle arises here with regard to property. If individuals are not able to have any intelligible property prior to the existence of a state, yet the state's role is to enforce property rights, where does the original assignment of property to individuals occur? John Locke had famously avoided this problem in his theory of property by making property a product of a single individual's activity. By "mixing" one's labor with an object in the commons, one comes to have property in the object. Kant objects to Locke's theory of property on the grounds that it makes property a relation between a person and a thing rather than between the wills of several persons (6:268-69). Since property is a relation of wills that can occur only in a civil condition under a common sovereign power, Kant suggests that prior to this civil condition property can be acquired only in anticipation of and in conformity with a civil condition. Provisional property is initial physical appropriation of objects with the intention of making them rightful property in a state (6:264, 267).

Property is of three types for Kant (6:247-48, 260). First is the right to a thing, to corporeal objects in space. Examples of these things include land. The second is the right against a person, the right to coerce that person to perform an action. This is contract right. The third is the "right to a person akin to a right to a thing", the most controversial of Kant's categories in which he includes spouses, children, and servants. Of these three types, the first has already been discussed in relation to acquisition. The middle of these, contract right, involves the possession by one person of the "deed" of another (6:274). One person is able to control the choice of another in order to apply the other's causal powers to some end. At first glance this contract right appears to violate the second formula of the categorical imperative which states that persons are to be treated always as ends and never merely as means.

A contract appears to be a case in which an individual is used merely as a means. A homeowner, for example, hires a repair specialist specifically as a means for repairing his house. Kant turns the tables on this problem by showing that a contract is "the united choice of two persons" and thus treats both parties to the contract as ends. For example, he notes that the repair specialist who is contracted to work on a house has agreed to the exchange in order to obtain an end of his own, namely, money (27:1319). Each party to the contract is both means for the other and an end. In the third category, the right to a person akin to a thing, Kant argues that some contracts or rightful obligations such as the parent-child relation allow one party to the contract to control not only the choice of the other, but also to possess some power over the body of the other, such as the power to insist that the other remain in the household. His discussion of the legal relation of marriage treats marriage as reciprocal access to the other's sexual organs; here, despite his personal sexism, he describes this legal relation as equal.

REBELLION AND REVOLUTION

The very idea of a right to rebel against the government is incoherent, Kant argued, because the source of all right is the actually existing state. By this he did not mean that any actually existing state is always completely just, or that merely by virtue of having power, the state could determine what justice is. He meant that a rightful condition, the opposite of the state of nature, is possible only when there is some means for individuals to be governed by the "general legislative will" (6:320). Any state embodies the general legislative will better than no state. While such reasoning seems pragmatic, it is not. It is instead based upon the claims above that a rightful condition requires the centralizing of coercive power in a state as the only means to bring about reciprocal coercion and obligation. Kant also argues that a right to rebel would require that a people be authorized to resist the state.

This kind of authorization for action, however, is an exercise of sovereign power, and to any people who claimed such a right would be claiming it (the people) rather than the state embodies sovereign power. It would thus "make the people, as subject, by one and the same judgment sovereign over him to whom it is subject" (6:320). This is a contradiction. The nature of sovereignty is such that sovereign power cannot be shared. Were it shared between the state and the people, then when a dispute arose between them, who would judge whether the state or the people are correct? There being no higher sovereign power to make such a judgment, all other means for resolving the dispute fall outside of rightful relations. This role of judgment relates to the judgment that Kant discusses with regard to the social contract.

Under the idea of a social contract, the sovereign legislator may not make a law that the people could not make for itself because it possesses irrational, non-universal form. The state, not the people, is the judge of when a law is rational (8:297). People who argue for a right to revolution, Kant claims, misunderstand the nature of a social contract. They claim that the social contract must have been an actual historical occurrence from which the people could withdraw (8:301-02). But since the social contact is only an idea of reason which sets moral limits to the sovereign's legislative acts, and the sovereign's judgment alone determines how these limits are to be interpreted, there is no independent contractual agreement to which the people could refer in its complaints. Citizens are still allowed to voice their grievances through their use of public reason, but they can do nothing more than attempt to persuade the sovereign to alter his decision.

While the people cannot rebel against the state, Kant does not insist that citizens always obey the state. He allows at least for passive civil disobedience. This comes in two forms: in a republican representative system such as England's, there can be "a negative resistance, that is, a refusal of the people (in parliament) to accede to every demand the government puts forth as necessary for administering the state" (6:322). In the context of this discussion it is clear that Kant is referring to the use of the power of the legislature to refuse funding, and therefore approval, of actions of the executive. He clarifies that the legislature is not allowed to dictate any positive action to the executive, its legitimate resistance is only negative. A second form of acceptable resistance applies to individuals. Kant mentions that citizens are obligated to obey the sovereign "in whatever does not conflict with inner morality" (6:371). He does not elaborate on the term "inner morality".

Nor does Kant always reject the actions of revolutionaries. If a revolution is successful, citizens have as much obligation to obey the new regime.as they had to obey the old one (6:323). Since the new regime is in fact a state authority, it now possesses the right to rule. Further, in his theory of history, Kant argues that progress in the long run will come about in part through violent and unjust actions such as wars. Kant even takes it as a sign of progress that spectators of the French Revolution have greeted it with "a wishful participation that borders closely on enthusiasm" (7:85). Kant is not pointing to the revolution itself as a sign of progress but to the reaction of people such as himself to news of the revolution. The spectators endorse the revolution not because it is legitimate but because it is aimed at the creation of a civil constitution. Revolution, then, is wrong but still contributes to progress.

In fact, Kant did believe that the French Revolution was legitimate, and a look at his argument illuminates some of his complex terminology. The French king possessed sovereignty until he convened the Estates General as representative of the people, at which time sovereignty "passed to the people" even though the king had intended for the assembly to resolve specific problems and then return the reins of power to him (6:341-2). Further, the king could not have any power to restrain the actions of the assembly as a condition for it being given the sovereign power, for there can be no restrictions on this sovereign power. This understanding of sovereignty shows the difference between a rebellion against authority and an election. In an election, sovereignty is passed back to the people, so there is nothing wrong with the people replacing the entire government. Without an election (or similar method of designating the return of sovereignty to the people), any action aimed at replacing the government is wrong.

PUNISHMENT

Kant was long considered to be an exemplar of the retributivist theory of punishment. While he does claim that the only proper justification of punishment is guilt for a crime, he does not limit the usefulness of punishment to retributivist matters. Punishment can have as its justification only the guilt of the criminal. All other uses of punishment, such as rehabilitation (the alleged good of the criminal) or deterrence (alleged good to society) uses the criminal merely as a means (6:331). Once this guilt is determined, however, Kant does not deny that something useful can be drawn from the punishment. In Feyerabend lectures on Natural Right, Kant is clear that the sovereign "must punish in order to obtain security", and even while using the law of retribution, "in such a way the best security is obtained" (27:1390-91). The state is authorized to use its coercive force to defend freedom against limitations to freedom; more particularly, since right does not entail that each citizen must limit his own freedom but only that "freedom is limited" by conditions of right, it is right for another, i.e. the state, to actively limit citizens freedom in accord with right (6:231). The state is authorized to use force to defend property rights (6:256). Kant's view, then, is that punishment of a particular individual can serve deterrent functions even when it cannot be based on deterrence as its justification.

Retributivist theory holds not only that criminal guilt is required for punishment, but that the appropriate type and amount of punishment is also determined by the crime itself. Traditionally this is the heart of the ancient injunction "an eye for an eye". Kant supports this measurement for punishment because all other measurements bring into consideration elements besides strict justice (6:332), such as the psychological states of others that would measure the effectiveness of various possible punishments on deterrence. As a principle, retribution grounds but does not specify the exact punishment. Kant recognizes that "like for like" is not always possible to the letter, but believes that justice requires that it be used as the principle for specific judgments of punishment.

The retributivist theory of punishment leads to Kant's insistence on capital punishment. He argues that the only punishment possibly equivalent to death, the amount of inflicted harm, is death. Death is qualitatively different from any kind of life, so no substitute could be found that would equal death. Kant rejects the argument against capital punishment offered earlier in his century by the Italian reformer, the Marchese Cesare Beccaria, who argued that in a social contract no one would willingly give to the state power of his own life, for the preservation of that life is the fundamental reason one enters a social contract at all. Kant objects to Beccaria's claim by distinguishing between the source of a social contract in "pure reason in me" as opposed to the source of the crime, myself as capable of criminal acts. The latter person wills the crime but not the punishments, but the former person wills in the abstract that anyone who is convicted of a capital crime will be punished by death. Hence one and the same individual both commits the crime and endorses the punishment of death. This solution mirrors the claim that individuals can be coerced to join a civil condition: reason dictates that entering the civil condition is mandatory even if one's particular arbitrary choice might be to remain outside it.

INTERNATIONAL RELATIONS AND HISTORY

Kant complains that the German word used to describe international right, "Völkerrecht", is misleading, for it means literally the right of nations or peoples. He distinguishes this kind of relation among groups of individuals, which he discusses as Cosmopolitan Right and will be covered in Section 9, from the relations among the political entities, which would better be called "Staatenrecht", the right of states. (Kant still uses the phrase "right of nations" and also discusses a "league of nations", although it is clear that he is referring not to nations as peoples but to states as organizations; this article will strictly adhere to the term "state" even when Kant did not.) States must be considered to be in a state of nature relative to one another. Like individuals in the state of nature, then, they must be considered to be in a state of war with each other. Like individuals, the states are obligated to leave this state of nature to form a union under a social contract, in this case, a league of states. Before the creation of such a league of states, states do have a right to go to war against other states if another state threatens it or actively aggresses against it (6:346).

But any declaration of war ought to be confirmed by the people "as colegislating members of a state" (6:345). Rulers who wage war without such consent are using their subjects as property, as mere means, rather than treating them as ends in themselves. This claim is one of Kant's strongest statements that actual voting by citizens is required: citizens "must therefore give their free assent, through their representatives, not only to waging war in general but also to each particular declaration of war" (6:345-46). Once war has been declared, states are obligated to conduct the war under principles that leave upon the possibility of an eventual league of states. Actions that undermine future trust between states, such as the use of assassination, are prohibited.

States are obligated to leave this state of nature among states and enter into a congress, or league, of states. In his 1797 *Metaphysics of Morals*, Kant argues that this organization must be a voluntary coalition among states rather than a federation, or state of states, which would be indissoluble. Hence Kant holds that the league among nations is only analogous, not equivalent, to a state created by citizens, since each particular civil state is indisolluble. But in his essay "Toward Perpetual Peace" two years earlier, Kant had advocated a state of nations as the best possible relation among states (8:357). This state of nations would entail states subjecting themselves to public coercive laws. Kant recognizes that states will balk at such a surrender of their sovereign power, so accepts that the second best option, a league of states in which each state retains the right to leave, must be adopted. In a league of states, wars are replaced with negotiated settlements of differences.

In the essay "Toward Perpetual Peace", Kant offers a set of six "preliminary articles" which aim to reduce the likelihood of war, but cannot by themselves establish permanent peace (8:343-47). These are a ban on making temporary peace treaties while still planning for future wars, the prohibition of annexation of one state by another, the abolition of standing armies, the refusal to take on national debts for external affairs, a ban on interference by one state in the internal affairs of another, and a set of limits on the conduct of war that disallows acts that would breed mistrust and make peace impossible. These six articles are negative laws that prohibit states from engaging in certain kinds of conduct. They are not sufficient by themselves to prevent states from lapsing back into their old habits of warring on one another.

To institute an international order that can genuinely bring about perpetual peace, Kant offers three "definitive articles". The first of these is that every state shall have a republican civil constitution (8:348, discussed in section 4 above). In a republican constitution, the people who decide whether there will be a war are the same people who would pay the price for the war, both in monetary terms (taxes and other financial burdens) and in flesh and blood. Republican states will therefore be very hesitant to go to war and will readily accept negotiations rather than resort to war. This consideration is Kant's most important contribution to the debate about securing peace. He believes that when states are ruled in accordance with the wishes of the people, their self-interest will provide a consistent basis for pacific relations among states. The second definitive article is that each state shall participate in a federalism of states. The third definitive article advocates a cosmopolitan right of universal hospitality.

Kant's view of historical progress is tied to his view of international relations. He actually presents several versions of his argument for the progress of humanity toward the ideal condition in which states, each governed by a republican civil constitution and thus each providing maximal consistent freedom for its citizens, all cooperate in a league of states. In his essay "Idea for a Universal

History from a Cosmopolitan Point of View" (8:15-31), he takes the basis of his claims for historical progress to be the culmination of the human ability to reason, which, as a natural property of human beings, must be worked out to perfection in the species. He argues that incessant wars will eventually lead rulers to recognize the benefits of peaceful negotiation. They will gradually increase the freedoms of their citizens, because freer citizens are economically more productive and hence make the state stronger in its international dealings. Importantly he claims that the creation of civil constitutions in particular states is dependent upon the creation of an international league of states, although he does not elaborate on this reasoning. In "Toward Perpetual Peace" Kant reverses that order, claiming that some particular state may, through "good fortune", become a republic and then act as a focal point for other states to join in peaceful relations, and that gradually such cooperation can spread to all states (8:356).

COSMOPOLITAN RIGHT

Relations among the states of the world, covered above, are not the same as relations among the peoples (nations, *Volk*) of the world. Individuals can relate to states of which they are not members and to other individuals who are members of other states. In this they are considered "citizens of a universal state of human beings" with corresponding "rights of citizens of the world" (8:349, footnote). Despite these lofty sounding pronouncements, Kant's particular discussion of cosmopolitan right is restricted to the right of hospitality. Since all peoples share a limited amount of living space due to the spherical shape of the earth, the totality of which they must be understood to have originally shared in common, they must be understood to have a right to possible interaction with one another. This cosmopolitan right is limited to a right to offer to engage in commerce, not a right to demand actual commerce. A citizen of one state may try to establish links with other peoples; no state is allowed to deny foreign citizens a right to travel in its land. Settlement is another matter entirely. Kant is strongly critical of the European colonization of other lands already inhabited by other peoples. Settlement in these cases is allowed only by uncoerced informed contract. Even land that appears empty might be used by shepherds or hunters and cannot be appropriated without their consent (6:354).

Cosmopolitan right is an important component of perpetual peace. Interaction among the peoples of the world, Kant notes, has increased in recent times. Now "a violation of right on one place of the earth is felt in all" as peoples depend upon one another and know about one another more and more. Violations of cosmopolitan right would make more difficult the trust and cooperation necessary for perpetual peace among states.

SOCIAL PHILOSOPHY

"Social philosophy," can be taken to mean the relationship of persons to institutions, and to each other via these institutions, that are not part of the state. Family is a clear example of a social institution that transcends the individual but has at least some elements that are not controlled by the state. Other examples would be economic institutions such as businesses and markets, religious institutions, social clubs and private associations created to advance interests or for mere enjoyment, education and university institutions, social systems and classifications such as race and gender, and endemic social problems like poverty.

It is worth noting a few particulars, if only as examples of the range of this topic. Kant advocated the duty of citizens to support those in society who could not support themselves, and even gave the state the power to arrange for this help (6:326). He offered a biological explanation of race in several essays and also, certainly into his "Critical" period, held that other races were inferior to Europeans. He supported a reform movement in education based on the principles presented by Rousseau in "Emile". I will not provide detailed treatement of Kant's views on these particular matters (some of which are scant, others of which are irrelevant to his main philosophy) but only focus on the nature of social philosophy for Kant. Kant had no comprehensive social philosophy. One might be tempted to claim that, in line with natural law theorists, Kant discusses natural rights related to some social institutions. One might read the first half of the "Doctrine of Right" as a social philosophy, since this half on "Private Right" discusses the rights of individuals relative to one another, in contrast to the second half on "Public Right" that discusses the rights of individuals relative to the state.

Kant even offers an explanation of this difference by claiming that the opposite of state of nature is not a social but the civil condition, that is, a state (6:306). The state of nature can include voluntary societies (Kant mentions domestic relations in general) where there is no a priori obligation for individuals to enter them. This claim of Kant's, however, is subject to some doubt, since he explicitly links all forms of property to the obligation to enter the civil condition (see section 5 above), and his discussion of marriage and family comes in the form of property relations akin to contract relations. It is thus not obvious how there can be any social institutions that can exist outside the civil condition, to the extent that social institutions presuppose property relations.

Another approach to the issue of social philosophy in Kant is to view it in terms of moral philosophy properly speaking, that is, the obligations human beings have to act under the proper maxims, as discussed in the "Doctrine of Virtue" (see section 1 above). In the "Doctrine of Virtue" Kant talks about the obligation to develop friendships and to participate in social intercourse (6:469-74). In the *Religion within the Boundaries of Mere Reason* Kant discusses the development of an "ethical commonwealth" in which human beings strengthen one another's moral resolve through their participation in the moral community of a church. He also holds that educational institutions, the subject of his book *On Pedagogy*, should be designed to provide for the development of morality in human beings, who lack a natural disposition for the moral good. In these cases Kant's social philosophy is treated as an arm of his theory of virtue, not as a freestanding topic in its own right.

A third approach to social philosophy comes through Kant's *Anthropology from a Pragmatic Point of View*. Kant had envisioned anthropology as an empirical application of ethics, akin to empirical psychology as a application of pure metaphysical principles of nature. Knowledge of the general characteristics of human being as well as particular characteristics of genders, races, nationalities, etc, can aid in determining one's precise duties toward particular individuals. Further, this knowledge can aid moral agents in their own task of motivating themselves to morality. These promises of anthropology in its practical application are disappointed, however, in the details of Kant's text. He does little critical assessment of social prejudices or practices to screen out stereotypes detrimental to moral development. His own personal views, considered sexist and racist universally today and even out of step with some of his more progressive colleagues, pervade his direct discussions of these social institutions. There are various theories about what can make power legitimate. Do you think that one theory is more convincing than others? To understand the fundamental principles of legitimate power and governance one must look at the period surrounding the Enlightenment because this is the time when the individual became an important entity, no longer was the individual part of a class on a hierarchical structure, with power relating to that class. The natural rights theorists aim was to show that *man* was born in a state of nature, and given the right to do as he/she wished, but this was sacrificed to the governance of the land, i.e. that the *rational man* would give up the state of freedom, for the security and safety of law, governance and sovereignty.

Locke, said instead of giving up the right to do absolutely anything to the sovereign entity, the rational man would put these rights in the hands of a government that holds the good of the people as supreme. Locke did not believe that man gives up all these natural rights, but each person retained rights that were regulated by a political government, to ensure a person would not use their rights in a way that would harm the rights of others. Locke's version of rights was one of the first models of inherent rights to life, liberty, freedom and property, where the king was there at the will of the people and benevolent in nature. The influence of John-Jacques Rousseau is also important, although not strictly speaking a natural law theorist, in the sense of earlier theorists. The most important difference that Rousseau discussed in his works was that government and reason has not protected *man* but enslaved *man*, whereas in the state of nature these rights were upheld in a paradisiacal state. One of Rousseau's most interesting critiques of government and law was in the Social Contract where man was originally free but in society 'everywhere in chains'. Therefore he believed instead of giving up one's freedom to a governing body, it needs to be reclaimed by man but this did not mean reclaiming the paradise of Rousseau's state of nature. Instead these rights should be inherent to each man and that the government created is not only for the good of the people but should be determined by the will of the people. Rousseau believed people should be part of the regulation of the government and law; otherwise the government that is essentially corrupt will take away these rights. Popular involvement makes it impossible for these rights to be taken away by the government.

There was an assumption of equality between *men* and basis rights to life, liberty, freedom, and protection from the corruption of absolute government (i.e. rights to freedom of speech and assembly) and the right to a fair trial and independent Court of law. This argument stems from the authors of the American Constitution where the rights embodied in the text were self-evident because all men were created equal and given certain inalienable rights, which are afforded to all persons of the globe, state borders have no impact on these rights. The writers claimed these rights came from God. Other theorists have argued we have these rights merely because we are human. This argument is still one used in the 20th/21st Century as it is the easiest to pass off, however there is no real moral justification for upholding these rights, therefore how can one say we must keeps these rights in the face of a breach or dissolution of them. Hobbes' state of nature sets up that; *Men by nature [are] equal: Nature hath made men so equal, in faculties of the body, and mind For as to the strength of body, the weakest has strength enough to kill the strongest, either by secret, machination, or by confederacy with others, that are in the same danger with himself;* hence all are equal in fear of death. Therefore if this fear was set forth by the monarch then this first law of nature legitimizes the citizens to revolt and set up a form of governance that ensures this equality and that their basic rights are upheld. Therefore if the citizens of Hobbes' state are able to get together to give the power of law and governance to a single individual they believe will uphold the common good; then in the same coalition they can depose this individual if in fact their powers of governance and over the law are misused. This state of nature is hypothetical in order to provide a theory justify the fair governance of a small section of society, or as Hobbes prefers a monarch. It is the equality of fear, the individual's right to everything in addition to subsequent laws of nature which provides the conditions for a social contract to ensure security and equality of mankind. There are some problems with Hobbes' social contract which is giving the power of rule and governance to a single individual; this is arguably giving this individual unchecked power. Therefore if every man has the *right to everything* and then if the state of nature's equality is no longer the case because the power of law lays in an individual's hands-where this individual has the wants and desires to obtain everything. Hence there will be a tyrannical government, rather than a government for the common good.

Utilitarianism is not a theory of individual rights, instead it views that the good of the community was a more important aim for the law and government ruled by the people. Theorists such as Edmund Burke believed that rights were natural, including life, liberty and freedom but this theory was in the abstract, therefore they should be given by society for the good of its people, because these rights cannot be universal otherwise there is no place for cultural diversity. Burke is one of the first theorists with the cultural relativism argument; the critics of universal justice have further advanced this in the 20th and 21st centuries. Burke's move to reject universalism was the first chip in these inherent rights that ensured legitimate power; how can rights be inherent if they not available for everyone, because a culture denies them. Jeremy Bentham advanced this. His theory held that were no natural rights-the government for the good of society-a form of utilitarianism, afforded rights. Therefore Bentham's rights were legal rights where one can do whatever one wants as long as the law does not prohibit it i.e., rights are not stemming from the individual but the states and the powers of governance (Positivism). The problem with positivism or this early form of rights from utility is that the law/governance are the basis of rights and because there is no greater principle of just and legitimate governance. The model of Marxism states that it does not regard the individual as having any human rights, instead it is for the state to set the needs of the individuals, i.e., it is not the good of the individual that the state upholds but the good and the needs of the state. Marx considered law, justice, freedom and democracy as ideas and concepts that are determined by historical and sociological circumstances and irrelevant. Instead a person's essence was the potential to use one's ability to the fullest and satisfy one's needs', therefore promoting fundamental rights as rights of well-being and satisfaction of the individual. These rights would involve social and economic rights, which is the only way to ensure legitimate power and justice. Marx's vision turned out to be idealistic and failed in reality.

The most legitimate version of power and governance seems to be a mixture of traditional utilitarianism that affords a method of human rights. Modern utilitarian theorists have extended the theory of Bentham, but have put it in more modern terms. Instead of maximising the pleasures and desires of the individual the government would be maximising the general welfare of individuals therefore minimising frustration of wants and preferences. Therefore what one can see is that the governing bodies must put the general welfare first, yet minimise the individual's needs-therefore causing a conflict of rights between what is in the name of the society and what the individual wants. The problems with this theory is it is socially constructed, there is no autonomy of being and no argument for universal rights that transcend all cultures and religions, therefore falling short of what is needed for an all-encompassing human rights theory, as the general welfare can be different for differing cultures.

Rawl's in his thesis for engendering human rights states that justice is the prime basis of all government and to ensure justice human rights are the obvious means and end to ensure justice is fulfilled. Rawl's theory is based on a few key ideas, which are the rights and duties of government/institution of society and the burdens and benefits of citizens co-operating. Rawls bases his theory that each individual has an inherent and inviolable being set in justice-this being cannot be overridden for the welfare of the society. This theory does not fall foul to the arguments against modern utilitarianism. Rawl's does use the social contract fiction of Hobbes and Locke, however the basis of moving from ignorance (state of nature) is reason and this reason set up on principles of justice that his social contract is based upon. These principles are; (1) that each person has basic rights and liberties in accordance with freedom; and (2) there is distributive justice, where inequalities are restrained by the greatest benefit of least advantaged and each person has the condition of fair equality of opportunity. These principles cannot be derogated for the public good and liberty is the supreme principle. Rawl's theory is very important when looking at human rights theories because it begins to tackle the universality of human rights based on justice, as well as the inequalities apparent in society. The theory does have flaws but it one of the more comprehensive theories setting up basis rights and freedoms and ensuring legitimate power because it protects the individual's democratic rights, because it is a more complex analysis of the nation-state and as Andrews and Sayward argue:

The modern Western approach to political legitimacy links it with the opportunities for democratic participation, so that democracy is now seen as a necessary condition of political legitimacy In theories of political legitimacy a stereotype of a domestic state with its 'own' domestic population can easily emerge. Yet the actual histories of state are much more complicated than that.

5

SOCIAL EXCLUSION

THE EUROPEAN APPROACH TO SOCIAL DISADVANTAGE

The United States is falling further behind the European Union in its conceptualization of poverty and its understanding of those living at the margins of society. The United States still imagines poverty strictly as a deficiency of income for basic necessities. In contrast, the European Union has continually revised its thinking about social deprivation, adopting a view of poverty relative to rising average living standards, and, more recently, a framework for thinking about nonmonetary aspects of deprivation. Europeans are now committed to include the "excluded," the outsiders, the people left out of mainstream society and left behind in a globalizing economy. The United States can learn much from the European fight against social exclusion.

Ironically, an Englishman, B. Seebohm Rowntree, pioneered the American method of counting the poor by estimating an absolute monetary threshold based upon bare subsistence requirements. Our poverty line reflects a convenient rule of thumb that a government economist, Mollie Orshansky, devised in 1964. It has since become a policy and social science fixture. Based on the value of an "economy food plan" times three (since families spent a third of their after tax earnings on food), this narrow approach persists, even though today, food, including restaurant meals, occupies a mere 15 percent of American budgets. The poverty threshold, adjusted only for inflation, identifies people living in the direst material circumstances, not those living below what John Kenneth Galbraith termed "the grades and standards" of society. Although in 1995, the National Academy of Sciences recommended limited changes to the poverty line to reflect real consumption relative to all money and nonmonetary resources, minus work-related expenses, there has been no official redefinition yet (see Miller and Oyen 1996). American poverty researchers have conducted longitudinal studies tracking incomes over time, but the U.S. government has not considered dynamic measures of income poverty either. In contrast, the European Union (EU) adopted as the official poverty line a *relative* poverty indicator of one-half of the national median disposable household income. It rises when Europeans grow richer. EU statistical reports provide data on 60 percent of median income, providing evidence of near poverty as well. Concern about rising income inequality, a problem much worse in the United States than in Europe, has also encouraged the development of income distribution measures, most notably with the Luxembourg Income Study.

The European Household Panel Survey and the longitudinal EU Statistics on Income and Living Conditions study now make it possible to develop dynamic indicators of poverty, tracking those who enter, leave, and stay mired in destitution. Thus, at the March 2001 Stockholm Summit, the European Commission's Synthesis Report on Social Inclusion proposed seven indicators of "social exclusion," three of which captured forms of "financial poverty": (1) the share of the population below 60 percent of national median equivalent income before and after social transfers; (2) the ratio of the share of the top 20 percent to the share of the bottom 20 percent of the income distribution; and (3) persistent poverty, or the share of the population below the 60 percent poverty line for three consecutive years (Atkinson et al. 2002).

But the real European innovation is the development of nonmonetary indicators of "social exclusion," transcending economists' focus on money. Mention of "social exclusion" in

European public and social science discourse has increased much faster than references to "poverty" or "the underclass" (Abrahamson 1998; Lievens 2000 in Mayes 2001, 9). Cognizant that deprivation is a multidimensional condition, Eurostat (the EU Statistical Office), national statistical agencies, and European social scientists have developed social and political benchmarks to track progress against exclusion. International agencies are now adopting this approach, too.

The Origins of "Social Exclusion"

Europeans conceive of social exclusion as distinct from income poverty. Poverty is a distributional outcome, whereas exclusion is a relational process of declining participation, solidarity, and access. For some, exclusion is a broader term encompassing poverty; for others, it is a cause or a consequence of poverty. The two may even be unrelated (Heady and Room 2002).

The meaning of social exclusion also varies across countries. The term originated in France, where the "Anglo-Saxon" idea of "poverty" is thought to patronize or denigrate equal citizens. In French Republican thought, social exclusion refers to a "rupture of the social bond" or "solidarity." The French social contract does not leave individuals to fend for themselves. Society owes its citizens the means to a livelihood, and citizens in turn have obligations to the larger society. European welfare states were supposed to do away with "charity" for "the poor," providing basic social assistance, and, hence, as a right of citizenship, eliminating absolute material deprivation. Although the United States flirted with the idea of a guaranteed annual income, notably under Nixon, even the Earned Income Tax Credit and Food Stamps have eligibility restrictions. Nor is there a right to housing, except under the New York State constitution.

Many sociological theories adumbrated the concept of exclusion, but French advocates for destitute groups, such as ATD-Fourth World, were among the first to employ the term in its contemporary sense. By the 1970s, references to "the excluded" became more frequent, especially to refer to the disabled. But after the Oil Shocks, unemployment began to mount, especially among youth, older workers, and immigrants. In the 1980s, as the problem groups "excluded" from economic growth multiplied, "exclusion" discourse helped cement a national movement of associations, ALERTE, urging France to launch a comprehensive war on exclusion. In 1988, with the support of the Right and the Left, France enacted a minimum "insertion" income (RMI).

The RMI entails signing an "insertion" contract specifying a trajectory for an assisted individual to follow to become a productive member of society, whether through work, volunteering, studying, family reunification, or the like. Social workers and nonprofits provide multifaceted, comprehensive, and personally tailored assistance, from health care to subsidized jobs, to help the excluded reenter social life in all its spheres. Thus, in France, social bonds are reknit in families and communities as well as in the workplace.

In 1990, homeless activists won a legal right to housing, and in June 1998, a full-blown French "law of prevention and combat of social exclusions" guaranteed universal access to fundamental rights. It mandated coordinated interventions in at least ten spheres: employment, training, social enterprise, social minima, housing, health, education, social services, culture, and "citizenship" (e.g., helping the homeless to vote) (Silver 1998; Choffe in Mayes 2001). Most policies promoting social inclusion or cohesion emphasize (1) multipronged interventions crossing traditional bureau cratic domains and tailored to the multidimensional problems of excluded individuals and groups; (2) a long-term process of insertion and integration moving through transitional stages; and (3) participation of the excluded in their own inclusion into economic and social life.

The latter is especially important since targeted and means-tested programs may unintentionally stigmatize their intended beneficiaries. Often, local nonprofit initiatives of disadvantaged residents become public-private partnerships supported by subsidies from municipal or national governments and the European Union Structural Funds.

From France, the "exclusion" approach dispersed throughout Europe. Central to this diffusion was Jacques Delors, president of the European Commission in the mid-1980s, who pressed for a "social dimension" to European integration. The European "Social Protocol" developed gradually from 1989 until 1997, when it became part of the Amsterdam Treaty. This delay was partly due to the principle of "subsidiarity" that assigned social protection responsibilities to the member states as well as to British refusal to ratify that section of the 1992 Maastricht Treaty. During this period, the third EU "poverty program" was gradually transformed into a fight against social exclusion, supporting over two dozen local Model Actions and Twelve Innova-tory Initiatives "to foster the economic and social integration of the least privileged groups." This terminological shift was partly political.

The euphemism appeased UK Conservatives and Christian Democrats in Germany who maintained that generous guaranteed minimum income had eradicated absolute poverty. If they rejected a relative poverty definition, they could not gainsay rising unemployment. The number of unemployed workers in the EU soared from 14 million in 1992 to 16.5 million in 1998, half of whom were out of work for over a year. These facts of economic life and the urging of countries like France forced the EU to recognize market integration had a "social dimension," too. In 1997, once the New Labour government accepted the Social Protocol and created a "Social Exclusion Unit" in Prime Minister Blair's office, the EU's fight against social exclusion could begin in earnest.

Drawing upon lessons from building monetary union and committed to "basic principles of solidarity which should remain the trademark of Europe," the "Luxembourg Process" coordinated a European Employment Strategy of nineteen guidelines into four pillars (1) improving employability; (2) developing entrepreneurship; (3) encouraging business and worker adaptability; and (4) providing equal employment opportunity. The Employment Strategy was "soft law," integrating EU, national, and local level efforts through peer pressure and without recourse to regulations with formal sanctions.

Multilevel iterative monitoring promotes learning from national best practices and modifications of goals and procedures over time. Explicit long-term employment targets were later adopted. In December 2000 at Nice, the EU applied this "open coordination method" to the Social Agenda, separating the fight against poverty and exclusion from employment strategy more generally. Every two years, nation-states produce "National Action Plans" on social inclusion, laying out their progress toward agreed-upon goals on a variety of social indicators.

Since the 2000 Lisbon meeting, the European Council has pursued a comprehensive strategy to become the "most competitive and dynamic knowledge-based economy" over the next decade, combining "sustainable economic growth with more and better jobs and greater social cohesion." To this end, the European Social Model explicitly aims to eradicate poverty, fight social exclusion, and enhance social cohesion. In October 2001, the Commission and the Council adopted the *Joint Inclusion Report*, based upon the first 2001 National Action Plans of Social Inclusion. The document, which strongly resembles the 1998 French law against social exclusion, specified four objectives:

1. facilitating participation in employment and access to resources and rights, goods and services for all citizens (e.g., social protection, housing, health care, education, justice, culture);
2. preventing the risks of exclusion by preserving family solidarity, preventing overindebtedness and homelessness, and promoting "inclusion";
3. helping the most vulnerable, for example, the persistently poor, children, residents of areas marked by exclusion; and
4. mobilizing all relevant bodies by promoting participation and self-expression of the excluded and partnerships and mainstreaming their concerns,

In March 2001 at Stockholm, the Commission called for explicit targets, and in December 2001 at the Laeken Summit, a revised list of social indicators was adopted. Most of these pertained to income, labor market status, access to public services, health, and education. Work on social and political indicators continues.

What Is Social Exclusion?

When the EU adopted "social exclusion" terminology from the French, its meaning subtly changed. British experts in the Poverty Programme, for example, tried to reconcile the French emphasis on social and cultural exclusion to their longstanding emphasis on material deprivation and social rights of citizenship, seeing poverty as an impediment to full participation in society. Deprivation could arise from insufficient income or directly from insufficient access to basic needs that allow people to actualize their social responsibilities (Townsend 1979). Conceptual work took a back seat to political compromise. Consider this definition of social exclusion (Vleminckx and Berghman 2001, 46) as "a concoction (or blend) of multidimensional and mutually reinforcing processes of deprivation, associated with progressive dissociation from social milieu, resulting in the isolation of individuals and groups from the mainstream of opportunities society has to offer!"

Simply put, the EU recast exclusion as an inability to exercise "the social rights of citizens" to a basic standard of living and as barriers to "participation" in the major social and occupational opportunities of the society (Mayes 2001). Methodologists (Atkinson et al. 2002) use the term as "shorthand for a range of concerns considered to be important in setting the European social agenda" and in "the fields that people have in mind when they talk about social rights." In contrast to poverty, which is exclusively economic, material, or resource-based, social exclusion offers a more holistic understanding of deprivation (de Haan 1999). Social exclusion is (1) multidimensional or socioeconomic, and encompasses collective as well as individual resources, (2) dynamic or processual, along a trajectory between full integration and multiple exclusions, (3) relational, in that exclusion entails social distance or isolation, rejection, humiliation, lack of social support networks, and denial of participation, (4) active, in that there is a clear agency doing the excluding, and (5) relative to context. Disrespect, discrimination, and degradation are as much at work as monetary poverty and physical need. In some versions, even the welfare state can exclude some citizens from protection or trap them in joblessness.

There may be consensus that exclusion is multidimensional, but that does not mean agreement on which dimensions are operative. EU social indicators are much better developed for material and labor market deprivation than for social, political, or cultural dimensions (Berger-Schmitt and Noll 2000). One approach is to ask people. The Poverty and Social Exclusion Survey (Gordon et al. 2000) not only asked people about their resources and participation in social activities, but also about whether they could afford them and even if they wanted them.

There is also disagreement over whether multidimensionality re fers to "cumulative" disadvantage or to any one of a wide range of deprivations that need not be material or economic. Britain's Social Exclusion Unit uses the term as "a shorthand label for what can happen when individuals or areas suffer from a combination of linked problems such as unemployment, poor skills, low incomes, poor housing, high crime environments, bad health and family breakdowns". In this definition, the excluded approximate a marginal, deviant "underclass." Multiple disadvantages obviously characterize fewer individuals and neighborhoods than those suffering from one of a number of disadvantages. Similarly, many more people suffer disadvantage at some point in their lives than those who remain disadvantaged for long periods.

French sociologists emphasize dynamics. Castel (1991) and Paugam (2000) trace a trajectory of "disaffiliation" and "disqualification" from a condition of economic and social integration through vulnerability or fragility to a breakdown of social ties. Both accounts emphasize social relations as well as labor market processes. While some say "social exclusion implies entrapment" and intergenerational transmission (Vleminckx and Berghman 2001, 136), persistent multiple disadvantage is infrequent (Burckart 2002; Leisering and Leibfried 1999; Room 2002). Exclusion exists along a continuum, rather than as an absolute condition of being an "outsider" or "pariah." Social exclusion is a relative, intrinsically social term also because it takes on different meanings, depending upon context or the point of reference for inclusion. When Americans speak of "exclusion," racial connotations often spring to mind: there are "exclusionary" institutions, like clubs or zoning, or "exclusive" prestigious resources, like neighborhoods or prep schools. When Bill Clinton spoke of inner city problems in 1993, he remarked "It's not an underclass anymore, it's an outer class." His Affirmative Action Report, calling to "mend it, don't end it," is full of calls for inclusion.

Other countries have different ideas about what belonging, membership, and full participation mean and about the benefits they bestow. Different histories, cultures, and demography shape national identities and criteria for citizenship and the salient types of inclusion (Silver 1996). While American race relations are central in defining the significance and common understanding of the term "integration" in the United States, Europeans feel uncomfortable with the word "race." Europe has few affirmative action policies, and avoids specific diversity targets. Equal opportunity policies apply mainly to women. Access to social rights traditionally comes through union representation.

French colonial history in North Africa or Germany's historical anti-Semitic and guest-worker policies are more central to how immigrant minorities are "integrated" or "incorporated" in France or Germany. While Europeans usually call the opposite of exclusion "insertion" or "solidarity," the preferred framework for cultural diversity issues is one of "citizenship," "nationality," or "cohesion." Speaking of cohesion can direct attention away from excluded groups and toward the responsibilities of the entire society. While the agents of exclusion can be impersonal institutions, dominant groups, and powerful individuals, the excluded must participate in their own inclusion. This means policies must provide them access, participation, and "voice" rather than making them passive recipients of material assistance. Many programs to combat exclusion build broad-based partnerships with representatives of excluded groups.

Measuring Social Exclusion

The complexity and relativity of social exclusion, its sensitivity to context and time, and its variation across salient dimensions, processes, and domains of social relations, have made it extremely difficult to define and measure "scientifically." Yet, driven by EU policy mandates, efforts to operationalize the concept separately from poverty have outpaced theoretical work. Most measurement efforts draw upon available data and are British-inspired, reflecting the forty or so output indicators of Blair's Social Exclusion Unit. However imperfect, these bench marks, more material than social, will offer "a toolbox of instruments" and a "common language for assessment" of National Action Plans to promote social inclusion. All approaches attempt to capture exclusion's multidimensionality, but, aside from low income and unemployment, they do not agree upon which dimensions are salient or causal. The most influential measurement report was by Tony Atkinson et al. (2002, 3) who proposed three levels of indicators of social exclusion. Level 1 has a small number of leading indicators, while Level 2 elaborates these, and Level 3 refers to nationally specific indicators.

Although this official list stresses consumption and production, work is under way to measure social and political dimensions of exclusion. European researchers are examining less tangible aspects like nonparticipation in civic life, poor future prospects, inability to participate in customary family and community activities, social crisis points in depressed regions and large cities, poor health, education, literacy/ numeracy, housing, and homelessness. Financial precariousness or indebtedness is also considered, as are measures of exclusion from public and private services, from social relations and activities, and from social support (e.g., Room 1995; Gordon et al. 2000; Gordon and Townsend 2000; Howarth et al. 1998; Robinson and Oppenheim 1998). Insofar as social exclusion is a relational concept associated with social isolation or civic participation, it overlaps with indicators of "social capital" taking account of associational membership, social network involvement, democratic inclusion, and access to rights. However, social capital indicators also refer to trust and treat social relations more instrumentally, as economic resources, rather than necessary aspects of social life. In this respect, even exclusion from leisure and culture are assessed as essentials of social membership. Regional disparities unrelated to unemployment also exist, including exposure to crime and other environmental conditions (Stewart 2002). Nongovernment organizations and the "social partners" are participating in this statistical process, giving a voice to the excluded. However, there are no indicators for exclusion by ethnicity or immigration. For example, Eurostat's fifteen nonmonetary indicators were grouped into seven dimensions of social exclusion, as well as their cumulation over time:

Implications

Americans have always resisted a relative definition of poverty. Poverty-line thinking has so dominated American social policy that "wel-fare" has narrowed its meaning to means-tested income transfers to lone parents. Now that welfare "reform" has mobilized multiple social supports to enable these parents to enter the paid labor force, the rhetoric of "inclusion"—the demand for access to jobs, respect, and a place at the table—may not be as foreign as it sounds. How many working Americans are "excluded" from health, unemployment, or disability insurance? How many are excluded from good jobs because of inadequate family support or child care or inferior public schools? How many are shut out of the housing market by unaffordable rents? Is segregation not about exclusion from white neighborhoods, schools, suburbs? Is the "glass ceiling" not a barrier to including women in the top echelon of jobs? Has the Americans with Disabilities Act really eliminated physical exclusion from all public facilities?

Are not formally equal citizens denied a say, while politicians listen only to campaign contributors, and school officials listen only to English? Americans have always had a populist, democratic impulse that rejects special privileges. If social exclusion and inclusion became important ideas in American policy alongside traditional concerns with absolute poverty, the political landscape might begin to change. Currently, groups concerned about neighborhoods (crime, services, education), the labor market (low wages, insecure employment, long-term unemployment, contingent work, unemployment insurance), social programs and services (Medicaid, Temporary Assistance to Needy Families [TANF], food stamps, child care), school performance, immigration, cultural expression, and many other issues are fragmented and even competitive.

A social exclusion/inclusion approach could serve as the rhetorical umbrella that brings the groups together. The role of symbolic discourse in building political alliances should not be underestimated.

Talking about "exclusion" connects people at all levels of the society through a common emotional experience found in social relations everywhere. No one can get through life without some rejection, humiliation, or unfair treatment. We have all been subjected to sanctions like gossip, or felt unwanted, left out, stigmatized, or "dissed." Conversely, the goal of inclusion appeals to our egali tarian impulses and common humanity, promoting solidarity with the excluded. Emma Lazarus's poem still strikes a deep chord with Americans whose ancestors were welcomed into our nation of immigrants. Citizens demand equal opportunity, even if they tolerate unequal rewards.

While the American emphasis on personal responsibility would seem to clash with the implication that insiders are the agents of exclusion, thinking dynamically as well as multidimensionally about disadvantage can also remind Americans that many of us have been down, but not out. Hard times can befall anyone. This thought too can help us empathize with the excluded. Just as "social exclusion" highlights the complex multidimensionality, cumulative and dynamic character of social disadvantage, so must inclusionary policies transcend traditional bureaucratic domains. Discrete programs and single-focus policies that now administer to people in need are, to put it euphemistically, disjointed. Service providers have little contact with one another. Families with multiple problems must make the rounds among many bureaucracies operating in different ways, each with scant understanding of families' overall situation, and with a lack of attention to improving their overall situation.

Americans need more comprehensive, "transversal," or what the British call "joined-up policies for joined-up problems" across social policy domains. Britain's Social Exclusion Unit or France's "interministerial" commissions coordinate national policy areas across ministries. Regional and local public-private partnerships collectively administer social assistance and service programs. One-stop service centers and casework that tailors packages of support and assistance to individual needs are back in vogue. In the United States, more progressive states now pursue similar strategies in their welfare-to-work policies, but integrating TANF with the Workforce Improvement Act and human services should be national policy. Since devolution, poverty in the United States should be thought of "relative" to state living standards. And if a few states adopt a policy of social inclusion, it may start things rolling at the federal level (Micklewright 2002).

The great divides of American society are not only economic but also based on racial-ethnic, gender, cultural, educational, and politi cal status lines. Discrimination and disrespect have material consequences, denying access to information, contacts, and resources, consigning minorities to low quality schools, dangerous neighborhoods, poorly paid jobs, and even joblessness. Americanizing the social exclusion perspective could put new wind in the sails of affirmative action. Calling for full inclusion would show that poverty, racism, and other forms of domination are integral to the functioning of American society, rather than accidental or unintended consequences easily addressed with an ameliorative program or financial adjustment here or there. To be sure, there is a danger of ghettoization and stigmatization whenever we introduce new labels for social problems.

Calling attention to spectacular forms of cumulative disadvantage may distract attention from widespread problems like rising inequality and family dissolution and undermine broader social programs. Indeed, some on the European Left worry that the "social exclusion" framework is replacing a "social class" perspective. Any discourse can serve a variety of political purposes, but ensuring widespread participation may overcome these downsides. Although people argue about the precise nature and measures of exclusion and cohesion, these ideas do provide a framework for discussing the new, complex forms of disadvantage. If appropriate, easily understood indicators could be found for these notions, benchmarking our progress as a society could go beyond the simple, intuitive, and familiar poverty line to track multiple forms of disadvantage.

6

The Social Exclusion Discourse: Ideas and Policy Change

This article explores the *political* discourse of social exclusion and its potential impact on social policy. The analysis suggests that in France, Britain, and the European Union at large, the growing political focus on social exclusion has helped to shift policy attention away from other forms of inequality, including income inequality. This logic and the reforms enacted in the name of social inclusion are compatible with moderate forms of economic liberalism distinct from Thatcherite neoliberalism. Theoretically, the article draws on the social science literature on the role of ideas to stress the possible consequences of the social exclusion discourse.

INTRODUCTION

Since the election of the first Blair government, the issue of social exclusion has become a major aspect of British social policy debates (Levitas, 2005). This issue has also gained much ground at the European Union level (Silver and Miller, 2003). Yet social exclusion is a contentious issue and scholars have debated the usefulness of this concept (eg Blanc, 1998).1 Because the concept of social exclusion first emerged in France and has long been a major policy issue there, it is appropriate to use France as the starting point for an inquiry into the meaning of that concept (eg Silver, 1994). The objective of this article is to draw extensively on the French case to shed new light on the *political* discourse about social exclusion and its potential impact on welfare state restructuring. Such an analysis suggests that the current political focus on social exclusion has helped to shift policy attention away from other forms of inequality, including income inequality between the wealthy and the rest of the population. This logic, as well as the content of many reforms enacted in the name of social inclusion (ie the fight against social exclusion and for citizenship integration), is compatible with moderate forms of economic liberalism distinct from Thatcherite neoliberalism. This fact partly explains the success of the concept of social exclusion among centre-left and Third Way politicians and public intellectuals, both in France and in Britain.

The argument here is not that the struggle against social exclusion can only take a liberal meaning, or that this concept should be discarded altogether. Indeed, the concept of social exclusion can take different meanings (Silver, 1994; Levitas, 2005), and it has the potential advantage of emphasising social problems that do not fall under the traditional concept of poverty. For example, this concept stresses the logic of 'cumulative disadvantage' that affects the most deprived segments of the population (Silver and Miller, 2003). But, as mobilised in centre-left and Third Way political discourse, the idea of social exclusion can become a powerful ideological tool that legitimises modest policy reforms entirely compatible with moderate understandings of economic liberalism and, ultimately, unable to fight the social evils this idea refers to. Theoretically, the article draws on the growing literature on the role of ideas in policy making to underline the three main ways in which the political discourse on social exclusion can impact policy making and welfare state reform. (i.e. serving as policy paradigm, reform blueprint, and justification device).

Three main sections comprise this article. First, a brief discussion about the role of ideas and discourse provides the necessary theoretical background to understanding the potential impact of the social exclusion discourse on welfare state reform. Second, an extended discussion of the French case traces the history of the concept of social exclusion before analysing the political discourse and the concrete social measures that have surrounded it since the late 1980s. Finally, a more concise section explores the similarities and the differences between the French and the British cases regarding the policy and ideological consequences of the social exclusion discourse. Because there is a lot of excellent scholarship already available about the British case (e.g. Levitas, 2005), this final section does not need to offer a comprehensive analysis of Third Way social policy but, instead, only comparative insight about the social exclusion discourse derived from the analysis of the French case.

THE IDEA OF SOCIAL EXCLUSION AND POLICY MAKING

Ideas impact political decisions in three main ways (Blyth, 2001, 2002). First, ideas can serve as 'cognitive locks' that help reproduce existing institutions and policies over time. This role of ideas corresponds to Peter Hall's widely cited work of policy paradigms and degrees of institutional change. For Hall, a policy paradigm is 'a framework of ideas and standards that specifies not only the goals of policy and kind of instruments that can be used to attain them, but also the very nature of the problems they are meant to be addressing' (Hall, 1993: 279) Second, ideas serve as policy blueprints that provide political actors with a model for reform. Offering a basic understanding of actors' interests, institutional opportunities and the economic pressures at stake, this model helps actors coordinate their efforts and build coalitions around common economic, social and political objectives.

Third, ideas constitute powerful ideological weapons that 'allow agents to challenge existing institutional arrangements and the patterns of distribution that they enshrine' (Blyth, 2001: 4) These ideas constitute a *political* discourse that, through framing processes (Campbell, 1998; Schmidt, 2001; Fischer, 2003), seek to convince decision makers, interest groups and the population at large that change is necessary. This is what Robert Cox labels 'the social construction of the need to reform'. 'In a political environment the advocates of reform need to employ strategies to overcome the scepticism of others and persuade them of the importance of reform. In other words, they must create a frame that changes the collective understanding of the welfare state, because doing so 'shapes the path' necessary to enact reform' (Cox, 2001: 475). Following this typology, the idea of social exclusion can contribute to three political tasks in the field of social policy reform. First, social exclusion constitutes a specific form of understanding that participates in the construction of both social problems and the policy responses to them.

From this perspective, the concept of social exclusion helps experts and policy makers make sense of the social world and design policies aimed at solving the social problems they deem important. But any policy paradigm comes with specific intellectual 'blind spots', as the focus on certain social problems relegates others to the periphery of the policy agenda. Second, this idea, and the related concept of social inclusion, can become the centrepiece of reform blueprints. This is especially true when social exclusion is tied to powerful concepts like solidarity and social citizenship. Centre-left and Third Way governments seeking to preserve references to social justice and national solidarity in the context of economic liberalism are especially prone to embrace a high-profile, yet ultimately modest, campaign against social exclusion.

The politics of social policy reform under the Rocard government in France and the Blair governments in Britain provides ground to this claim. Finally, the discourse about social exclusion and inclusion can become an effective framing tool to justify the 'need to reform' and promote specific policy alternatives. As suggested above, the explicit quest for social inclusion and 'national solidarity' in France legitimised the enactment of social programmes that reduced the fiscal reliance on social insurance contributions, which is one of the core policy imperatives of contemporary economic liberalism in continental Europe.3 In Britain, an increasingly moralistic social exclusion discourse constructed the need for workfare, a policy idea 'imported' from the US during the Clinton years (Daguerre, 2004).

The following section on France will first trace the emergence of the social exclusion paradigm before analysing the formulation of an exclusion-centred reform blueprint and, finally, the framing of a justification discourse about social exclusion that participates in the construction of the 'need to reform' the French welfare state.

SOCIAL EXCLUSION AND SOCIAL POLICY REFORM IN FRANCE

As it emerged after the Second World War, the modern French welfare state was embedded in a social insurance model that prominently featured 'occupational solidarity' (*solidarité professionnelle*). This means that, despite efforts to unite existing pre-war social insurance schemes, the French welfare state has largely remained fragmented among occupational lines. In addition to the *régime général* protecting private sector workers, dozens of autonomous insurance schemes cover about 20% of the workforce (eg Béland and Hansen, 2000). Occupational categories participating in these schemes include independent workers, farmers and civil servants. Despite this high level of fragmentation, the post-war French social insurance system offered earnings-related benefits to the vast majority of the working population. Furthermore, employers and labour unions participated in the administration of the social insurance system. Yet, with the exception of unemployment insurance, the French state maintained a central role in the governance of this system. Although that system represented the centrepiece of the welfare state, social assistance programmes granting genuine social rights existed to help those excluded from the labour market (Bec, 1998).

THE EMERGENCE OF THE SOCIAL EXCLUSION PARADIGM

In France, as in most other advanced industrial countries, the expansion of the post-war welfare state coincided with almost three decades of economic prosperity that ended with the 1973 oil crisis and the following stagflation era. It was during the last of these three decades of prosperity that the term 'exclusion' emerged in the

French social and academic discourse.4 As early as 1965, social commentator Jean Klanfer published a book entitled *L'Exclusion sociale: Étude de la marginalité dans les sociétés occidentales* [Social exclusion: The study of marginality in western societies]. In this moralistic book emphasising personal responsibility, the term 'social exclusion' refers to people who cannot enjoy the positive consequences of economic progress due to irresponsible behaviour (Klanfer, 1965).

Less than a decade later, René Lenoir published *Les exclus: Un français sur dix* [The excluded: One Frenchman out of ten]. For Lenoir, the excluded are those citizens who are separated from mainstream society because of factors like disability, mental illness and poverty. According to Lenoir who, as a civil servant, had studied French social problems for more than 15 years, as much as 10% of the population suffered from social exclusion. Focusing on social and economic conditions rather than personal responsibility to explain social problems, Lenoir thus defines social exclusion in an extremely broad manner (Lenoir, 1974). Although the meaning of the term 'exclusion' has changed since the mid-1970s, Lenoir's book is widely regarded as the 'founding document' of the modern discourse about exclusion in French society (Frétigné, 1999: 63).

During the 1980s and 1990s, the prevalence of long-term unemployment and growing concerns about racism and discrimination altered the meaning of social exclusion, a concept that increasingly – yet not exclusively – defined the lack of social integration related to limited access to labour market opportunities. From the perspective of the emerging social exclusion paradigm, long-term unemployment is a major source of social isolation. This is why social exclusion constitutes a threat to France's Republican model of integration based on the ideas of citizenship and social solidarity. Although evidence suggests that there is no strong relationship between unemployment and social isolation (Gallie et al, 2003), the belief that long-term unemployment and, consequently, social exclusion represent a major threat to social order is featured prominently in the discourse about the deprived suburbs of France. To a certain extent, the geographical isolation of these suburbs reinforces the idea that France was witnessing the advent of a divided society that betrayed the egalitarian model of citizenship and social integration at the centre of the French republican tradition.

'The very word *la banlieue*, which creates an image of crime and indigence, graffiti and burned-down cars cut off from Paris and other French cities highlights the extent to which the extreme deprivation of segments of French society is marginal to the majority's daily existence and life chances' (Béland and Hansen, 2000: 54). Economic and urban problems bred ethnic tensions as a portion of the population of African descent felt increasingly left behind. The emergence of the racist Front National in the mid-1980s exacerbated such tensions. This situation triggered a debate over the efficiency of the 'French model of integration' based on secularism and colourblind public policy (Schnapper, 1998). Furthermore, although the excluded were generally described as the victims of unfavourable economic and social conditions, the growing discourse about 'urban insecurity' suggested that those excluded from mainstream society could become a menace to ordinary citizens, and even to the Republican order as a whole.

The suburban riots of October and November 2005, France's 'worst unrest since the student uprisings of 1968', exacerbated fears of 'urban violence' and led Prime Minister Dominique de Villepin to declare a state of emergency (Associated Press, 2005). At the cognitive and paradigmatic level, there are two original things that distinguish the term 'social exclusion' from other concepts used to define contemporary social problems. First, this term has a strong biographical meaning because it refers to the personal experience of social and economic isolation supposedly related to unemployment, discrimination and other social problems (Goguel d'Allondans, 2003: 43). Second, social exclusion is based on a horizontal, spatial metaphor rather than a vertical model of inequality focusing mainly on income disparities. From the perspective of the social exclusion paradigm, people are more 'in' or 'out' of mainstream society than 'up' or down' the class or the income distribution structure. Because of that, it is possible to argue that, in France, the growing emphasis on social exclusion during the 1980s and 1990s helped move the social and political debate away from class inequality and income redistribution at large (eg Friot, 1998).

When long-term unemployment and social isolation become the centre of attention, class and income inequality increasingly moves to the outskirts of the policy agenda.5 From this perspective, the focus on social exclusion is compatible with moderate interpretations of economic liberalism, which are grounded in the assumption that the state should fight deprivation but not income inequality at large, a phenomenon described as a condition of economic prosperity. Furthermore, in France as elsewhere, the struggle against long-term unemployment and social exclusion has mainly favoured the enactment of fiscally modest measures financed through general revenues of the state, not payroll taxes. This is important for two reasons: first, comparatively high payroll taxes, like the ones existing in France, are perceived as an obstacle to economic competitiveness in the era of economic globalisation and European integration; second, and consequently, social policy reforms enacted in France since the late 1980s have attempted to reduce the relative role of payroll taxes within the French welfare state in part by referring to a great patriotic struggle against social exclusion (Béland and Hansen, 2000; Palier, 2002; Barbier and Théret, 2004).

Before exploring the social exclusion blueprint and the welfare reforms stemming from it, one can formulate a few cautionary remarks about the impact of economic liberalism in France. As opposed to countries like Britain and the US, explicitly neoliberal political discourse against the welfare state is hardly popular in France, where Thatcherite reforms are viewed with suspicion. And, when blatantly neoliberal reforms are pushed forward, waves of protest like the strikes of December 1995 can put those in power into a difficult situation (e.g. Béland and Hansen, 2000). Furthermore, post-war economic legacies make Thatcherite neoliberalism impossible to implement in France. This means that, in this country, the triumph of economic liberalism during the 1980s took a more moderate form than in Britain and the US, for example (Prasad,

2005).6 Finally, as underlined below, the moralistic side of Thatcherite neoliberalism grounded in the idea of workfare enjoys little political support in France. These cautionary remarks are crucial to understand the ideological background of France's policies dealing with social exclusion.

THE SOCIAL EXCLUSION BLUEPRINT AND POLICY CHANGE

It was only in the late 1980s and early 1990s that the idea of 'exclusion' became a central *political* issue in France. From this perspective, references to social exclusion and inclusion emerged as a coherent blueprint for social policy reform. Two factors helped transform the fight against social exclusion into a policy blueprint capable of guiding policy change. First, the increase of long-term unemployment and the growing public debate about racism in French society pushed this issue onto the policy agenda. Second, political actors began to identify themselves with the struggle against social exclusion in an era of fiscal austerity and economic deception. In a macro-economic context that had witnessed a shift from Keynesianism to a moderate form of economic liberalism during François Mitterrand's first presidential mandate (Jobert, 1994; Schmidt, 1996), elected officials, especially those on the left, found in the struggle against exclusion a vehicle to reaffirm their strong commitment to the ever popular Republican model of integration while showing their generosity towards the unemployed.

Politically, the Rocard years (1988–91) represented a turning point in French social policy development as the Socialist government attempted to significantly restructure the welfare state in a manner compatible with both the liberal economic paradigm and the Republican social solidarity imperative that one can trace back to the work of Émile Durkheim and his followers (Bourgeois, 1998; Humphreys, 1999). Retrospectively, one could argue that the Rocard government attempted to articulate a new centre-left policy blueprint and agenda compatible with moderate forms of economic liberalism.7 Two crucial measures were adopted under the Rocard government:

the *Revenu minimum d'insertion* (RMI) [Minimum Integration Income] and the *Contribution sociale généralisée* (CSG) [Universal Social Contribution]. Favouring a partial shift from social insurance and 'occupational solidarity' to universal social assistance rights and 'national solidarity', these measures would have a long-term impact on the French welfare state (Palier, 2002; Barbier and Théret, 2004).

Unanimously adopted by the National Assembly in December 1988, the RMI is a social assistance programme that provides modest financial support to unemployed individuals aged 25 and older who have exhausted their unemployment insurance benefits.8 Grounded in the Republican idea of 'national solidarity', this programme therefore assumes that 'family solidarity' (ie parental help) would provide minimum support to the unemployed aged between 18 and 24. Yet the RMI defines social assistance as a right of citizenship – at least for those older than 24. More importantly, the RMI is not defined as a traditional, 'passive' form of assistance but as an 'active' one. This means that one of the main objectives of the RMI is to help those who face long-term unemployment to reintegrate into the labour market.

While rejecting the punitive concept of workfare which was then becoming more popular in the US, French policy makers promoted the concept of *insertion*, which is featured in the programme's very name (Barbier and Théret, 2001). In the French social and political discourse, insertion refers to a participatory model of 'activation' based on a contractual model rather than the punitive logic that later triumphed in the US with the enactment of the controversial 1996 welfare reform (Personal Responsibility and Work Opportunity Reconciliation Act). This provides more ground to the idea that France's policy makers have rejected the moralistic and neoliberal logic of workfare that became dominant in the US and, later, in Britain (Morel, 2000; Daguerre, 2004).

Within the French Republican model, the state has the *obligation* to provide assistance to citizens (Bec, 1998). Yet what the RMI introduces is a *contrat d'insertion* that creates a sense of reciprocal obligations between the state and the beneficiary. Such a contract enumerates the tasks the beneficiary should undertake in order to reintegrate the labour market (e.g. returning to school, undertaking occupational training). Although this contract is more symbolic than constraining, it lays the foundation for a more individualised form of social protection and economic integration (Rosanvallon, 2000). In this context, the role of the state is not only to provide minimum financial support but to help the long-term unemployed return to the labour market. In contrast with the optimistic rhetoric about insertion surrounding the enactment of the RMI in 1988, this programme has been criticised for its modest benefits and limited success regarding the actual proportion of beneficiaries who find a permanent job after spending months or even years on welfare. From this perspective, the RMI does not strongly reduce economic insecurity as a large proportion of beneficiaries spend their time moving in and out of the labour market between precarious, short-term contracts and 'passive' assistance (Bec, 1998).

A second major social policy measure passed during the Rocard years is the Contribution Sociale Généralisée (CSG). Enacted in 1991, the CSG is the first among a series of policies that have favoured a partial shift from contributionfinancing to tax-financing in the French welfare state. Initially, the CSG proved relatively modest, with a tax rate of 1.1% levied on all incomes. Over the years, however, successive governments have increased that rate (Levy, 1999; Palier, 2002), which, in 2005, varied between 3.8 and 8.2% (French Government, 2005). One of the rationales of the CSG is to limit the level of social insurance contributions that, from the perspective of economic liberalism, are perceived as a strong obstacle to job creation and, consequently, the fight against long-term unemployment (Jobert, 1994). In order to promote job creation and reduce social exclusion, the French government has thus offered targeted reductions in social insurance contributions affecting low-paid workers.

It was during the 1990s that social exclusion, both as a policy blueprint and a political discourse, became truly dominant in France. Considering the neoliberal context of fiscal austerity related to

European monetary integration and global competitiveness, however, successive French governments could hardly launch bold social programmes to fight social exclusion and long-term unemployment. Perhaps because of that, the social inclusion blueprint essentially led to the enactment of symbolic measures like the *Loi d'orientation de lutte contre les exclusions* [Guidelines for the Struggle against Social Exclusions] of May 1998. Marginal in its concrete policy effects, this legislation appeared as a mere political statement of the Socialist Jospin government (1997–2002) regarding its commitment to fight all forms of social exclusion and to help needy citizens. Yet this commitment led to a few significant measures, like the 1999 legislation that made health coverage truly universal for the first time. Following the adoption of this measure, the French state provided health coverage to deprived individuals who were not participating in existing social insurance schemes. Although modest, this measure constitutes a highly symbolic legislation adopted in order to fight social exclusion.

The social exclusion discourse and the construction of the 'need to reform'

In France, as elsewhere, social exclusion is not only a term that refers to a set of social and economic problems; it also constitutes a powerful political and normative discourse about the welfare state and the reforms necessary to adapt it to changing social and economic conditions. For this reason, the discourse on social exclusion participates in the 'social construction of the need to reform' (Cox, 2001) and can legitimise path-departing reforms in the name of 'national solidarity' and social citizenship (Béland and Hansen, 2000). Yet, because these reforms reduce the role of social insurance schemes and focus mainly on the 'truly needy' at the expense of other forms of inequality, they are compatible with neoliberal assumptions about economic and social regulation. Seldom criticised directly, such discourse on social exclusion has become dominant in mainstream French political circles, especially with the Socialist Party. During the 1990s, the struggle against social exclusion became one of the most central aspects of the Socialist Party's centre-left platform (eg Jospin, 1998). Still, moderate right-wing politicians like Jacques Chirac have also embraced the struggle against exclusion, for example during the 1995 presidential campaign, making it the central element of his electoral platform for a strategic reason (ie the need to seduce moderate and Socialist voters). A few months after his election to the presidency, he made sure to remind the public about his commitment to fight social exclusion (Chirac, 1995). Although an example of political opportunism that faded away after the 1995 presidential election, this discourse suggests that, during the 1990s at least, one witnessed a convergence of both the moderate left and the moderate right around the issue of social exclusion. A moral issue surrounded by references to the Republican tradition, the war on exclusion represented a fiscally affordable yet highly symbolic (Republican) form of social policy restructuring.

Beyond the political field, centre-left public intellectuals depicted the war on social exclusion as a major objective of French public policy that would mean the end of the traditional social insurance model that had dominated France's social policy arena since the beginning of the 20th century. The most prominent of these public intellectuals is probably Pierre Rosanvallon, a scholar who has been associated with the Socialist Party and the centrist labour union CFDT (*Confédération Française Démocratique du Travail*). In his 1995 best-seller *La nouvelle question sociale: Repenser l'état-providence* [translated in 2000 as The new social question: Rethinking the welfare state], Rosanvallon offers a theoretical and ideological justification for the reforms enacted under the Rocard government (CSG, RMI). Furthermore, this author argues that more reforms are needed in order to adequately fight social exclusion and long-term unemployment while pushing the French welfare state further away from the traditional social insurance model.

According to him, the 'passive welfare state' should become less central as the 'active welfare state' emerges as a new tool of social integration and insertion. For Rosanvallon, the social insurance model implemented decades ago is less and less consistent with the new structure of risk that characterises contemporary society. Among the new social risks, social exclusion is certainly the most crucial one. In part because of that, the RMI is described as a model for future social programmes, whose goal would be to promote active economic citizenship. As for the CSG, it is depicted as an innovative fiscal model that could bring about genuine 'national solidarity' while moving beyond the fiscally regressive aspect (and the economic burden) of social insurance contributions (Rosanvallon, 2000). In the name of inclusion and social citizenship, Rosanvallon is advocating path-departing reforms that would reduce the relative weight of social insurance. Although this project remains largely unfinished, his ideas show how concerns about social exclusion can help construct the need to restructure social insurance schemes compatible with economic liberalism.

In France, such a frontal ideological attack against social insurance provoked a strong reaction from the far left, especially from supporters of 'old left' labour unions like FO (*Force Ouvrière*) and the CGT (*Confédération Générale du Travail*). Interestingly, these unions seldom address the issue of social exclusion, perhaps because it may underline the limits of the social insurance model with which they identify. This is true because labour unions participate in the management of the French social insurance system, and this participation provides them with significant material and symbolic benefits (eg Bonoli, 2000). Opinion polls also suggest that the public support the maintenance of business and labour participation in social insurance governance. Furthermore, elected officials rarely attack the idea of social insurance publicly, as they fear negative reactions from social partners (Clasen and Clegg, 2003: 372–3). Finally, on the far left, public intellectuals like Bernard Friot oppose the discourse on social exclusion and 'national solidarity'. According to Friot, the CSG and the struggle against social exclusion constitute an attack against the protected wage system based on social insurance principles and the traditional class distinction between workers and employers. Consequently, this author explicitly opposes British-style, universalistic welfare to 'occupational solidarity' based on class relations (Friot, 1998).

Overall, this section showed that, in France, social exclusion gradually became an influential paradigm in the 1970s and 1980s, before emerging in the early 1990s as a centre-left reform blueprint and a political discourse participating in the 'social construction of the need to reform' (Cox, 2001) post-war policy legacies.

FROM FRANCE TO BRITAIN

Social exclusion as a paradigm, a blueprint and a political discourse has been dispersed throughout Europe and beyond. This diffusion process began in the mid-1980s, when Jacques Delors, then president of the European Commission, stressed the need for a strong 'social dimension' to the European project. From this perspective, the fight against social exclusion gradually became a *European* policy paradigm and justification discourse. Following this logic, during the 1990s, 'the third EU "poverty programme" was gradually transformed into a fight against social exclusion' (Silver and Miller, 2003: 5). The 2000 Lisbon and Nice European Councils reinforced this commitment in the struggle against exclusion, which had gradually become a major feature of the European blueprint about social welfare, especially employment policy (eg Begg and Berghman, 2002; van Berkel and Hornemann Møller, 2002). The fight against exclusion is now a major aspect of the so-called 'open method of coordination', and the European Union and other European organisations have published numerous reports and studies about social exclusion (eg Fernández de la Hoz, 2001).

Although the transmission of the idea of social exclusion throughout Europe came to the attention of some British policy makers, it was the advent of the Third Way and, more specifically, the 1997 electoral victory of 'New Labour' that pushed the issue of social exclusion into the centre of the policy agenda. The first symbol of this new focus was the Social Exclusion Unit (SEU), an organisation created in December 1997. Less than three years later, Melissa Benn could even write that 'To many government insiders, the SEU is the jewel in Labour's policy crown, its favoured administrative son' (Benn, 2000: 309). In his various speeches, the

Prime Minister emphasised the need for an ambitious social inclusion blueprint: 'I have always said that turning the tide of social exclusion is a ten-year project. We have made a start but there are still far too many areas where people have no job, no shop, no bank account, no links to the mainstream economy.

Bringing people into the economy and giving them access to the opportunities that others take for granted requires us to make a new connection between economic opportunity and social renewal' (Blair, 1999). Yet, as Benn points out, the gap between the Prime Minister's blueprint and the actual measures enacted 'in the name of inclusion' – for example the various 'New Deals' – is striking (Benn, 2000). Regarding the social exclusion blueprint, this is certainly something that the French and the British situations have in common: powerful rhetoric about social justice yet modest resources allocated to social inclusion programmes. This remark points to another striking similarity between France, Britain and the European Union at large: the compatibility between some forms of economic liberalism and the social exclusion paradigm that provides the intellectual and ideological background for centrist policy making. In the case of New Labour, its Third Way approach to social and economic problems is grounded in the explicit recognition that the new government should preserve most of Thatcher's economic and social policy legacy (Hefferman, 2000: 65).

Like in France, the official, centrist discourse about social exclusion helps to shift the policy attention away from broad forms of income inequality, particularly the one between the wealthy and the rest of the population. This is true in part because the Third Way's agenda is rooted in the assumption that the citizen's capacity to participate in social and economic life is a better measure 'of social justice than income inequality alone' (Davies, 2005: 13). The recent work of Anthony Giddens provides an ideological justification to that paradigm shift (Giddens, 2001). Concretely, income inequality is increasing in Britain and 'between 1996 and 2001 Britain moved from sixth to fourth most unequal in the European Union, passing Ireland and Italy' (Davies, 2005: 22). At the social policy level, the fight against exclusion has justified the moving away from unconditional social rights to conditional entitlements related to the idea of 'activation' (Dwyer, 2004).

This model of 'activation' involves the imposition of work-related conditions to entitlements, which is compatible with the transformation of social assistance witnessed in the US and in other European nations (Cox, 1998).12 Among the many British measures enacted to fight social exclusion and to bring 'activation' about are the 1999 Welfare Reform and Pensions Act, the 2002 Job Centre Plus initiative, and the various New Deals for the youth and the unemployed (Dwyer, 2004). Overall, the push for 'activation' has proved stronger in Britain than in France, where the RMI's *contrat d'insertion* is distinct from the workfare model the first Blair government borrowed from the Clinton administration (King, 1999; Clasen and Clegg, 2003: 366; Daguerre, 2004).

From this perspective, the official New Labour discourse about social exclusion justifies conditional entitlements in the name of an increasingly moralistic vision of social inclusion (Levitas, 2005). Although it emphasises a convergence between the French and the British social policy discourse about social exclusion, this comparison does not suggest that the situation in these two countries is identical.

First, Thatcherite neoliberalism has never become prominent in France, where economic liberalism has a more moderate character than in Britain. Second, the French discourse on social exclusion is centred on the notion of social solidarity, which is not a prominent feature of the British political discourse. Third, the British discourse on 'activation' is increasingly grounded in moralistic claims about personal responsibility that are less apparent in France. In that country, it is politically risky to 'blame the victim', an approach perceived as an attack against the idea of social solidarity so central in the French Republican model. The late 2005 social and political backlash against the harsh and moralistic 'law and order' discourse of the French Minister of the Interior Nicolas Sarkozy provides ground to this claim (eg Ridet, 2006).

Fourth, in France, social exclusion had long existed as a widely debated concept and paradigm before becoming the centrepiece of a prominent policy blueprint, which was not the case in Britain. There, the Blair government suddenly transformed it into a prominent policy blueprint and discourse before it emerged as a shared paradigm (eg Marsh, 2004: 19). In other words, as opposed to the situation prevailing in France, social exclusion became a blueprint and a justification discourse before academics, journalists and public intellectuals began to discuss its meaning seriously as a cognitive category. In such a context, it is the transformation of social exclusion into a major Third Way blueprint and discourse that forced many British academics and public intellectuals to embrace the social exclusion paradigm or, at the very least, to engage critically with it.

CONCLUSION

The political debate over social exclusion is still raging in France, Britain and elsewhere in Europe, so it is perhaps too early to derive definitive conclusions about the policy impact of the political discourse on social exclusion and inclusion. Drawing extensively from the French case, this article suggests that social exclusion can become a policy paradigm, the centrepiece of influential reform blueprints and a justification discourse. From this perspective, the politics of social policy surrounding the issue of social exclusion features the three main ways in which ideas can impact policy development: the crystallisation of policy paradigms that affect the perception of social problems, the elaboration of reform blueprints and, finally, the construction of the 'need to reform' and the related justification of relevant policy options.

Regarding the social exclusion debate, these three types of ideational processes helped move policy attention away from other forms of social inequality while legitimising specific policy alternatives compatible with moderate interpretations of economic liberalism and, consequently, with centre-left and Third Way agendas. Yet, the above discussion about the French and the British cases should not suggest that social exclusion is in itself a liberal idea, or that scholars should get rid of this potentially meaningful concept altogether. Social exclusion can become a useful intellectual tool, and perhaps references to this idea could draw the public's attention towards major social problems not associated with traditional concepts such as poverty and the 'underclass' (Silver and Miller, 2003). Yet, in the current context, the dominant political discourse about social exclusion has done little more than legitimise modest social programmes that seldom challenge the liberal logic seeking to limit social spending while encouraging citizens to become increasingly dependent on market outcomes (ie 'recommodification').

All in all, this article points to the crucial fact that the politics of ideas involves major symbolic struggles, and scholars, although they are not always aware of it, participate in them on a regular basis. As the French and the British cases suggest, academic debates about social exclusion have a *political* meaning, and students of social policy should keep in mind that *their* discourse about this issue can matter a great deal.

7

Social Inclusion, Social Exclusion and Social Closure

INTRODUCTION

Theories of social exclusion focus on the shortcomings and barriers that prevent members of disadvantaged groups improving their life circumstances. Their failure to match the social capital advantages of other sectors of society perpetuates social inequalities through generations. In recent decades inequality and social exclusion have become more noticeably concentrated in neighbourhoods, a process of 'ghetto-isation'. The UK Labour government has sought to address this growth of inequality and social exclusion. Neighbourhood renewal has become a major policy concern. The Social Exclusion Unit was a central, Cabinet level organisation in the 1990s and neighbourhood renewal was a major government priority (Great Britain, Social Exclusion Unit 1998). Utilisation of social capital and community capacity building are seen as community interventions able to break the cycle of disadvantage.

This paper began from interest in social networking and social capital. However, I have studied these processes among privileged groups: corporate executives and business leaders (Alexander 2003, 2004) By contrast, most practitioner interest in social capital comes from community workers and government departments concerned with ameliorating social disadvantage. My initial aim was to see whether the social network formations I observed among privileged groups are models for community development networks. What I discovered, however, is that it is not the form of social networks that matters but the values that animate them. 'Networking' in these settings is very different. I will return to this initial question in my conclusion. The main task of this paper, however, will be to offer a social theory framework for observations of similarity and contrast between these two settings.

Social exclusion is the main theoretical idea I will discuss. The practitioner and ameliorative vision highlights social exclusion at the outcome level. Inequality and disadvantage are visible and measurable. But what is happening at the process level? What are the forms of social interaction that produce social exclusion and how is it perpetuated? The answers to these questions turn out to be surprising. The social processes that produce social exclusion are actually the ones that are also presented as the tactics to overcome it. It is the utilisation of social capital and the community capacity building of advantaged sectors of the community that, on the platform of accumulated privileges, permit them to maintain and expand their social capital and move even further ahead of the disadvantaged communities.

Community capacity building, empowerment, collective action, and cooperation are aspects of the general concept of social capital. Robert Putnam's (1993) seminal comparison of Northern and Southern Italy argued that differences in their current prosperity and wellbeing were due to the North's traditions and institutions of civic engagement and community cooperation. In the corporate world, management theory sees successful corporations as those that develop their human assets to create the intellectual and social capital resources and contribute to nnovation.

The 'communities of practice' of the major professions such as medicine and law are seen as repositories of social capital (Bourdieu 1996). They sustain that social capital through the sharing of theoretical and technical knowledge and collective action to maintain their public prestige, status and market value.

Defined in this framework social exclusion flows from a lack of action. We may blame the advantaged groups for a failure to reach out and include the disadvantaged communities. Or we may blame the disadvantaged communities for a failure to develop and utilise their social resources in ways that allow them to compete with the advantaged communities.

This is not the language commonly associated with discussions of social exclusion however. Social exclusion, inequality and disadvantage are usually discussed as outcomes of power relations. At a process level this becomes personal when inequality is linked to an active process of discrimination, stereotyping and intolerance. At this process level, social exclusion is easily visualised as social closure. The in-group consolidates and defines its identity as superior to other groups. 'Power structures' perpetuate inequality and work to continually undermine the empowerment attempts of disadvantaged groups.

What then makes community work or civic activity empowering, whether it be interventions sponsored by governments to improve disadvantaged communities or the self-generated and self-sustaining activities of successful communities? Standard definitions of social capital focus on trust, norms and networks (Field 2003, pp. 1-5). My own research work involves the study of networks and this will be the direction of this paper. However, the study of networks can be an abstract exercise looking at networks from above and seeing overall patterns of connection, density and so forth. My own research is mostly in this tradition of network analysis. The other side of social network analysis looks at networks from within, seeing how individuals build their personal relationships to create, collectively but unintentionally, networks. Networks are objects of scientific excitement when viewed from the special vantage point of the omniscient outsider observer (Buchanan 2002) but 'personal communities' when understood from the perspective of the social actors (Wellman 1999, pp. 18-23 and passim). This inside view of networks also permits us to focus on the processes inside networks, the activity of 'networking' (Gilchrist 2004).

This paper addresses the gap between the internal and external views of networks through discussion of the neo-Weberian concept of social closure and links this concept to issues of power and empowerment. Social closure is a concept that embraces elements of process — exclusion — and outcomes — social inequality. Neo-Weberian theory takes account of the pervasive public concern with structure of power as a process of *exclusionary* social closure but does not insist that social exclusion is the only possible outcome of social closure. In the first section of the paper I give the background and principal ideas of neo-Weberian theory. In the second part of the paper I discuss its perspective on the emergence of 'class' conflict in the situation of the 1970s and its prescient view of the way that situation could change. I then show how contemporary views of community engagement and community work in the UK have indeed shifted prevailing perceptions of class conflict and social amelioration in directions prefigured by the neo-Weberian theory.

This paper began from the idea of looking at networks and networking among successful communities and groups ('social elites') to see what aspects of their practice might be of interest to community workers and policy makers seeking to ameliorate inequality and social exclusion. The concept of social closure provides a social theoretical framework to consider these issues and I explore this concept in the body of the paper. Finally I conclude the paper by looking at our initial question in light of the framework discussion.

NEO-WEBERIAN THEORY OF SOCIAL CLOSURE

Neo-Weberian theory was the label for a group of British sociologists in the 1970s. They were concerned with studies of stratification and mobility but chose to keep themselves apart from the Marxist and Foucauldian theories that dominated British sociological discourses of the era. The major theorist of the group was Frank Parkin. Parkin produced only two books of theory, however, an account of Weber's sociology (Parkin 2002) and a small, densely argued tract structured as a critique of the academic Marxist writings of the era (Parkin 1979). While each of these books contains the essential elements of his theoretical position, his statement of neo-Weberian theory emerges only as a subtext to the actual foci of the books.

Parkin derives his theory from Weber's discussions of social closure, particularly those in the famous essay on *Class, Status and Power* (Weber 1946). Neo-Weberian theory involves taking the central concept of social closure and developing its principles beyond the point that Weber had done and, indeed, in ways that are incompatible with Weber's separate discussion of power.

Social closure is defined as: "the process by which social collectivities seek to maximize rewards by restricting access to resources and opportunities to a limited circle of eligibles" (Parkin 1979, p. 44).

Weber's essay gives examples of social closure and exclusivity as status hierarchies, competition for 'honour' and standards of 'good taste'. These are also issues explored by Pierre Bourdieu (1996). Weber used the term 'status-groups' to designate the social entities created by social closure. The notion of party in the essay extends this idea of social closure to the point where the social mechanisms of closure and exclusion allow the status-group to act collectively to gain political, economic and material rewards from its ability to undertake collective action.

Parkin designates this process *exclusionary* social closure. He suggests that it is a universal tendency that results in systems of stratification. The system of aristocracy is the most obvious system based on exclusionary social closure. In an aristocratic society the status-group controls political power and also institutionalises its right to pass on that power and privilege directly to its offspring.

The liberal revolutions of the nineteenth century overturned aristocratic privilege and fought to purge it from the constitutions of liberal democracies. However it was only the principle of hereditary privilege that they objected to, not the process of social closure or the continuation of stratification and inequality. The liberal ideal thus posits a system where the transmission of privilege and, hence, the maintenance of the stratification system and inequality is, in theory, based on an individual's merit and personal abilities, not on family, birth or 'breeding'.

However, like aristocratic families before them, the successful status-groups of liberal democracies want to pass on their privileges to their offspring. They do this through mechanisms that help their offspring gain the personal abilities and meritorious achievements that will be recognised in the status system. Thus, in Parkin's view, liberal democracies espouse principles of equal opportunity and meritocracy while turning a blind eye to the de facto mechanisms that allow for the transmission of accumulated privilege. Bourdieu's analysis of culture, taste and privilege is a fuller description of the same process.

Parkin suggests that while social closure and status-group formation can lead to a uni-dimensional, layered system of stratification, such as the Indian caste system, the characteristic system of stratification in western, capitalist societies develops around binary oppositions of social class. Social differences become perceived as 'class' differences when the subordinate groups define their identity in terms of their subordinate position and direct their collective action toward changing the system rather than simply seeking to accumulate advantages over less well placed status-groups within a given system of stratification. Marxist theory located all social conflicts around the binary opposition of the working class and the bourgeoisie. Parkin argues, however, that 'class' conflict can also arise when ethnic groups see themselves as oppressed. Here the identifier of 'class', understood as the principle of classification, is not social position but ethnic identity.

Britain in the late 1970s was a society where class was defined and understood in an oppositional way. The struggles between the union movement and the Thatcher government created a climate of social conflict. The embedded concepts of social class and the intensity of social conflict thus combined to make it an era of 'class struggle'. The point of neo-Weberian theory is to suggest that this was a historically specific configuration. A consequence of its position is that the conditions of class conflict may moderate and become less oppositional, changing the grounds of political identity, party programs and class conflict. The prescience of the neo-Weberian theory is that such change has occurred since the 1970s. Thus some of the less remarked upon theoretical issues raised by neo-Weberian theory are now more salient than at the time of its original formulation.

THE DECLASSING OF SOCIAL CONFLICT AND SOCIAL CLOSURE

Neo-Weberian theory suggested that there is an enduring tension within liberal democracy between the formal commitment to equal opportunity and advancement on merit, and the de facto privilege that wealthy and professional families are able to pass on to their offspring. The neo-Weberian school was active in the 1970s. Neo-liberal reforms to social institutions were only beginning in that era. The salience of their theoretical insights was not apparent at that time.

The neo-liberal policies of the 1980s and 1990s produced sweeping changes in public policy frameworks and fundamental institutional reforms. Much commentary focuses on the social disruptions and economic restructuring that these changes entailed. This concern means that attention focuses on the groups who were disadvantaged and displaced and little attention is given to other social impacts.

Neo-liberal reforms had a profound impact, however, on the institutional structures involved in the de facto perpetuation of status and privilege. This came through the systematic and continuing concern of neo-liberal policy makers with competition policy. Competition policy has been the weapon with which neo-liberal policy makers selectively attack areas of entrenched privilege and the status-groups formed around them. To some extent this has even affected corporate elites. In Australia there has been a significant and effective campaign to wipe out the restrictive trade practices (i.e.

price-fixing) of local oligopolies that prevailed till the 1970s. This has been accompanied by trade liberalisation (tariff reduction) and open entry for foreign investment, forcing local companies to match world producers in productive efficiency.

One of the further concerns of competition policy, broadly conceived, is to break down the perceived 'monopolies' that professions create through systems of state regulation, licensing and credentials. Government managed systems for medical and pharmaceutical regulation are continually subject to scrutiny. Australia has instituted systems forcing State governments to recognise overseas and interstate professionals. Professional associations that regulated practitioners by prohibiting them from charging less than the standard fees or advertising have been required to disband these regulations. There is continuing jockeying between professional associations (and unions) claiming to protect service standards and governments seeking to 'protect' consumers. The comfortable security of professional elites has thus been shaken and their practices of exclusionary social closure subject to public scrutiny. At the same time however, neo-liberalism has been happy to provide greater freedom to inherited wealth on the grounds that it is legitimately 'earned'.

The second area that neo-Weberian theory saw as contributing to heightened levels of class conflict was the degree to which subordinated groups viewed their position of inequality in oppositional terms thus creating a revolutionary status-group (or 'class' in the Marxist sense) identity. Here too the changes since the 1970s have been dramatic.

In the 1970s, labour parties in Britain and Australia were closely linked to their industrial base and tended to support union resistance to neo-liberal reforms. In the 1980s the ALP became the party of modernisation and globalisation working closely with the leadership of the union movement to bring about economic reforms, which they saw as necessary. In Britain the shift occurred later with the re-formulation of the Labour Party as 'New Labour' and the ideological proposition of the 'Third Way'. The Third Way allowed

Labour to move away from the oppositional definition of status-group identity, and see the improvement of social conditions for less privileged as possible within the social institutions of competitive capitalism.

Neo-liberalism thus pushed through significant restructuring of key institutions of liberal democracy. These changes impact on the patterns and practices through which professional groups had previously maintained their de facto perpetuation of privilege. Through competition policy there is a scrutiny of unearned privilege and scepticism about licensing and entrenching professional 'monopolies'. Parallel with this selective attack on professional privileges has been the lessened recognition of 'the underprivileged' in status-group (i.e. social 'class') terms.

SOCIAL CLOSURE ON THE GROUND: THE ETHICS OF COMMUNITY WORK

The impact of neo-liberal reforms for social policy thinking has been profound. While the level of social inequality has increased, neo-liberals point to the greater openness of the system as the significant change. This highlights process rather than outcome as the goal of social policy. It also de-legitimates any tendency to think of disadvantage in oppositional terms and attacks the traditional Marxist view of the solidarity of the working class.

Even if they are swept up by neo-liberal reformist zeal governments cannot ignore social policy. Social democratic parties also have their own traditions and constituencies that counter-balance the siren calls of neo-liberal ideology. Defining social policy as the amelioration of social exclusion fits social policy into the framework of neo-liberal ideals. Within this framework, however, social democratic and conservative governments can then distinguish their approaches in terms of the energy they put into dealing with social exclusion and the social units that they favour as the vehicles of improvement. The Labour government in the UK has made the amelioration of social exclusion a major priority for action and sees local communities as the main vehicle of empowerment. The Liberal-

National government in Australia places less emphasis on social amelioration. In contrast to the Blair Labour government, its rhetoric and programs emphasise the family rather than the community or neighbourhood as the vehicle of social policy.

The UK policy setting produces a strong level of demand for community workers who must implement the ideals of community engagement, community capacity building and empowerment on the ground. There is a growing body of practitioners working in these areas who are working to build networks in disadvantaged communities to marshal their collective resources. This assumes that these communities can emulate or even match the established networking practices of advantaged status-groups, communities and the professions. The Standing Conference for Community Development (now the Community Development Exchange — CDA) is the umbrella organisation for these practitioners, providing key definitions of community development and its practices in its seminal statement, *The Strategic Framework for Community Development.* (SCCD 2001) Similarly, the Federation for Community Work Training Groups (FCWTG 2003) has development national standards and a system of training and accreditation for community workers and trainers.

This collective scrutiny of community development activity among disadvantaged groups makes explicit issues around the ethics and practice of networking that are simply not addressed in the discussion of networking, social capital building and social closure among successful groups. Among business people and professionals 'networking' has been seen as an important aspect of career for many years. However, in these circles, there is seldom any discussion of its ethics and social effects. In the world of community development, by contrast, there is constant attention to the ethics of networking and its potentially exclusive effects (Gilchrist 2004).

In community development practice, networking has to be socially *inclusive.* Indeed it often has to work to correct the effects of *exclusionary* social closure among disadvantaged groups. This is the case, for instance, when building networks involving different ethnic and religious groups. These groups may have previously sustained themselves through in-group solidarity and suspicion of other groups. The community development worker has to create bridges between these groups and initiate communication among them. What is the rationale for such network bridges however? If they are seen as simply avenues of formal negotiation between the groups, they may actually enhance the internal solidarity and exclusiveness of those groups. The task of the community worker, Gilchrist suggests, is to create network bridges that allow for meaningful personal communications between people in these separate groups. It is personal networking that lessens the barriers between groups.

A second, less immediate, ethical dimension of active community networking is attention to the outcome of community empowerment. If the community succeeds in creating the networks and community capacity that facilitates action of some kind, does it matter what that action is? If advantaged status-groups and professions can utilise their community power in ways that are not compatible with liberal ideals is it possible that networks of community empowerment among underprivileged groups could also do so?

The community work standards and statements of principle place enormous emphasis on social justice. This draws attention to the outcomes of action, not just the process. The ethics of community work thus deal with the issue of outcomes in a way that the 'personal advancement' approach to networking does not.

CONCLUSIONS

This paper began from the idea of studying social capital and networking amongst social elites as a model for networking practices by community workers and others working to ameliorate social conditions among disadvantaged groups and communities. The reality is, however, that the ethics and practices of community workers have more to teach about creating socially inclusive networks than do the practices of professional status-groups or the narrowly self-seeking manuals of business and career networking. In theoretical debate, however, the activity of networking in each arena and the networks and social capital it creates can be sensibly compared and contrasted.

This paper has argued that the sociological discussion of social closure provides a framework to understand both the operation of networks and networking in each domain and the broader setting of both types of activity. The paper resurrected the concept of 'social closure' from the sectarian debates of the 1970s and repositioned it to understand the shifting grounds of 'class' identities and class conflict between the 1970s and the present. Our discussion has drawn attention to aspects of the concept beyond those discussed by the original neo-Weberian theory. Whereas theorists of the 1970s assumed that social closure was nearly always driven by *exclusionary* status-group formation and self-interest, the policy changes and practitioner experiences of the last two or three decades make it necessary to consider the real possibility of practices of social closure (or 'networking') that are *inclusionary* and, potentially, increase social justice outcomes.

The intended audience for this paper was community work practitioners. Here the message from this paper is mixed. On the one hand the sociological study of social elites reinforces the basic assumption of ameliorative community work: advantaged status-groups and professions are built on active networks and social capital and group identity. They are networks of an inclusive kind that foster personal and professional relations and trust. There are also examples of community capacity building to show that collective action leads to status-group betterment. The relation between networking, social closure, social status and power remains uncontested. In principle, therefore, similar arrangements can foster the empowerment of disadvantaged communities. The critical question is how to balance and manage exclusionary and inclusionary social closure.

I would argue therefore that there are important similarities in networking practice for activists working in both disadvantaged and successful communities and status-groups. In both settings networking needs to be inclusive. It needs to connect people across barriers of difference of distance and to breakdown any internal in-groups. Active and successful networking needs to breakdown any legacy of exclusionary social closure within the community or status-group of activity.

The broader ethical question about the goals toward which status-group or community capacity is directed is harder to address. Calls for 'social justice' although meaningful for those working with disadvantaged groups do not translate to conditions of successful communities and status-groups. Neo-liberal competition policy is largely concerned with perceived 'abuses' of status-group power and mobilise public concern around on the basis of popular resentments of professional groups rather than positive claims about the social benefits of competition. Neo-Weberian theory offers little guidance at this level since it largely described the processes and outcomes of exclusionary social closure. But the identification of inclusionary social closure and networking at the process level does offer grounds for a project that takes this idea to a higher level. That is the task for another paper however.

8

Critical Theory

INTRODUCTION OF CRITICAL THEORY AS META-PHILOSOPHY: PHILOSOPHY, IDEOLOGY AND TRUTH

The best way to show how Critical Theory offers a distinctive philosophical approach is to locate it historically in German Idealism and its aftermath. For Karl Marx and his generation, Hegel was the last in the grand tradition of philosophical thought able to give us secure knowledge of humanity and history on its own. The issue for Left Hegelians and Marx was then somehow to overcome Hegelian "theoretical" philosophy, and Marx argues that it can do so only by making philosophy "practical," in the sense of changing practices by which societies realize their ideals. Once reason was thoroughly socialized and made historical, historicist skepticism emerged at the same time, attempting to relativize philosophical claims about norms and reason to historically and culturally variable forms of life.

Critical Theory developed a nonskeptical version of this conception, linking philosophy closely to the human and social sciences. In so doing, it can link empirical and interpretive social science to normative claims of truth, morality and justice, traditionally the purview of philosophy. While it defends the emphasis on normativity and universalist ambitions found in the philosophical tradition, it does so within the context of particular sorts of empirical social research, with which it has to cooperate if it is to understand such normative claims within the current historical context. After presenting the two main versions of this conception of philosophy, I turn to an illuminating example of how this cooperative relation between philosophy and the social sciences works from the point of view of the main figures in Critical Theory who sought to develop it: the critique of ideology, a form of criticism which if generalized threatens to undermine the critical stance itself as one more ideology. Even if Critical Theorists are united in a common philosophical project, this example shows the large differences between the first and second generation concerning the normative justification of social criticism.

In the modern era, Philosophy defines its distinctive role in relation to the sciences. While for Locke philosophy was a mere "underlaborer," for Immanuel Kant it had a loftier status. As Rorty and others have put it, transcendental philosophy has two distinct roles: first, as the tribunal of Reason, the ultimate court of appeal before which disciplines stand and must justify themselves and secondly, as the domain for normative questions left out of naturalistic inquiry. In light of this ability to judge the results of the sciences, philosophy can also organize knowledge, assigning to each of them their proper sphere and scope. The Kantian solution denies the need for direct cooperation with the sciences on issues related to normativity, since these were determined independently through transcendental analysis of the universal and necessary conditions for reason in its theoretical and practical employment. Echoes of the subsequent post-Hegelian criticisms of Kantian transcendental philosophy are found in the early work of Horkheimer and Marcuse.

Indeed, Horkheimer criticizes "traditional theory" in light of the rejection of its representational view of knowledge and its nonhistorical subject. Echoing Marx in *The German Ideology*, Horkheimer insists that for a critical theory "*the world and subjectivity in all its forms have developed with the life processes of society*" (Horkheimer 1982, 245). Much like certain naturalists today, he argued that "materialism requires the unification of philosophy and science," thus denying any substantive distinction between science and philosophy (Horkheimer1993, 34). As Horkheimer understood the task of Critical Theory, philosophical problems are preserved by taking a role in defining problems for research, and philosophical reflection retains a privileged role in organizing the results of empirical research into a unified whole.

This understanding of the relation of philosophy and the sciences remains broadly Kantian. Even while rejecting the role of philosophy as transcendental judge, he still endorses its normative role, to the extent that it still has the capacity to organize the claims of empirical forms of knowledge and to assign each a role in the normative enterprise of reflection on historically and socially contextualized reason. This unstable mixture of naturalism with a normative philosophical orientation informed much of the critical social science of the Frankfurt School in the 1930s.

According to this conception of materialism, Critical Theory could operate with a theoretical division of labor in which philosophy's normative stance could criticize the embodiments of reason and morality according to their internal criteria. At least for modern societies, such an enterprise of "immanent critique" was possible (see, for example, Horkheimer 1993, 39). However, Horkheimer and Marcuse saw the skeptical and relativist stance of the emerging sociology of knowledge, particularly that of Karl Mannheim, as precisely opposed to that of Critical Theory. As Marcuse puts it, "sociology that is only interested in the dependent and limited nature of consciousness has nothing to do with truth. While useful in many ways it has falsified the interest and goal of any critical theory" (Marcuse 1969 152). As opposed to merely debunking criticism, "a critical theory is concerned with preventing the loss of truth that past knowledge has labored to attain." Given Critical Theory's orientation to human emancipation, it seeks to contextualize philosophical claims to truth and moral universality without reducing them to social and historical conditions.

Horkheimer formulates this skeptical fallacy that informed much of the sociologically informed relativism of his time in this way: "That all our thoughts, true or false, depend on conditions that can change in no way affects the validity of science. It is not clear why the conditioned character of thought should affect the truth of a judgment—why shouldn't insight be just as conditioned as error?" (Horkheimer 1993, 141). The core claim here is that fallibilism is different from relativism, suggesting that it is possible to distinguish between truth and the context of justification of claims to truth.

Faced with a sociological naturalism that relativized claims to truth and justice are necessary for social criticism, the challenge could be answered by detranscendentalizing truth without losing its normativity (Horkheimer 1993, 6; McCarthy, in McCarthy and Hoy 1994, 10). Indeed it is relativism that depends on an implausible and ahistorical form of detachment and impartiality, especially expressed in its methodological commitments to "reverential empathy and description." The skepticism offered by historicism and the sociology of knowledge is ultimately merely theoretical, the skepticism of an observer who takes the disengaged view from nowhere. Once the skeptic has to take up the practical stance, alternatives to such paper doubt become inevitable. Indeed, the critic must identify just whose practical stance best reveals these possibilities as agents for social transformation of current circumstances. As I point out in the next section, the Frankfurt School most often applied ideology critique to liberal individualism, pointing out its contextual limitations that lead to reductionist and pernicious interpretations of democratic ideals.

Despite the force of these antirelativist and antiskeptical arguments, two problems emerge in claims made by Horkheimer and Marcuse to underwrite some "emphatic" conception of truth or justice. *First,* philosophy is given the task of organizing social research and providing its practical aims even in the absence of the justification of its superior capacities. A more modest and thoroughly empirical approach would be more appropriate and defensible. *Second,* the source of this confidence seems to be practical, that critics must immanently discover those transformative agents whose struggles take up these normative contents of philosophy and attempt to realize them. But once this practical possibility no longer seems feasible, then this approach would either be purely philosophical or it would turn against the potentialities of the present. Indeed, during the rise of fascism in the Second World War and the commodified culture afterwards, the Frankfurt School became skeptical of the possibility of agency, as the subjective conditions for social transformation were on their view undermined.

It is clear that in *Dialectic of Enlightenment* Horkheimer and Adorno abandoned this interdisciplinary materialist approach with its emphasis on cooperation with the social sciences (1982, xi). Adorno and Horkheimer did not to deny the achievements of the Enlightenment, but rather wanted to show that it had "self-destructive tendencies," that its specific social, cultural and conceptual forms realized in modern Europe "contained its own possibility of a reversal that is universally apparent today" (Adorno and Horkheimer 1982, xiii). Since Adorno and Horkheimer planned to offer a positive way out of the dialectic of Enlightenment at the time they wrote these words, this reversal is by no means inevitable. Even if their specific historical story of the emergence of Enlightenment reason out of myth is no longer so convincing, it is not enough to say with Habermas that *The Dialectic of Enlightenment* did not "do justice to the rational content of cultural modernity" (Habermas 1987, 103). For the positive task of avoiding the reversal of Enlightenment, reconstructing the rational content of modernity is not enough, since the issue is not to affirm its universalism, but its self-critical and emancipatory capacity.

If the issue is the self-correcting capacity of the Enlightenment, two questions emerge: how is it undermined? Where do we locate the exercise of this capacity? This is the "Enlightenment problem," the solution to which is twofold: to reconstruct those human capacities that have such reflexivity built into them and to tie the operation of Enlightenment institutions to the conditions of their successful exercise.

Against this skeptical predicament of the first generation of Critical Theory, it could be said without exaggeration that Habermas's basic philosophical endeavor from *Knowledge and Human Interests* to

The Theory of Communicative Action has been to develop a more modest, fallibilist, empirical account of the philosophical claim to universality and rationality. This more modest approach rids Critical Theory of its vestiges of transcendental philosophy, pushing it in a naturalistic direction. Such naturalism identifies more specific forms of social scientific knowledge that help in developing an analysis of the general conditions of rationality manifested in various human capacities and powers. Thus, Habermas's alternative sees practical knowledge, or reason in the robust sense, as it is "embodied in cognition, speech and action" (Habermas 1984, 10). Habermas's calls for particular "reconstructive sciences," whose aim it is to render theoretically explicit the intuitive, pretheoretical know-how underlying such basic human competences as speaking and understanding, judging, and acting. Unlike Kant's transcendental analysis of the conditions of rationality, such sciences yield knowledge that is not necessary but hypothetical, not a priori but empirical, not certain but fallible.

They are nevertheless directed to universal structures and conditions and raise universal, but defeasible claims to an account of practical reason. In this way, Habermas undermines both of the traditional Kantian roles for philosophy and brings them into a fully cooperative relation to the social sciences. This can be seen in the clear differences between his account of the critique of ideology, which is at once contextualist and antirelativist but also underwrites its own normativity in ways that Horkheimer and Marcuse's more nearly transcendental account could not, given the inevitable tension between philosophical ideals and the historical conditions of current societies and their practices.

Like many other such theories, the theory of communicative action offers its own distinctive definition of rationality. In good pragmatist fashion, Habermas's definition is epistemic, practical, and intersubjective. For Habermas, rationality consists not so much in the possession of knowledge and thus primarily concerned with the consistency and content of one's beliefs, but rather in "how speaking and acting subjects acquire and use knowledge" (Habermas, 1984, 11).

Such a broad definition suggests that the theory could be developed through explicating the general and formal conditions of validity in knowing and reaching understanding through language, and this task falls primarily on "formal pragmatics."

As one among many different "reconstructive sciences," such a reconstruction of speech is inherently normative, in the sense that it is one of the disciplines that reconstructs a common domain: "the know-how of subjects who are capable of speech and action, who are attributed the capacity to produce valid utterances, and who consider themselves capable of distinguishing (at least intuitively) between valid and invalid expressions" (Habermas 1990, 31). The positive goal of such a theory is not only to provide an account of rationality based on this know-how that is rich enough to grasp uses of reason in all their variety, yet also normative enough to be able to clarify the necessary conditions for its practical employment as well as a critical analysis of the "pathologies" that occur when these conditions fail to obtain.

More than just reconstructing an implicitly normative know-how, Habermas is clear that such reconstructive sciences have a "quasi-transcendental" status by specifying very general and formal conditions of successful communication. In this way, their concern with normativity and with the abilities needed for rationality in Habermas's practical and social sense permits them to acquire a critical role. Certainly, the goal of the reconstructive sciences is theoretical knowledge: they make such practical know-how explicit. But insofar as they are capable of explicating the conditions for valid or correct utterances, they also explain why some utterances are invalid, some speech acts unsuccessful, and some argumentation inadequate.

Thus, such sciences "also explain deviant cases and through this indirect authority acquire a *critical* function as well" (Habermas, 1990, 32). This authority then permits the theory of rationality to underwrite critical claims about social and political practices, to show how their functioning violates not only the espoused rules but also the conditions of rationality.

Such an approach can be applied to normative features of democratic practices. Rather than only providing a set of explicit principles of justification and institutional decision rules, *democracy* is also a particular structure of free and open communication. *Ideology* restricts or limits such processes of communication and undermines the conditions of success within them. Ideology as distorted communication affects both the social conditions in which democratic discussion takes place and the processes of communication that go on within them.

The theory of ideology, therefore, analyzes the ways in which linguistic-symbolic meanings are used to encode, produce, and reproduce relations of power and domination, even within institutional spheres of communication and interaction governed by norms that make democratic ideals explicit in normative procedures and constraints. As a reconstruction of the potentially correct insights behind Marx's exaggerated rejection of liberalism, the theory of distorted communication is therefore especially suited to the ways in which meanings are used to reproduce power even under explicit rules of equality and freedom. This is not to say that explicit rules are unimportant: they make it possible for overt forms of coercion and power to be constrained, the illegitimacy of which requires no appeal to norms implicit in practices.

Democratic norms of freedom can be made explicit in various rights, including civil rights of participation and free expression. Such norms are often violated explicitly in exercises of power for various ends, such as wealth, security, or cultural survival. Besides these explicit rights, such coercion also violates the communicative freedom expressed in ignoring the need to pass decisions through the taking of yes/no attitudes by participants in communication. Habermas calls such speech that is not dependent on these conditions of communicative rationality "distorted communication." For example, powerful economic groups have historically been able to attain their agency goals without explicitly excluding topics from democratic discussion but by implied threats and other nondeliberative means (Przworski and Wallerstein 1988, 12-29;

Bohman 1997, 338-339). Threats of declining investments block redistributive schemes, so that credible threats circumvent the need to convince others of the reasons for such policies or to put some issue under democratic control. Similarly, biases in agenda setting within organizations and institutions limit scope of deliberation and restrict political communication by defining those topics that can be successfully become the subject of public agreement (Bohman 1990). In this way, it is easy to see how such a reconstructive approach connects directly to social scientific analyses of the consistency of democratic norms with actual political behavior.

This theory of ideology as distorted communication opens up the possibility of a different relation of theoretical and practical knowledge than Habermas has suggested so far. His approach uses formal pragmatics philosophically to reflect upon norms and practices that are already explicit in justifications in various sorts of argumentation or second-order communication. Such reflection has genuine practical significance in yielding explicit rules governing discursive communication (such as rules of argumentation), which in turn can be used for the purpose of designing and reforming deliberative and discursive institutions (Habermas 1996, 230). It is easily overlooked that such rules are only part of the story; they make explicit and institutionalize norms that are already operative in correct language use. Such implicit norms of well-formed and communicatively successful utterances are not identical with the explicit rules of argumentation.

These claims about norms raise two difficulties. *First*, there is a potential regress of rules, that is, that explicit rules requires further rules to apply them, and so on. *Second*, this approach cannot capture how norms are often only implicit in practices rather than explicitly expressed (Brandom 1994, 18-30). Here Habermas sides with Pettit in seeing the central function of explicit norms as creating a commons that can serve as the basis for institutionalizing norms, a space in which the content of norms and concepts can be put up for rational reflection and revision (Pettit 1992, Habermas 1990). Making such implicit norms explicit is thus also the main task of the interpretive social scientist and is a potential source of social criticism; it is then the task of the participant-critic in the democratic public sphere to change them. There is one more possible role for the philosophically informed social critic. As we have seen in the case of ideological speech, the reconstructive sciences "also explain deviant cases and through this indirect authority acquire a *critical* function as well" (Habermas, 1990, 32).

In this section, I have discussed claims that are distinctive of the metaphilosophy of Critical Theorists of both generations of the Frankfurt School and illustrated the ways in which critical normativity can be exercised in their differing models of the critique of ideology. Critical Theorists attempt to fulfill potentially two factors at the same time: first, they want to maintain the normativity of philosophical conceptions such as truth or justice, while at the same time they want to examine the contexts in which they have developed and may best be promoted practically. I argued that the first generation theorists avoided the relativism of sociologies of knowledge such as Mannheim's only to fall into a practical skepticism about the feasibility of agents acting upon such norms in current contexts.

Habermas's conception of the cooperation between philosophy and the social sciences in rational reconstruction of practical knowledge allows him to articulate a normative conception of "*real democracy*" more fully and to develop a social scientifically informed conception of democracy that is an alternative to current liberal practices. This project shifts the goal of critical social inquiry from human emancipation as such, to the primary concern with democratic institutions as the location for the realization of ideals of freedom and equality. The limits on any such realization may prove to be not merely ideological: Critical Theory is also interested in those social facts and circumstances that constrain the realization of the ideal democracy and force us to reconsider its normative content. While such an account of the relation between facts and norms answers the sociological skepticism of Weber and others about the future of democracy, it may be based on an overly limited account of social facts.

DEMOCRACY AS A PRACTICAL GOAL OF CRITIQUE: FROM IDEOLOGY TO SOCIAL FACTS

In its initial phases Critical Theory attempted to develop a normative notion of "real democracy" that was contrasted with actual political forms in liberal societies. A democratic society would be rational, because in it individuals could gain "conscious control" over social processes that affect them and their life chances. To the extent that such an aim is possible at all, it required that human beings become "producers of their social life in its totality" (Horkheimer 1982, 244). Such a society then becomes a "true" or expressive totality, overcoming the current "false totality," an antagonistic whole in which the genuine social needs and interests cannot be expressed or developed (Jay 1984). Such a positive, expressivist ideal of a social whole is not, however, antiliberal, since it shares with liberalism the commitment to rationalism and universalism. The next phase in the development of Critical Theory took up the question of antidemocratic trends. This development of the Frankfurt School interpretation of the limits on democracy as an ideal of human freedom was greatly influenced by the emergence of fascism in the 1930s, one of the primary objects of their social research.

Much of this research was concerned with antidemocratic trends, including increasingly tighter connections between states and the market in advanced capitalist societies, the emergence of the fascist state and the authoritarian personality. Horkheimer came to see that these antidemocratic trends gradually undermined the realization of an expressive whole, with the consequence that "the situation of the individual is hopeless," that the subjective conditions for exercising freedom and achieving solidarity were being eroded by an increasingly totalizing social reification.

As first generation Critical Theorists saw it in the 1940s, this process of reification occurs at two different levels. First, it concerned a sophisticated analysis of the contrary psychological conditions underlying democracy and authoritarianism; second, this analysis was linked to a social theory that produced an account of objective, large-scale, and long-term historical processes of reification. If these facts and trends are true, then the idea of a "true totality" is a plausible critical category.

However, this concept is ill suited for democratic theory due to a lack of clarity with regard to the underlying positive political ideal of Critical Theory. Finally, in reaction to these normative failures, Habermas seeks to develop an intermediate level of analysis and a new normative conception in the historical analysis of the emergence of the "public sphere" (*Öffentlichbkeit*). As his later and more fully developed normative theory of democracy based on macrosociological social facts about modern societies shows, Habermas offers a modest and liberal democratic ideal based on the public use of reason within the empirical constraints of modern complexity and differentiation.

This social theory may make it difficult for him to maintain some aspects of radical democracy as an expressive and rational ideal that first generation critical theorists saw as a genuine alternative to liberalism.

CRITIQUE OF LIBERALISM TO THE DIALECTIC OF ENLIGHTENMENT

Except for passages on "real democracy" as the achievement of a rational society, many of the Frankfurt School's writings on democracy are concerned with developing a critique of liberal ideology reminiscent of "The Jewish Question." Horkheimer puts his criticism of bourgeois negative liberty in these terms: "The limited freedom of the bourgeois individual puts on the illusory form of perfect freedom and autonomy" (Horkheimer 1982, 241). Horkheimer criticizes the modern philosophical and legal subject as abstract, detached, and ahistorical; whatever freedom and autonomy actors have, they are best understood as "definite individuals" whose freedom in exercised in relation others and in historically specific societies. The freedom of real individuals can only be thought of in a holistic way, "in the resultant web of relationships with the social totality and with nature."

Like all good ideology critiques, then, this criticism of liberalism is immanent, using the liberal norms and values against their historical realization in specific institutions. Nonetheless, this ideology critique recognized that liberalism was still, as Marcuse put it, a "rationalist theory of society." Whatever its successor, the new form would have to pass the normative tests that fascism and other emerging forms of antiliberalism do not: this new unity "would have to prove itself before the tribunal of individuals, to show that their needs and potentialities are realized within it" (Marcuse 1968, 7). Using Hegelian terminology, Critical Theorists came to regard advanced capitalist societies as a "totality," in which the tight integration of states and markets threatened to eliminate the space for freedom. While the emergence of fascism is possible evidence for this fact, it is also an obvious instance in which reliance on the internal criticism of liberalism is no longer adequate.

The shift in the Frankfurt School to such external forms of criticism from 1940 onwards is not confined to the fascist state. With the development of capitalism in its monopoly form, the liberal heritage loses its rational potential as the political sphere increasingly functionalized to the market and its reified social relationships. In this way the critique of liberalism shifts away from the normative underpinnings of current democratic practices to the ways in which the objective conditions of reification undermine the psychological and cultural presuppositions of democratic change and opposition. Such a society is now a "wholly false totality." The work of Adorno and Horkheimer in this period shows the philosophical consequences of this shift, especially in *Dialectic of Enlightenment* (1944) and The *Eclipse of Reason* (1947).

One of the central claims of *Dialectic of Enlightenment* concerns the "entwinement of myth and Enlightenment," as providing a deep historical treatment of the genesis of modern reason and freedom and how they turn into their opposites. Rather than being liberating and progressive, reason has become dominating and controlling with the spread of instrumental reason. Liberal institutions do not escape this process and are indeed part of it with their institutionalization of self-interest and self-preservation, tending toward a "totally administered society." In *Eclipse of Reason* Horkheimer turns this critique of instrumental reason against liberal democracy. He argues that the liberal tradition that Marcuse argued needed to be preserved only retained its normative force on the metaphysical foundation of "objective reason." However grounded, liberalism depended on subjectivizing reason and objective moral principles; subjects are proclaimed "autonomous" all the while they sink into the heteronomy of market relations. The "inevitable" tendency of liberalism to collapse into fascism "can be derived, apart from any economic causes, from the inner contradiction between the subjectivist principle of self-interest and the idea of reason that it is supposed to express" (Horkheimer 1987, 21). Shorn of its objective content, democracy is reduced to mere majority rule and public opinion to some measurable quantity.

The argument here is primarily genealogical (thus based on a story of historical origin and development) and not grounded in social science; it is a reconstruction of the history of Western reason or of liberalism in which calculative, instrumental reason drives out the utopian content of universal solidarity. Some nondominating, alternative conception is exhibited in Horkheimer's religiously influenced ideal of identification with all suffering creatures or Adorno's idea of mimetic reconciliation with the other found primarily in art (Horkheimer 1972; Adorno 1973). These analyses were also complemented by an analysis of the emergence of state capitalism and of the culture industry that replaces the need for consent and even the pseudo-consent of ideology.

Some of the more interesting social scientific analyses of fascism that the Frankfurt School produced in this period were relatively independent of such a genealogy of reason. The first is the analysis of political economy of advanced, administered capitalist societies, with Franz Neumann providing a dissenting view that no state can completely control social and economic processes in the ways that might be more consistent with Horkheimer and Adorno's critique of instrumental reason. Especially interesting were empirical investigations into the "authoritarian" and "democratic" personalities, which provided a microsociology of democratic and antidemocratic character traits (Adorno et al 1953). Perhaps one of more striking results of this study is that the core of the democratic personality is a particular emotional or affective organization: "if fear and destructiveness are the major emotional sources of fascism, eros belongs mainly to democracy" (Adorno et al 1953, 480).

Thus, long-term historical cultural development and macro- and micro-sociological trends work against the democratic ideal. The sources of resistance to these trends are increasingly found at the level of what Foucault would call "micropolitics."

Whatever the merits of such general historical frameworks for critical interpretations of the present, the internal difficulty for a critical theory is that "real democracy," the goal of emancipatory criticism, demands a richer set of practical and theoretical resources, including institutional possibilities. What was needed was an alternative conception of rationality that is not exhausted by the decline of objective reason into subjective self-interest. This basic problem of first generation Critical Theory has been the life-long theme of the work of Jürgen Habermas, for whom the publicity and more generally the public sphere (*Öffentlichkeit*), occupies precisely the right conceptual space. Habermas also replaces the expressive totality of a fully democratic society with the ideal of "undamaged intersubjectivity" and of universal solidarity established through "communication free from domination." On the social theoretical side, totality is replaced by a conception of social complexity, which is not necessarily false or reifying. These shifts permit a more positive reassessment of the liberal tradition and its existing political institutions and open up the possibility of a critical sociology of the legitimation problems of the modern state.

On the whole, Habermas marked the return to normative theory united with a broader use of empirical, reconstructive and interpretive social science. Above all, this version of Critical Theory required fully developing the alternative to instrumental reason, only sketched by Adorno or Horkheimer in religious and aesthetic form;

for Habermas criticism is instead grounded in everyday communicative action. Indeed, he cam to argue that the social theory of the first generation, with its commitments to holism, could no long be reconciled with the historical story at the core of Critical Theory: the possible emergence of a more robust and genuine form of democracy

THE STRUCTURAL TRANSFORMATION OF DEMOCRACY: HABERMAS ON POLITICS AND DISCURSIVE RATIONALITY

Habermas's rejection of the explanatory holism of the first generation of the Frankfurt School has both explanatory and normative implications. First, he brings categories of meaning and agency back into critical social theory, both of which were absent in the macro-sociological and depth psychological approaches that were favored in the post war period. This brings democratic potentials back into view, since democracy makes sense only within specific forms of interaction and association, from the public forum to various political institutions. Indeed, Habermas's first and perhaps most enduring work, *The Structural Transformation of the Public Sphere* (Habermas 1989/1961), traced the historical emergence of new forms of public interaction from the intimate sphere of the family, to coffee houses, salons, and finally to parliamentary debates.

While linked ultimately to a narrative of its decline through the market and the administrative state, the core of such interaction and the critical and egalitarian potential of being part of a public whose members address one another as equals had for Habermas a nonideological, even "utopian" core (Habermas 1989, 88). Second, Habermas also developed an alternative sociology of modernity, in which social differentiation and pluralization are not pathological but positive features of modern societies (Habermas 1982, 1986). Indeed, the positive conception of complexity permits an analysis of the ways in which modern societies and their functional differentiation opens up democratic forms of self-organization independently of some possible expressively integrated totality. Such an ideal of an expressive totality and conscious self control over the production of the conditions of social life is replaced with publicity and mutual recognition within feasible discursive institutions.

This emphasis on the normative potential of modernity does not mean that modern political forms such as the state are not to be criticized. In *Legitimation Crisis* (1969), for example, Habermas argues not only that the demands of advanced capitalism restrict the scope and significance of democracy, but also that the state is "crisis ridden" and unable to solve structural problems of unemployment, economic growth, and environmental destruction. These crisis tendencies open up a space for contestation and deliberation by citizens and their involvement in new social movements. This criticism of the contemporary state is put in the context of a larger account of the relation between democracy and rationality. Contrary to "formal" democracy understood as majority rule, Habermas opposes "substantive democracy," which emphasizes the "genuine participation of citizens in political will formation" (Habermas 1975, 32). The relevant notion of rationality that can be applied to such a process is procedural and discursive; it is developed in terms of the procedural properties of communication necessary to make public will formation rational and thus for it to issue in a genuine rather than merely de facto consensus.

With such an expansion of Kantian practical reason, democracy is now grounded in the intersubjective structure of communication exhibited in the special form of reflective and reciprocal communication and public testing of claims to validity that Habermas calls "discourse." As communication about communication, discourse emerges in problematic situations in which new solutions must be sought in order to continue social cooperation. Democratic institutions have the proper reflexive structure and are thus discursive in this sense. In them, citizens deliberate as free and equal persons, for whom the legitimacy of the decision is related to the achievement of a "rational consensus." That is, a consensus is rational to the extent that it is based on a norm that could under ideal conditions be justified to all those who are affected by a decision. Early on

Habermas called the full list of these counterfactual conditions "the ideal speech situation," although later it is clear that it is meant to provide a principled basis by which to assess the quality of agreements reached discursively.

One philosophical purpose of such a procedural conception of rationality is to refute value skeptics, who reduce politics to what Weber called the struggle between "gods and demons" (Weber 1949). Its purpose in social theory is to provide the basis for an account of cultural rationalization and learning in modernity. In normative theory proper, Habermas has from the start been suspicious of attempts to apply this fundamentally epistemological criterion of rationality directly to the structure of political institutions. As early as *Theory and Practice* (1966), Habermas distanced himself from Rousseau's claim that the general will can only be achieved in a direct, republican form of democracy.

By failing to see that the ideal agreement of the social contract specifies only a certain procedural and reflexive level of justification, Rousseau confused "the introduction of a new principle of legitimacy with proposals for institutionalizing just rule" (Habermas 1979, 186). Indeed democratic principles need not be applied everywhere in the same way (Habermas 1973, 32-40). Instead, the realization of such norms has to take into account various social facts, including facts of pluralism and complexity (Habermas 1996, 474). For Habermas, no normative conception of democracy or law could be developed independently of a descriptively adequate model of contemporary society, lest it become a mere ought. Without this empirical and descriptive component, democratic norms become merely empty ideals and not the reconstruction of the rationality inherent in actual practices. I shall return to the problematic relation of social facts to democratic ideals in the next section in discussing Habermas's account of the philosophy of critical social science.

Another way in which this point about democratic legitimacy can be made is to distinguish the various uses to which practical reason may be put in various forms of discourse. Contrary to the account of legitimacy offered in *Legitimation Crisis*, Habermas later explicitly abandons the analogy between the justification of moral norms and democratic decision-making. Moral discourses are clearly restricted to questions of justice that can be settled impartially through a procedure of universalization (Habermas 1990, 43ff). The moral point of view abstracts from the particular identities of persons, including their political identities, and encompasses an ideally universal audience of all humanity. Although politics and law include moral concerns within their scope, such as issues of basic human rights, the scope of justification in such practices can be restricted to the specific community of associated citizens and thus may appeal to culturally specific values shared by the participants.

There are at least three aspects of practical reason relevant to democratic deliberation: pragmatic, ethical, and moral uses of reason are employed with different objects (pragmatic ends, the interpretation of common values, and the just resolution of conflicts) and thus also different forms of validity (Habermas 1993, 1-18). Because of this variety, democratic discourses are often mixed and complex, often including various asymmetries of knowledge and information. Democratic deliberation is thus not a special case of moral judgment with all of its idealizing assumptions, but a complex discursive network with various sorts of argumentation, bargaining, and compromise (Habermas 1996, 286). What regulates their use is a principle at a different level: the public use of practical reason is self-referential and recursive in examining the conditions of its own employment. Given the social circumstances of large-scale and pluralistic modern societies, distinctively democratic deliberation requires the "medium of law," so that the results of deliberation must be expressed through law.

Habermas expresses the relevant differences among the uses of practical reason in morality and politics as sub-principles of the same principle of discursive justification, which he calls "*D*." *D* simply names a discursive procedure: "just those norms of action are valid if all persons affected could agree as participants in rational discourse" (Habermas 1996, 107). The moral principle "*U*" specifies that the rule of argumentation for moral discourse is univeralizability

(Habermas 1990, 65-66). The more specific principle of democracy states that "only those laws may claim legitimacy that can meet with the agreement of all citizens in a discursive lawmaking procedure that is itself legally constituted" (Habermas 1996, 110). He argues that such a principle is at a different level than the moral principle, to the extent that its aim is primarily to establish a discursive procedure of legitimate law making and is a much weaker standard of agreement.

Nonetheless, even this democratic principle may still be too demanding, to the extent that it requires the agreement of all citizens (counterfactually) as a criterion of legitimacy. Habermas admits that in the case of cultural values we need not expect such agreement, and he even introduces compromise as a possible discursive outcome of democratic procedures. One way to genuinely weaken the principle would be to substitute cooperation for consensus and the outcome of the procedure: "a law then would be legitimate only if it could be agreed to in a fair and open deliberative process in which all citizens may freely continue to participate whatever the outcome" (Bohman 1996, 89). In this way, what is crucial is not the agreement as such, but how citizens reason together within a common public sphere. The democratic principle in this form expresses an ideal of citizenship rather than a standard of liberal legitimacy.

The internal complexity of democratic discourse does not overcome the problem of the application of the democratic principle to contemporary social circumstances. As Habermas puts it, "unavoidable social complexity makes it necessary to apply the criteria of democracy in a differentiated way" (Habermas 1996, 486). Such complexity restricts the application of fully democratic justification for a number of reasons: first, it is not possible for the sovereign will of the people by their democratic decision-making powers to constitute the whole of society; and, second, a society formed by merely associative and communicative means of coordination and cooperation is no longer possible. This objection to radical democracy is thus directed to those theories that do not figure out how such principles can be institutionally mediated given current social facts. Indeed, institutional mediation can overcome deficits in communicative self-organization, in so far as they compensate for "the cognitive indeterminacy, motivational insecurity, and the limiting coordinating power of moral norms and informal norms of action in general" (Habermas 1996, 323).

This approach to law has important consequences for a critical theory, since it changes how we appeal to democratic norms in criticizing current institutions: it is not clear exactly what the difference is between a radical and a liberal democracy, since some of the limitations on participation are due to the constraints of social facts and not to power asymmetries.

By insisting upon popular sovereignty as the outcome of the generation of "communicative power" in the public sphere, Habermas tries to save the substance of radical democracy. The unresolved difficulty is that in a complex society, as Habermas asserts, "public opinion does not rule" but rather points administrative power in particular directions; or, as he puts it, it does not "steer" but "countersteers" institutional complexity (Habermas 1996, chapter 8). That is, members of the public do not control social processes; qua members of a public, they may exercise influence through particular institutionalized mechanisms and channels of communication.

The open question for current Critical Theory (although not all critical theories) is then whether or not "real democracy" is still the goal of social criticism given these putatively "unavoidable" facts about the structure of modern society. Even given the limits of social complexity, there is still room for judgments of greater or lesser democracy, particularly with regard to the democratic value of freedom from domination. For example, a critical theory of globalization could show that the democratic potential of modern societies is being undermined by neoliberal globalization and denationalization of economic policy. Such a theory sees the solution here to be the achievement of more democracy at the international level. It is also possible that the critical use of democratic concepts may require reconceptualizing the democratic theory that has informed much of Enlightenment criticism in European societies. Here critical theorists are then simply one sort of participant in the ongoing internal work of redefining the democratic ideal, not simply in showing the lack of its full realization.

Either way, radical democracy may no longer be the only means to social transformation, and indeed we may, with Marcuse, think that preserving the truths of the past, such as democratic constitutional achievements, to be as important as imagining a new future. Given the new situation, Critical Theory could now return to empirical social inquiry to discover new potentials for improving democracy, especially in understanding how it may increase the scope and effectiveness of public deliberation. In these various roles, critical theorists are participants in the democratic public sphere. One of the main continuing legacies of Critical Theory has been to see that democracy is "the unfinished project of modernity" (Habermas 1986, xi) and its further realization and transformation a genuine goal even in complex and globalizing societies. To do so would entail a different, perhaps more reflexive notion of critical social inquiry, in which democracy is not only the object of study but is itself understood as a form of social inquiry. Critical Theory would then have to change its conception of what makes it practical and democratic.

In the next two sections, I will discuss two aspects of this transformed conception of Critical Theory. First, I turn to the role of social theory in this more pragmatic account of critical social inquiry. Contrary to its origins in Marxian theoretical realism, I argue for methodological and theoretical pluralism as the best form of practical social science aimed at human emancipation. Second, I illustrate this conception in developing the outlines of a critical theory of globalization, in which greater democracy and nondomination are its goals. This theory also has a normative side, which is inquiry into democracy itself outside of its familiar social container of the nation state. In this sense, it attempts not just to show constraints but also open possibilities. Critical Theorists have failed not only to take up the challenge of such new social circumstances but also thereby to reformulate democratic ideals in novel ways. I shift first to the understanding of the philosophy of social science that would help in this rearticulation of Critical Theory as critical social inquiry as a practical and normative enterprise.

CRITICAL THEORY, PRAGMATIC EPISTEMOLOGY AND THE SOCIAL SCIENCES

Such a practical account of social inquiry has much in common with pragmatism, old and new (Bohman 1999a, 1999b). As with pragmatism, Critical Theory came gradually to reject the demand for a scientific or objective basis of criticism grounded in a grand theory. This demand proved hard to square with the demands of social criticism directed to particular audiences at particular times with their own distinct demands and needs for liberation or emancipation.

The first step was to move the critical social scientist away from seeking a single unifying theory to employing many theories in diverse historical situations. Rather, it is better to start with agents' own pretheoretical knowledge and self-understandings. The issue for critical social inquiry is not only how to relate pretheoretical and theoretical knowledge of the social world, but also how to move among different irreducible perspectives. The second step is to show that such a practical alternative not only provides the basis for robust social criticism, but also that it better accounts for and makes use of the pluralism inherent in various methods and theories of social inquiry. While it is far from clear that all critical theorists understand themselves in this way, most agree that only a practical form of critical inquiry can meet the epistemic and normative challenges of social criticism and thus provide an adequate philosophical basis fulfilling the goals of a critical theory.

CRITICS, OBSERVERS, AND PARTICIPANTS: TWO FORMS OF CRITICAL THEORY

The philosophical problem that emerges in critical social inquiry is to identify precisely those features of its theories, methods, and norms that are sufficient to underwrite social criticism. A closer examination of paradigmatic works across the whole tradition from Marx's *Capital* (1871) to the Frankfurt School's *Studies in Authority and the Family* (1939) and Habermas's *Theory of Communicative Action* (1982) reveals neither some distinctive form of explanation nor a special methodology that provides the necessary and sufficient conditions for such inquiry. Rather, the best such works employ a variety of methods and styles of explanation and are often interdisciplinary in their mode of research. What then gives them their common orientation and makes them all works of critical social science?

There are two common, general answers to the question of what defines these distinctive features of critical social inquiry: one practical and the other theoretical. The latter claims that critical social inquiry ought to employ a distinctive theory that unifies such diverse approaches and explanations. On this view, Critical Theory constitutes a comprehensive social theory that will unify the social sciences and underwrite the superiority of the critic. The first generation of Frankfurt School Critical Theory sought such a theory in vain before dropping claims to social science as central to their program in the late 1940s (Wiggershaus 1994). By contrast, according to the practical approach, theories are distinguished by the form of politics in which they can be embedded and the method of verification that this politics entails. But to claim that critical social science is best unified practically and politically rather than theoretically or epistemically is not to reduce it simply to democratic politics. It becomes rather the mode of inquiry that participants may adopt in their social relations to others. The latter approach has been developed by Habermas and is now favored by Critical Theorists.

Before turning to such a practical interpretation of critical social inquiry, it is first necessary to consider why the theoretical approach was favored for so long and by so many Critical Theorists. First, it has been long held that only a comprehensive social theory could unify critical social science and thus underwrite a "scientific" basis for criticism that goes beyond the limits of lay knowledge. Second, not only must the epistemic basis of criticism be independent of agents' practical knowledge, but it might also be claimed that the correctness of any explanation is independent of its desirable or undesirable political effects on a specific audience. So conceived, social criticism is then a two-stage affair: first, inquirers independently discover the best explanation using the available comprehensive theory; then, second, they persuasively communicate its critical consequences to participants who may have false beliefs about their practices.

Starting with Marx's historical materialism, large-scale macrosociological and historical theories have long been held to be the most appropriate explanatory basis for critical social science. However, one problem is that comprehensiveness does not ensure explanatory power. Indeed, there are many such large-scale theories, each with its own distinctive and exemplary social phenomena that guide an attempt at unification. A second problem is that a close examination of standard critical explanations, such as the theory of ideology, shows that they typically appeal to a variety of different social theories (Bohman 1999b). Habermas's actual employment of critical explanations bears this out. His criticism of modern societies turns on the explanation of the relationship between two very different theoretical terms: a micro-theory of rationality based on communicative coordination and a macro-theory of the systemic integration of modern societies in such mechanisms as the market (Habermas 1987).

Not only does the idea of a comprehensive theory presuppose that there is one preferred mode of critical explanation, it also presupposes that there is one preferred goal of social criticism, a socialist society that fulfills the norm of human emancipation. Only with such a goal in the background does the two-step process of employing historical materialism to establish an epistemically and normatively independent stance make sense. The validity of social criticism does not merely depend on its being accepted or rejected by those to whom it is addressed. Pluralistic inquiry suggests a different norm of correctness: that criticism must be verified by those participating in the practice and that this demand for practical verification is part of the process of inquiry itself. Despite his ambivalence between theoretical and practical pluralism, Habermas has given good reasons to accept the practical and pluralist approach. Just as in the analysis of modes of inquiry tied to distinct knowledge-constitutive interests, Habermas accepts that various theories and methods each have "a relative legitimacy." Indeed, like Dewey he goes so far as to argue that the logic of social explanation is pluralistic and elides the "apparatus of general theories." In the absence of any such general theories, the most fruitful approach to social scientific knowledge is to bring all the various methods and theories into relation to each other: "Whereas the natural and the cultural or hermeneutic sciences are capable of living in mutually indifferent, albeit more hostile than peaceful coexistence, the social sciences must bear the tension of divergent approaches under one roof ..." (Habermas 1988, 3). In *The Theory of Communicative Action*, Habermas casts critical social theory in a similar pluralistic, yet unifying way. In discussing various accounts of societal modernization, for example, Habermas argues that the main existing theories have their own "particular legitimacy" as developed lines of empirical research, and that Critical Theory takes on the task of critically unifying the various theories and their heterogeneous methods and presuppositions. "Critical Theory does not relate to established lines of research as a competitor; rather, starting from its concept of the rise of modern societies, it attempts to explain the specific limitations and relative rights of those approaches" (Habermas 1987, 375).

This tension between unity and plurality leads in two different directions, one practical and the other theoretical. What might be called the "Kantian" approach proceeds case by case, seeing the way in which these theories run up against their limits in trying to extend beyond the core phenomena of their domain of validity (Bohman 1991, chapter 2). This approach is not theoretical in orientation, but more akin to "social science with a practical intent" to use Habermas's older vocabulary (Habermas 1971). The "Kantian" answer is given sharpest formulation by Weber in his philosophy of social science. While recognizing the hybrid nature of social science as causal and interpretive, he sought explanations of particular phenomena that united both dimensions. For example, in his *Protestant Ethic and the Spirit of Capitalism* he brought the macroanalysis of institutional structures together with the micro-analysis of economic rationality and religious belief (Weber 1958). According to this contrasting approach, "the relative rights and specific limitations" of each theory and method are recognized by assigning them to their own particular (and hence limited) empirical domain rather than establishing these judgments of scope and domain through a more comprehensive theory that encompasses all others.

The second approach may be termed "Hegelian." Here theorists seek to unify social scientific knowledge in broad comprehensive theories that produce a general history of modern societies. But general theories provide "general interpretive frameworks" on which it is possible to construct "critical histories of the present" (McCarthy in Hoy and McCarthy 1994, 229-230). Even this account of a comprehensive theory hardly eliminates competing histories that bring together different theories and methods. Rather than aiming at a single best history, "Hegelian" theories of this sort are seen as practical proposals whose critical purchase is seen in offering a comprehensive interpretation of the present situation. They do not rely on the criteria of a theory of rationality often appealed to in the Kantian approach, but still seem to justify particular moral claims, such as claims concerning justice and injustice.

Habermas wants to straddle the divide between the Kantian and the Hegelian approaches in his social theory of modernity. Why not see Habermas's theory of rationality as providing both a theoretical and practical basis for Critical Theory? Certainly, this is how Habermas sees the purpose of such a theory (Habermas 1984, chapter 1). Yet even if this theory of rationality has to be understood in this way, it would still have to avoid what Rorty calls "the ambiguity of rationality," between its statuses as "a cognitive faculty and a moral virtue." For this reason, Rorty keeps them distinct. "The epistemological notion of rationality concerns our relation to something nonhuman, whereas the moral notion concerns our relations to our fellow human beings" (Rorty 1996, 74). In a way similar to recent arguments in Putnam, Habermas now more strongly distinguishes between claims to truth and the context of justification in which they are made, even as he also wants to reject moral realism.

The problem for the practical conception of critical social inquiry is then to escape the horns of a dilemma: it should be neither purely epistemic and thus overly cognitivist, nor purely moralistic. Neither provides sufficient critical purchase. In the case of the observer, there is too much distance, so much so that it is hard to see how the theory can motivate criticism; in the case of the pure participant perspective, there is too little distance to motivate or justify any criticism at all. It is also the same general theoretical and methodological dilemma that characterizes the debates between naturalist and anti-naturalist approaches. While the former sees terms such as rationality as explanans to explain away such phenomena as norms, the latter argues that normative terms are not so reducible and thus figure in both explanans and explanandum. The best practical account here reconciles Rorty's ambiguity by putting the epistemological component in the social world, in our various cognitive perspectives towards it that include the normative perspectives of others. The ambiguity is then the practical problem of adopting different points of view, something that reflective participants in self-critical practices must already be able to do by virtue of their competence.

SOCIAL INQUIRY AS PRACTICAL KNOWLEDGE

This shift to "perspective taking" is already implicit in the reflexivity of practical forms of Critical Theory. Rather than look for the universal and necessary features of social scientific knowledge, Critical Theory has instead focused on the social relationships between inquirers and other actors in the social sciences. Such relationships can be specified epistemically in terms of the perspective taken by the inquirer on the actors who figure in their explanations or interpretations. Seen in this way, the two dominant and opposed approaches to social science adopt quite different perspectives. On the one hand, naturalism gives priority to the third-person or explanatory perspective; on the other hand, the anti-reductionism of interpretive social science argues for the priority of first-and second-person understanding and so for an essential methodological dualism. Critical Theory since Horkheimer has long attempted to offer an alternative to both views.

Habermas and other Critical Theorists rightly call "technocratic" any social inquiry that only develops optimal problem-solving strategies in light of purely third-person knowledge of the impersonal consequences of all available courses of action. Pragmatists from Mead to Dewey offer similar criticisms (Habermas 1971, 1973; Dewey 1988). This conception of practical knowledge would model the role of the social scientist in politics on the engineer, who masterfully chooses the optimal solution to a problem of design. For the social scientist *qua* an ideally rational and informed actor, "the range of permissible solutions is clearly delimited, the relevant probabilities and utilities precisely specified, and even the criteria of rationality to be employed (e.g., maximization of expected utilities) is clearly stated" (Hempel 1965, 481). This technocratic model of the social scientist as detached observer (rather than reflective participant) always needs to be contextualized in the social relationships it constitutes as a form of socially distributed practical knowledge.

By contrast with the engineering model, interpretive social science takes up the first-person perspective in making explicit the meaningfulness of an action or expression. Interpretations as practical knowledge are not based on some general theory (no matter how helpful or explanatory these may be when interpretation is difficult), but reconstruct agent's own reasons, or at least how these reasons might seem to be good ones from a first-person perspective. This leaves an interpreter in a peculiar epistemic predicament: what started as the enterprise of seeing things from others' points of view can at best provide the best interpretation *for us* of how things are *for them*. As a matter of interpretive responsibility, there is no getting around the fact that ethnography or history is our attempt "to see another form of life in the categories of our own" (Geertz 1971, 16-17; Bohman 1991, 132). The only way out of this problem is to see that there is more than one form of practical knowledge.

Naturalistic and hermeneutic approaches see the relationship of the subject and object of inquiry as forcing the social scientist to take either the third-person or first-person perspective. However, critical social science necessarily requires complex perspective taking and the coordination of various points of view, minimally that of social scientists with the subjects under study. The "second-person perspective" differs from both third-person observer and the first-person participant perspectives in its specific form of practical knowledge. It employs the know-how of a participant in dialogue or communication (Bohman 2000). This perspective provides the alternative to opposing perspectives especially when our first-person knowledge or third-person theories get it wrong. When faced with interpreting others' behavior we quickly run into the limits of first-person knowledge *simpliciter*. Third-person accounts face the same "gerrymandering problem" as made clear in the private language argument (Brandom 1994, 28ff). Neither the interpreter's nor the observer's perspectives are sufficient to specify these opaque intentional contexts for others. For social scientists as well as participants in practices more generally, the adjudication of such conflicts requires mutual perspective taking, which is its own mode of practical reasoning.

Theories of many different sorts locate interpretation as a practice, that is, in acts and processes of ongoing communication. Communication is seen from this perspective as the exercise of a distinctive form of practical rationality. A critical theory of communicative action offers its own distinctive definition of rationality, one that is epistemic, practical, and intersubjective. For Habermas, for example, rationality consists not so much in the possession of particular knowledge, but rather in "how speaking and acting subjects acquire and use knowledge" (Habermas 1984, 11). Any such account is "pragmatic" because it shares a number of distinctive features with other views that see interpreters as competent and knowledgeable agents. Most importantly, a pragmatic approach develops an account of practical knowledge in the "performative attitude," that is, from the point of view of a competent speaker. A theory of rationality can be a reconstruction of the practical knowledge necessary for establishing social relationships. This reconstruction is essential to understanding the commitments of the reflective participant, including the critic.

There are two general arguments for a theory that assumes the irreducibility of such a perspective. The first is that interpreting is not merely describing something. Rather, it establishes commitments and entitlements between the interpreter and the one interpreted. Second, in doing so the interpreter takes up particular *normative* attitudes. These "normative attitudes" must be those of the interpreted. In interpreting one is not just reporting, but rather expressing and establishing one's attitude toward a claim, such as when the interpreter takes the interpreted to say something to be true, or to perform an act that is appropriate according to social norms. Some such attitudes are essentially two-person attitudes: the interpreter does not just express an attitude in the first-person perspective alone, but rather incurs a commitment or obligation to others by interpreting what others are doing (Brandom 1994, 79). To offer an interpretation that is accepted is to make explicit the operative social norms and thus to establish the normative terms of a social relationship.

The critical attitude shares with the interpretive stance a structure derived from the second-person perspective. Here an agent's beliefs, attitudes, and practices cannot only be interpreted as meaningful or not, but must also be assessed as correct, incorrect, or inconclusive. Nonetheless, the second-person perspective is not yet sufficient for criticism. In order for an act of criticism itself to be assessed as correct or incorrect, it must often resort to tests from the first-and third-person perspectives as well. The reflective participant must take up all stances; she assumes no single normative attitude as proper for all critical inquiry. Only such an "interperspectival" stance is fully dialogical, giving the inquirer and agent equal standing. If indeed all cooperative social activities "involve a moment of inquiry" (Putnam 1994, 174), then they also need a moment of self-reflection on the assumptions of such inquiry itself. It is this type of reflection that calls for a distinctively practical form of critical perspective taking. If critical social inquiry is inquiry into the basis of cooperative practices as such, it takes practical inquiry one reflective step further. The inquirer does not carry out this step alone, but rather with the public whom the inquirer addresses. As in Kuhn's distinction between normal and revolutionary science, second-order critical reflection considers whether or not the framework for cooperation itself needs to be changed, thus whether new terms of cooperation are necessary to solve problems.

Various perspectives for inquiry are appropriate in different critical situations. If it is to identify all the problems with cooperative practices of inquiry, it must be able to occupy and account for a variety of perspectives. Only then will it enable public reflection among free and equal participants. Such problems have emerged for example in the practices of inquiry surrounding the treatment of AIDS. The continued spread of the epidemic and lack of effective treatments brought about a crisis in expert authority, an "existential problematic situation" in Dewey's sense (Dewey 1986, 492). By defining expert activity through its social consequences and by making explicit the terms of social cooperation between researchers and patients, lay participants reshape the practices of gaining medical knowledge and authority (Epstein 1996, Part II).

The affected public changed the normative terms of cooperation and inquiry in this area in order that institutions could engage in acceptable first-order problem solving. If expertise is to be brought under democratic control, reflective inquiry into scientific practices and their operative norms is necessary (Bohman 1999a). This public challenge to the norms on which expert authority is based may be generalized to all forms of research in cooperative activity. It suggests the transformation of some of the epistemological problems of the social sciences into the practical question of how to make their forms of inquiry and research open to public testing and public accountability. This demand also means that some sort of "practical verification" of critical social inquiry is necessary.

Pluralism and Critical Inquiry

A practical approach to Critical Theory responds to pluralism in the social sciences in two ways, once again embracing and reconciling both sides of the traditional opposition between epistemic (explanatory) and non-epistemic (interpretive) approaches to normative claims. On the one hand, it affirms the need for general theories, while weakening the strong epistemic claims made for them in underwriting criticism. On the other hand, it situates the critical inquirer in the pragmatic situation of communication, seeing the critic as making a strong claim for the truth or rightness of his critical analysis. This is a presupposition of the critic's discourse, without which it would make no sense to engage in criticism of others.

A good test case for the practical and pluralist conception of Critical Theory based on perspective taking would be to give a more precise account of the role of general theories and social scientific methods in social criticism, including moral theories or theories of norms. Rather than serving a justifying role in criticisms for their transperspectival comprehensiveness, theories are better seen as interpretations that are validated by the extent to which they open up new possibilities of action that are themselves to be verified in democratic inquiry.

Not only that, but every such theory is itself formulated from within a particular perspective. General theories are then best seen as practical proposals whose critical purchase is not moral and epistemic independence but practical and public testing according to criteria of interpretive adequacy. This means that it is not the theoretical or interpretive framework that is decisive, but the practical ability in employing such frameworks to cross various perspectives in acts of social criticism. In the above example, it is accomplished in taking the patients' perspectives seriously in altering practices of medical inquiry into AIDS.

Why is this practical dimension decisive for democratizing scientific authority? There seems to be an indefinite number of perspectives from which to formulate possible general histories of the present. Merely to identify a number of different methods and a number of different theories connected with a variety of different purposes and interests leaves the social scientist in a rather hopeless epistemological dilemma. *Either* the choice among theories, methods, and interests seems utterly arbitrary, *or* the Critical Theorist has some special epistemic claim to survey the domain and make the proper choice for the right reason. The skeptical horn of the dilemma is embraced by "new pragmatists" like Richard Rorty (Rorty 1991) and Max Weber (1949) alike, who see all such knowledge as purpose-relative.

The latter, perhaps Hegelian horn demands objectivist claims for social science generally and for the epistemic superiority of the Critical Theorist in particular—claims that Habermas and other Critical Theorists have been at pains to reject (Weber 1949; Habermas 1973, 38). Is there any way out of the epistemic dilemma of pluralism that would preserve the possibility of criticism without endorsing epistemic superiority?

The way out of this dilemma has already been indicated by a reflexive emphasis on the social context of critical inquiry and the practical character of social knowledge it employs. It addresses the subjects of inquiry as equal reflective participants, as knowledgeable social agents. In this way, the asymmetries of the context of technical control are suspended; this means that critical social inquiry must be judged by a different set of practical consequences, appealing to an increase in the "reflective knowledge" that agents already possess to a greater or lesser degree. As agents in the social world themselves, social scientists participate in the creation of the contexts in which their theories are publicly verified. The goal of critical inquiry is then not to control social processes or even to influence the decisions that agents might make in any determinate sort of way. Instead, its goal is to initiate public processes of self-reflection (Habermas, 1971, 40-41).

Such a process of deliberation is not guaranteed success in virtue of some comprehensive theory. Rather, the critic seeks to promote just those conditions of democracy that make it the best available process upon the adequate reflection of all those affected. This would include reflection of the democratic process itself. When understood as solely dependent upon the superiority of theoretical knowledge, the critic has no foothold in the social world and no way to choose among the many competing approaches and methods. The publicity of a process of practical verification entails its own particular standards of critical success or failure that are related to social criticism as an act of interpretation addressed to those who are being criticized. An account of such standards then has to be developed in terms of the sort of abilities and competences that successful critics exhibit in their criticism.

Once more this reveals a dimension of pluralism in the social sciences: the pluralism of social perspectives. As addressed to others in a public by a speaker as a reflective participant in a practice, criticism certainly entails the ability to take up the normative attitudes of multiple pragmatic perspectives in the communication in which acts of criticism are embedded.

Reflexivity, Perspective Taking and Practical Verification

If the argument of the last section is correct, a pragmatic account is inevitably methodologically, theoretically, and perspectivally pluralistic. Any kind of social scientific method or explanation-producing theory can be potentially critical. There are no specific or definitive social scientific methods of criticism or theories that uniquely justify the critical perspective. One reason for this is that there is no unique critical perspective, nor should there be one for a reflexive theory that provides a social scientific account of acts of social criticism and their conditions of pragmatic success.

The standard ideas of ideology critique exhibit the problems with a solely third-person model of criticism dependent on some idea of the theorists being able to discern the "real interests" of participants (Geuss 1981). Rather than claiming objectivity in a transperspectival sense, most practically oriented Critical Theorists have always insisted that their form of social inquiry takes a "dual perspective" (Habermas 1996, chapter 1; Bohman 1991, chapter 4). This dual perspective has been expressed in many different ways. Critical Theorists have always insisted that critical approaches have dual methods and aims: they are both explanatory and normative at the same time, adequate both as empirical descriptions of the social context and as practical proposals for social change. This dual perspective has been consistently maintained by Critical Theorists in their debates about social scientific knowledge, whether it is with regard to the positivism dispute, universal hermeneutics, or micro- or macro-sociological explanations.

In the dispute about positivist social science, Critical Theorists rejected all forms of reductionism and insisted on the explanatory role of practical reason. In disputes about interpretation, Critical Theorists have insisted that social science not make a forced choice between explanation and understanding. Even if social scientists can only gain epistemic access to social reality through interpretation, they cannot merely repeat what agents know practically in their "explanatory understanding." Here we might think of explanations that create micro-and macro linkages, as between intentional actions pursued by actors for their own purposes and their unintended effects due to interdependencies of various sorts. Such dual perspective explanations and criticism both allow the reflective distance of criticism and the possibility of mediating the epistemic gap between the participants' more internal and the critics' more external point of view. Given the rich diversity of possible explanations and stances, contemporary social science has developed a variety of possible ways to enhance critical perspective taking.

Such a dual perspective provides a more modest conception of objectivity: it is neither transperspectival objectivity nor a theoretical metaperspective, but always operates across the range of possible practical perspectives that knowledgeable and reflective social agents are capable of taking up and employing practically in their social activity. It is achieved in various combinations of available explanations and interpretive stances. With respect to diverse social phenomena at many different levels, critical social inquiry has employed various explanations and explanatory strategies. Marx's historical social theory permitted him to relate functional explanations of the instability of profit-maximizing capitalism to the first-person experiences of workers. In detailed historical analyses, feminist and ethnomethodological studies of the history of science have been able to show the contingency of normative practices (Epstein 1996; Longino 1990). They have also adopted various interpretive stances.

Feminists have shown how supposedly neutral or impartial norms have built-in biases that limit their putatively universal character with respect to race, gender, and disability (Mills 1997; Minnow 1990, Young 2002). In all these cases, claims to scientific objectivity or moral neutrality are exposed by showing how they fail to pass the test of public verification by showing how the contours of their experiences do not fit the self-understanding of institutional standards of justice (Mills 1997; Mansbridge 1991). Such criticism requires holding both one's own experience and the normative self-understanding of the tradition or institution together at the same time, in order to expose bias or cognitive dissonance. It uses expressions of vivid first-person experiences to bring about cross-perspectival insights in actors who could not otherwise see the limits of their cognitive and communicative activities.

In these cases, why is it so important to cross perspectives? Here the second-person perspective has a special and self-reflexive status for criticism. Consider the act of crossing from the first-person plural or "we perspective" to the second-person perspective in two reflexive practices: science and democracy. In the case of science the community of experts operates according to the norm of objectivity, the purpose of which is to guide scientific inquiry and justify its claims to communal epistemic authority. The biases inherent in these operative norms have been unmasked in various critical science studies and by many social movements. For Longino, such criticism suggests the need for a better norm of objectivity, "measured against the cognitive needs of a genuinely democratic community" (Longino 1990, 236). This connection can be quite direct, as when empirical studies show that existing forms of participation are highly correlated with high status and income, that lower income and status citizens were often unwilling to participate in a public forum for fear of public humiliation (Verba, et al 1995, Mansbridge 1991, Kelly 2000). Adopting the second-person perspective of those who cannot effectively participate does not simply unmask egalitarian or meritocratic claims about political participation, but rather also suggests why critical inquiry ought to seek new forums and modes of public expression (Young 2002, Bohman 1996).

The practical alternative offers a solution to this problem by taking critical social theory in the direction of a pragmatic reinterpretation of the verification of critical inquiry that turns seemingly intractable epistemic problems into practical ones. The role of critical social science is to supply methods for making explicit just the sort of self-examination necessary for on-going normative regulation of social life. This practical regulation includes the governing norms of critical social science itself. Here the relation of theory to practice is a different one than among the original pragmatists: more than simply clarifying the relation of means and ends for decisions on particular issues, these social sciences demand reflection upon institutionalized practices and their norms of cooperation. Reflective practices cannot remain so without critical social inquiry, and critical social inquiry can only be tested in such practices. One possible epistemic improvement is the transformation of social relations of power and authority into contexts of democratic accountability among political equals (Bohman 1999a; Epstein 1996).

Properly reconstructed, critical social inquiry is the basis for a better understanding of the social sciences as the distinctive form of practical knowledge in modern societies. Their capacity to initiate criticism not only makes them the democratic moment in modern practices of inquiry; that is, the social are democratic to the extent that they are sufficiently reflexive and can initiate discussion of the social basis of inquiry within a variety of institutional contexts.

Normative criticism is thus not only based on the moral and cognitive distance created by relating and crossing various perspectives; it also has a practical goal. It seeks to expand each normative perspective in dialogical reflection and in this way make human beings more aware of the circumstances that restrict their freedom and inhibit the full, public use of their practical knowledge.

One such salient circumstance is the long-term historical process of globalization. What is a distinctively critical theory of globalization that aims at such a form of practical knowledge? How might such a theory contribute to wishes and struggles of the age, now that such problematic situations are transnational and even global? What normative standards can critics appeal to, if not those immanent in liberalism? While in the next section I will certainly talk about critical theorists, I will also attempt to do critical social inquiry that combines normative and empirical perspectives with the aim of realizing greater and perhaps novel forms of democracy where none presently exist.

A Critical Theory of Globalization: Democratic Inquiry, Transnational Critical Theory

While the standard theories of globalization deal with large scale and macrosociological processes, the social fact of globalization is not uniform; differently situated actors experience it differently. This makes it exemplary for pluralist and multiperspectival social inquiry. It is also exemplary in another sense. As a social fact that is not uniform in its consequences, globalization cannot be reconstructed from the internal perspective of any single democratic political community, it requires a certain kind of practically oriented knowledge about the possibilities of realising norms and ideals in *praxis* and is thus a theory of democratization, of creating a political space where none now exists. Adopting a term of Andrew Linklater, we may call this practical theory of praxis a "praxeology" (Linklater 2001, 38), the purpose of which is inquiry into the "knowing how" of practical normative knowledge, that is, how it is that norms are ongoingly interpreted, realized, and enacted under particular social and historical circumstances. A critical and praxeological theory of globalization must therefore solve two pressing internal problems: first, how to organize social inquiry within and among transnational institutions more democratically; and, second, it must show the salient differences between national and transnational institutions and public spheres so that the democratic influence over globalization becomes a more tractable problem with feasible solutions.

Current theories of globalization are primarily macro-sociological and focus primarily on globalization as imposing constraints on democratic institutions. While not denying that globalization is such a fact, its explanations can become more critical and practical by also showing how globalizing processes open up new institutional possibilities and new forms of publicity (Bohman 2003). In order to test these possibilities, this theory must make itself a more open and multiperspectival practice; it must become a global critical theory. It is in this context that we can press the questions of the normative adequacy of the democratic ideal that has been inherited from modern liberalism. Indeed, many critical theorists who defend a "cosmopolitan" conception of democracy have a surprisingly standard conception of how democracy is best organized discursively and deliberatively. For this reason, they have not asked the question whether such practices are able to sustain a sufficiently robust and cooperative form of inquiry under the new global circumstances of political interdependence.

Social Facts, Normative Ideals and Multiperspectival Theory

In what respect can it be said that this novel sort of practical and critical social science should be concerned with social facts? A social scientific praxeology understands facts in relation to human agency rather than independent of it. Pragmatic social science is concerned not merely with elaborating an ideal in convincing normative arguments, but also with its realizability and its feasibility. In this regard, any political ideal must take into account general social facts if it is to be feasible; but it must also be able to respond to a series of social facts that ground skeptical challenges suggesting that circumstances make such an ideal impossible.

With respect to democracy, these facts include, expertise and the division of labor, cultural pluralism and conflict, social complexity and differentiation, and globalization and increasing social interdependence, to name a few. In cases where "facts" challenge the very institutional basis of modern political integration, normative practical inquiry must seek to extend the scope of political possibilities rather than simply accept the facts as fixing the limits of political possibilities once and for all. For this reason, social science is practical to the extent that it is able to show how political ideals that have informed these institutions in question are not only still possible, but also feasible under current conditions or modification of those conditions. As I have been arguing, the ideal in question for pragmatism and recent critical social theory inspired by pragmatism is a robust and deliberative form of self-rule—also a key aspect of Critical Theory's wider historical ideal of human emancipation and freedom from domination.

The issue of realizability has to do with a variety of constraints. On the one hand, democracy requires voluntary constraints on action, such as commitments to basic rights and to constitutional limits on political power. Social facts, on the other hand, are non-voluntary constraints, or within our problematic, constraints that condition the scope of the application of democratic principles. Taken up in a practical social theory oriented to suggesting actions that might realize the ideal of democracy in modern society, social facts no longer operate simply as constraints. For Rawls, "the fact of pluralism" (or the diversity of moral doctrines in modern societies) is just one such permanent feature of modern society that is directly relevant to political order, because its conditions "profoundly affect the requirements of a workable conception of justice" (Rawls 1999, 424).

This is not yet a complete story. Social facts such as pluralism have become "permanent" only to the extent that modern institutions and ideals developed after the Wars of Religion, including constitutional democracy and freedom of expression, promote rather than inhibit their development. This fact of pluralism thus alters how we are to think of the *feasibility* of a political ideal, but does not touch on its realizability or possibility. Similarly, the "fact of coercion," understood as the fact that any political order created around a single doctrine would require oppressive use of state power, concerns not the realizability or possibility of a particular ideal, but its feasibility as "a stable and unified order," under the conditions of pluralism (Rawls 1999, 225). Thus, for Rawls, regardless of whether they unclear referent, that are considered in terms of possibility or feasibility, they are only considered as *constraints*, as restricting what is politically possible or what can be brought about by political action and power. In keeping with the nature and scope of entrenched pluralism, not all actors and groups experience the constraints of pluralism in the same way: from the perspective of some groups, pluralism enables their flourishing; for others, it may be an obstacle.

If this were the only role of putative "facts" in Rawls' political theory of modernity, then it would not be a full practical theory in the sense that I am using the term here. Rawls' contribution is that social facts differ in kind, so that some, such as the fact of pluralism, are "permanent" and not merely to be considered in narrow terms of functional stability. Social facts related to stability may indeed constrain feasibility without being limits on the possibility or realizability of an ideal as such; in the case of pluralism, for example, democratic political ideals other than liberalism might be possible. Without locating a necessary connection between its relations to feasibility and possibility, describing a social fact as "permanent" is not entirely accurate. It is better instead to think of such facts as "institutional facts" that are deeply entrenched in some historically contingent, specific social order rather than as universal normative constraints on democratic institutions.

This approach allows us to see the "facts" of modern societies as practical: they are precisely those determinations that are embedded in relatively long-term social processes, whose consequences cannot be reversed in a short period of time—such as a generation— by political action. Practical theories thus have to consider the ways in which such facts become part of a constructive process that might be called "generative entrenchment" (Wimstatt 1974, 67-86). By "entrenchment of social facts," I mean that the relevant democratic institutions promote the very conditions that make the institutional social fact possible in assuming those conditions for their own possibility. When the processes at work in the social fact then begin to outstrip particular institutional feedback mechanisms that maintain it within the institution, then the institution must be transformed if it is to stand in the appropriate relation to the facts that make it feasible and realizable. All institutions, including democratic ones, entrench some social facts in realizing their conditions of possibility.

Consider Habermas' similar use of social facts with respect to institutions. As with Rawls, for Habermas pluralism and the need for coercive political power make the constitutional state necessary, so that the democratic process of law making is governed by a system of personal, social, and civil rights. However, Habermas introduces a more fundamental social fact for the possibility and feasibility of democracy: the structural fact of social complexity. Complex societies are "polycentric," with a variety of forms of order, some of which, such as non-intentional market coordination, do not necessarily have to answer to the ideals of democracy. This fact of complexity limits political participation and changes the nature of our understanding of democratic institutions. Indeed, this fact makes it such that the principles of democratic self-rule and the criteria of public agreement cannot be asserted simply as the proper norms for all social and political institutions, and this seems ideally suited to understanding how globalization limits the capacity of democracy to entrench itself.

As Habermas puts it, "unavoidable social complexity makes it impossible to apply the criteria [of democratic legitimacy] in an undifferentiated way" (Habermas 1996, 305). This fact makes a certain kind of structure ineluctable; since complexity means that democracy can "no longer control the conditions under which it is realized." In this case, the social fact has become "unavoidable," and certain institutions are necessary for the social integration to which there is "no feasible alternative" (Habermas 2001 122).

While plausible, this claim lacks empirical evidence. Habermas here overestimates the constraining character of this "fact," which does little to restrict a whole range of indirect, institutionally mediated institutional designs. These mediated forms of democracy would in turn affect the conditions that produce social complexity itself and thus stand in a feedback relation to them. The consequences of the "fact" of social complexity is thus not the same across all feasible, self-entrenching institutional realizations of democracy, and some ideals of democracy may rightly encourage the preservation of aspects of complexity, such as the ways in which the epistemic division of labour may promote wider and more collaborative problem solving and deliberation on ends. How might this alternative conception of social facts guide a critical and praxeological theory of globalization?

When seen in light of the requirements of practical social science and the entrenchment of facts and conditions by institutions, constructivists are right to emphasise how agents produce and maintain social realities, even if not under conditions of their own making. In this context an important contribution of pragmatism is precisely its interpretation of the practical status of social facts. Thus, Dewey sees social facts as always related to "problematic situations," even if these are more felt or suffered than fully recognised as such. The way to avoid turning problematic situations into empirical-normative dilemmas is, as Dewey suggests, to see even facts practically: "facts are such in a logical sense only as they serve to delimit a problem in a way that affords indication and test of proposed solutions" (Dewey, 1986, 499). They may serve this practical role only if they are seen in interaction with our understanding of the ideals that guide the practices in which such problems emerge, thus where neither fact nor ideal is fixed and neither is given justificatory or theoretical priority.

The debate between Dewey and Lippmann about the public sphere and its role in democracy is precisely praxeological in the sense that I defined the term earlier. In response to Lippmann's insistence on the preeminence of expertise, Dewey criticised "existing political practice" for the reason that it largely ignored "occupational groups and the organized knowledge and purposes that are involved in the existence of such groups, manifests a dependence upon a summation of individuals quantitatively" (Dewey 1991, 50-51). At the same time, he recognised that existing institutions were obstacles to the emergence of such a form of participatory democracy in an era when "the machine age has enormously expanded, multiplied, intensified, and complicated the scope of indirect consequences" of collective action and where the collectives—affected by actions of such a scope—are so large and diverse "that the resultant public cannot identify and distinguish itself" (Dewey 1988, 314). Dewey saw the solution in a transformation both of what it is to be a public and of the institutions with which the public interacts. Such interaction will provide the basis for determining how the functions of the new form of political organization will be limited and expanded, the scope of which is "something to be critically and experimentally determined" in democracy as a mode of practical inquiry (Dewey 1988 281).

The question is not just one of current political feasibility, but also of possibility, given that we want to remain committed in some broad sense to democratic principles of self-rule even if not to the set of possibilities provided by current institutions. How do we identify such fundamentally unsettling facts? I turn next to the discussion of a specific social fact, the "fact of globalization" and interpret it not as a uniform and aggregative process but as a problematic situation that is experienced in different and even contradictory ways at different locations and from a variety of perspectives, and is differently assessed with respect to different normative ideals of democracy. Since this is a relatively recent and unsettled debate, through this example we can see Critical Theory in the making.

THE FACT OF GLOBALIZATION AND THE POSSIBILITY OF DEMOCRACY

For some critical theorists, the relatively "new" fact of globalization permits a direct inference to the need for new and more cosmopolitan forms of democracy and citizenship. Whatever the specific form these assume in future institutions, the usual arguments for political cosmopolitanism are relatively simple despite the fact that the social scientific analyses employed in them are highly complex and empirically differentiated in their factual claims. In discussions of theories of globalization, the fact of global interdependence refers to the unprecedented extent, intensity, and speed of social interactions across borders, encompassing diverse dimensions of human conduct from trade and cultural exchange to migration (Held, et al 1999). The inference from these facts of interdependence is that existing forms of democracy within the nation-state must be transformed and that institutions ought to be established that solve problems that transcend national boundaries (Held 1995, 98-101). Thus, globalization is taken to be a macro-sociological, aggregative fact that constrains the realization of democracy so long as the proper congruence between decision makers and decision takers is lacking. Globalization is thus taken as a constraint on democracy as it is realized in existing liberal representative systems.

The Deweyan alternative is to see that facts "have to be determined in their dual function as obstacles and as resources," as problems that also hold out the conditions that make the transformation of the situation possible (Dewey 1986, 399-400). The "mere" fact of the wider scale of interaction is thus inadequate on its own and does not capture what role globalization may play as a problematic situation for the emergence of new democratic possibilities.

A pragmatic interpretation of social facts in this way encourages us to see globalization as Janus-faced, as an obstacle and as a resource for the realization of democratic ideals. This sort of theory sees globalization not as a unitary but rather as a multidimensional process. Even the notion of "complex interdependence" can be misleading insofar as it falsely suggests the telos of an increasingly integrated world or an increasingly homogeneous culture or political community (Keohane 2000, 117). A pragmatic analysis is better served by a concept such as "interconnectedness" as opposed to interdependence to the extent that interdependence suggests convergence and levels the differences in the ways in which globalization is experienced. Rather, it is important here, as in the case of the fact of pluralism, to see that this process can be experienced in different ways by different peoples or political communities, given that it is a multifaceted and multidimensional process producing "differential interconnectedness in different domains" (Held et al 1999, 27).

In some domains such as global financial markets, globalization is profoundly uneven and deeply stratified reinforcing hierarchies and distributive inequalities. Inequalities of access to and control over aspects of globalizing processes may reflect older patterns of subordination and order, even while the process produces new ones by excluding some communities from financial markets and by making others more vulnerable to its increased volatility (Hurrell and Woods 1999).

If these descriptions are correct, the fact of globalization is a new sort of social fact whose structure of enablement and constraint is not easily captured at the aggregative level. It is even experienced in contradictory ways looking at its consequences and impacts that differ across various domains and at various locations. Institutions can only manage the problems of globalization in ways that consider the interests of everyone by having mechanisms that ensure that the full range of perspectives is available for inquiry. This requires that international financial institutions extent their forms of inquiry to include issues such as the social disintegration and domination produced by their policies (Rodrik 1994, Woods 2001).

One further question about the fact of globalization must be raised in order to understand the inherent possibilities for democracy in it. Is globalization a "permanent" fact for democracy as Rawls described the fact of pluralism for liberalism in that it is deeply embedded in its possible realizations? As many social theorists have argued, globalization is part of interlocking and long-term social processes beginning in early modernity; as Anthony Giddens put it, "modernity is inherently globalizing" (Giddens 1990, 63). Even if reversing such processes were possible, it is not feasible in any short time span and under the democratic constraints. As with Rawls' fact of pluralism, so long as "globalizing" societies are democratic, we can expect such processes to continue. This is not to say that globalization in its current form is somehow permanent or unalterable if we want to realize democratic ideals. Indeed, just how globalization will continue, and under what legitimate normative constraints, become the proper questions for democratic politics, as citizens and public vigorously interact with those institutions that make globalization a deeply entrenched and temporally stable social fact. However entrenched, the social fact of globalization still remains open to democratic reconstruction, should creative reinterpretation of democracy come about. In the next section, I examine recent debates among Critical Theorists about the significance of the European Union as a model for a genuine transformation of democracy.

The Emerging Ideal of a Multiperspectival Democracy: The European Union

The analysis thus far has taken a robust ideal of democracy for granted consisting of self-rule by the public deliberation of free and equal citizens—the ideal of deliberative democracy that informs both pragmatism and Critical Theory (Bohman 2004). Given the uneven and potentially contradictory consequences of globalization, it seems clear that current democratic institutions themselves cannot be responsive to all the dimensions of domination and subordination that are possible considering the scale and intensity of interconnectedness. What are the alternatives? It is not just a matter of exercising an institutional imagination within broadly understood democratic norms and ideals. Informed by democratic ideals of non-domination, the practical knowledge needed to promote the democratising of uneven and hierarchical social relations requires an empirical analysis of current transformations and its embedded possibilities. The democratic ideal of autonomy leads David Held and others to emphasise the emerging structures of international law that produce a kind of binding power of collective decisions. Others look to ways of reforming the structures of representation of current international institutions (Pogge 1997, Habermas 2001). Still others look to the emergence of various institutions in the European Union (EU) to discuss the trend toward international constitutionalism or supranational deliberation.

According to the sort of plurality of perspectives endorsed by a pragmatist philosophy of social science, a historical account of the emergence of single and multiple institutions would be helpful. In Gerald Ruggie's masterful analysis of the development of a global order beyond the nation-state, he shows that the modern sovereign state and the social empowerment of citizens emerged within the same epistemic era as the single point perspective in painting, cartography, or optics. "The concept of sovereignty then represented merely the doctrinal counterpart of the application of single point perspective to the organization of political space" (Ruggie, 2000, 186). Unbundling sovereignty would lead to new political possibilities, including the re-articulation of international political space in a new way that cannot be anticipated in dominant theories of international relations. Focusing on the shifts in the authority of states and the development of the European Union, Ruggie sees the "EU as the first multiperspectival polity to emerge in the modern era" and thus the emergence of a new political form. The concept of "the multiperspectival form" does seem to offer "a lens through which to view other possible instances of international transformation today" (Ruggie 2000, 196). Such an account also applies to the theory of practical knowledge that might inform reflection on the possibilities of democracy in an era of uneven globalization.

If the political authority that now promotes globalization is to answer to democratic will formation, the institutions in which such public deliberation takes place must seek to become explicitly multiperspectival in Ruggie's sense. The positive conditions for such an extension of current political possibilities already exist in the fact of interdependence—the emergence of greater social interaction among citizens who participate in vibrant interaction across transnational civil society and within emerging global public spheres. In order to develop the framework for such a normative-practical praxeology for emerging multiperspectival institutions, pragmatism and Critical Theory once again suggest themselves: here Dewey's testable claim that it is the interaction of public and institutions that promotes democracy and democratic inquiry.

However important giving greater powers to the European Parliament may be, parliamentary politics at best serves a mediating role among transnational and national institutions and is not the sole means to democratisation (Habermas 2001). Given that such institutions cannot easily be scaled up and retain their full democratic character, it is necessary to look to a different institutional level: to the possibility of new forms of social inquiry that may be developing in the problem-solving mechanisms of the European Union.

The Multiperspectival Public Sphere: The Critical and Innovative Potential of Transnational Interaction

How might new forms of inquiry emerge that are able to accommodate a greater number of perspectives and also remain democratic? Here we need again to distinguish between first-and second-order forms of deliberation, where the latter develops in order to accommodate an emergent public with new perspectives and interests. Dewey sees the normal, problem-solving functioning of democratic institutions as based on robust interaction between publics and institutions within a set of constrained alternatives. When the institutional alternatives implicitly address a different public than is currently constituted by evolving institutional practice and its consequences, the public may act indirectly and self-referentially by forming a new public with which the institutions must interact.

This interaction initiates a process of democratic renewal in which publics organise and are organised by new emerging institutions with a different alternative set of political possibilities. Of course, this is a difficult process: "to form itself the public has to break existing political forms; this is hard to do because these forms are themselves the regular means for instituting political change" (Dewey, 1988, 255). This sort of innovative process describes the emergence of those transnational publics that are indirectly affected by the new sorts of authoritative institutions brought about by managing "deregulation" and globalization. This account of democratic learning and innovation seems not to be limited by the scope of the institutions, even as the potential for domination also increases under current arrangements.

What sort of public sphere could play such a normative role? In differentiated modern societies (that is, societies divided into multiple economic and social spheres such as markets, a state, civil society and so on), one role of the distinctive communication that goes on in the public sphere is to raise topics or express concerns that cut across social spheres: it not only circulates information about the state and the economy, but it also establishes a forum for criticism in which the boundaries of these spheres are crossed, primarily in citizen's demands for mutual accountability. But the other side of this generalization is a requirement for communication that crosses social domains: such a generalization is necessary precisely because the public sphere has become less socially and culturally homogeneous and more internally differentiated than its early modern form (Habermas 1989).

Instead of appealing to an assumed common norm of "publicity" or a set of culturally specific practices of communication, a *cosmopolitan* public sphere is created when at least two culturally rooted public spheres begin to overlap and intersect, as when translations and conferences create a cosmopolitan public sphere in various academic disciplines. Instead of relying on the intrinsic features of the medium to expand communicative interaction, networks that are global in scope become publics only with the development and expansion of transnational civil society. The creation of such a civil society is a slow and difficult process that requires the highly reflexive forms of communication and boundary crossing and accountability typical of developed public spheres. On the basis of their common knowledge of violations of publicity, their members will develop the capacities of public reason to cross and negotiate boundaries and differences between persons, groups, and cultures.

In such boundary-crossing publics, the speed, scale, and intensity of communicative interaction facilitated by networks such as the Internet provides a positive and enabling condition for democratic deliberation and thus creates a potential space for cosmopolitan democracy. Such a development hardly demands that the public sphere be "integrated with media systems of matching scale that occupy the same social space as that over which economic and political decision will have an impact" (Garnham 1995, 265). But if the way to do this is through disaggregated networks (such as the Internet) rather than mass media, then we cannot expect that the global public sphere will no longer exhibit features of the form of the national public sphere. Rather, it will be a public of publics, of disaggregated networks embedded in a variety of institutions rather than an assumed unified national public sphere.

The emergence of transnational public spheres is informative for the practical goals of a critical theory of globalization. Once we examine the potential ways in which the Internet can expand the features of communicative interaction, whether or not the Internet is a public sphere is a practical question of possibility rather than a theoretical question about the fact of the matter. It depends not only on which institutions shape its framework but also on how participants contest and change these institutions and on how they interpret the Internet as a public space. It depends on the mediation of agency, not on technology. With the proliferation of non-governmental organizations (NGOs) and other forms of transnational civil society organization, it is plausible to expect that two different and interacting levels of multiperspectival innovation may emerge: first, new institutions such as the European Union that are more adapted to multiple jurisdictions and levels of governance; and, second, a vibrant transnational civil society that produces public spheres around various institutions with the goal of making their forms of inquiry more transparent, accessible and open to a greater variety of actors and perspectives. This approach does not limit the sources of the democratic impulse to transnational civil society. Rather, the better alternative is to reject both bottom-up and top-down approaches in favour of vigorous interaction between publics and institutions as the ongoing source of democratization and institutional innovation.

According to a pragmatically inspired democratic experimentalism, attempts at democratisation and reform need not wait for publics to emerge; they can be constructed in various practices. Consultative NGOs may generally become too intertwined with institutions and thus do not generatively entrench their own conditions in this way. This practical difficulty is evident in the official civil society organizations of the European Union that fail to promote public deliberation. Without further conceptual and normative clarification, the appeal to various "bottom up" strategies of democratization remains normatively underdeveloped (Dryzek 1996, Jagger, 2004). Even when informed by democratic aims, this form of politics cannot capture the complex interrelationships of civil society, the state and the market, especially given the background of inequalities and asymmetries that operate in processes of globalization. Apart from powerful corporate actors in civil society, NGOs from economically advantaged regions possess significant resources to influence and shape the formation of civil society in other contexts. A critical theory of such activity asks about the possibility of a strong connection between their powers in civil society with market forces (Silliman 1998).

Besides the spontaneous emergence of publics out of transnational associations, it is also possible to make use of self-consciously constructed publics of relevant stakeholders to act as "mini-publics" that are empowered to deliberate and make decisions (Fung 2003). Here we can include a variety of experiments, from participatory budgets to citizen boards and juries that have a variety of decision-making powers. Properly empowered and self-consciously constructed, mini-publics offer a strategy to get beyond the dilemma of insider consultation and outsider contestation that is a structural feature of civil society activity in currently existing international institutions.

Since self-consciously created minipublics seek to include all relevant stakeholders, they do not rely on representation as the mode of communicating interests, or even the inclusion of well-organized actors as a way of achieving effective implementation. Instead they open up a directly deliberative process within the institution that includes as many perspectives as possible and can be repeated when necessary.

The minipublic is then an institutionally constructed intermediary, although it could act in such a way as to become an agent for the creation of a larger public with normative powers. In this capacity, minipublics may become open and expandable spaces for democratic experimentation. While many are issue or domain specific, such experiments often become models for democratic governance in dispersed and diverse polities.

As Cohen and Rogers put it, the more specific and episodic practices aim at mutual benefits through improved coordination, experimental deliberative practices tied to larger political projects may redistribute power and advantage and in this way secure the conditions of democracy more generally (Cohen and Rogers 2003, 251).

The same point could be made about taking existing democratic institutions as the proper model for democratization. To look only at the constraints of size in relation to a particular form of political community begs the question of whether or not there are alternative linkages between democracy and the public sphere that are not simply scaled up. Such linkages might be more decentralized and polycentric than the national community requires. The issue here is the standard of evaluation, not whether some other public sphere or form of community "is totally or completely democratic, but whether it is adequately democratic given the kind of entity we take it to be" (McCormick 1996, 345).

For a nation state to be democratic it requires a certain sort of public sphere sufficient to create a strong public via its connections to parliamentary debate. A transnational and thus polycentric and pluralist community, such as the European Union, requires a different sort of public sphere in order to promote sufficient democratic deliberation. Once a transnational and post-territorial polity rejects the assumption that it must be what Rawls calls "a single cooperative scheme in perpetuity," a more fluid and negotiable order might emerge with plural authority structures along a number of different dimensions rather than a single location for public authority and power.

Without a single location of public power, a unified public sphere becomes an impediment to democracy rather than an enabling condition for mass participation in decisions at a single location of authority. The problem for an experimental institutional design of directly deliberative democracy is to create precisely the appropriate feedback relation between disaggregated publics and such a polycentric decision making process.

The lesson for a critical theory of globalization is to see the extension of political space and the redistribution of political power not only as a constraint similar to complexity but also as an open field of opportunities for innovative, distributive, and multiperspectival forms of publicity and democracy.

A critical theory of globalization is a practical or praxeologically oriented theory that sees the "fact of globalization" in relation to the goal of realizing the norms of human emancipation and democracy. The central and still open questions for such a practically oriented social science are the following: what available forms of *praxis* are able to promote the transformations that could lead to new forms of democracy? What sort of practical knowledge is needed to make this possible and how might this knowledge be stabilised in institutionalised forms of democratic inquiry? What are the possibilities and opportunities for democracy at a higher level of aggregation that globalization makes possible? How might the public sphere be realized at the global level?

The argument here suggests that such inquiry and institutions must go beyond single perspective understandings of democracy that dominate national political life as well as the various administrative *techne* that are common in the international sphere. A critical praxeology of realizing norms in multiperspectival institutions might add that it is also a reflexive question of putting such organization in the larger context of a project of human emancipation. Such an interactive account of publics and institutions gives a plausible practical meaning to the extending of the project of democracy to the global level.

It also models in its own form of social science the mode of inquiry that this and other publics may employ in creating and assessing the possibilities for realizing democracy. A critical theory of globalization does not only point out the deficits of current practices, but shows the potential for properly organized publics to create new ones. Since the new practices need not be modeled on the old ones, it is not a theory of democracy as such, but of democratization.

CONCLUSION: CRITICAL THEORY AND NORMATIVE INQUIRY

In facing the challenges of new social facts, Critical Theory remains a vital philosophical tradition in normative disciplines of social and political philosophy. Furthermore, this vitality is enhanced when it considers a range of democratic claims not discussed here, all of which equally challenge the fundamental frameworks of conceptions of democracy, justice, and their interrelationship: these include the struggles of aboriginal peoples, the disabled, women, and more. One great advantage of the practical account is that it makes it easier to see why there are many different critical theories in different historical contexts, what Marx called the "wishes and struggles of the age." On a practical account, critical inquiry aims at creating the reflective conditions necessary for the practical verification of its inquiry, and these conditions are not confined only to democratic institutions, but wherever publics employ critical social theories and methods as the moment of inquiry of their democratic politics.

As new forms of critical theory emerge related to racism, sexism, and colonialism, reflective social agents have transformed these same democratic ideals and practices in the interest of emancipation. In entrenching new social facts, agents transform the ideals themselves as well as their institutional form.

This critical and practical orientation gives rise to three different questions about critical social inquiry. First, does Critical Theory suggest a distinctive form of social inquiry? Second, what sort of knowledge does such inquiry provide in order to provide insight into social circumstances and justify social criticism of current ideals and institutions? Finally, what sort of verification does critical inquiry require? In light of the answers to these questions on the practical, democratic, and multiperspectival interpretation defended here, it is likely that Critical Theory is no longer a unique approach. Methodologically, it becomes more thoroughly pluralistic. Politically, it loses its capital letters as the aims and struggles of the age of globalization become more diverse and not automatically connected by the commitment to any particular holistic social theory. Given its own democratic aims, it would be hard to justify any other interpretation.

In a period in which philosophy cooperates with empirical sciences and disciplines, Critical Theory offers an approach to distinctly normative issues that cooperates with the social sciences in a nonreductive way. Its domain is inquiry into the normative dimension of social activity, in particular how actors employ their practical knowledge and normative attitudes from complex perspectives in various sorts of contexts. It also must consider social facts as problematic situations from the point of view of variously situated agents.

This kind of normative practical knowledge is thus reflexive and finds its foothold in those ongoing, self-transforming normative enterprises such as democracy that are similarly reflexive in practice. By discussing democracy in this way, I have also tried to show just how deep the connections are between it and critical social science: critical theories are not democratic theories, but their practical consequences are assessed and verified in democratic practice and solved by inquiry into better democratic practice. Perhaps one of the more pernicious forms of ideology now is embodied in the appeal of the claim that there are no alternatives to present institutions. In this age of diminishing expectations, one important role that remains for the social scientifically informed, and normatively oriented democratic critic is to offer novel alternatives and creative possibilities in place of the defeatist claim that we are at the end of history. That would not only mean the end of inquiry, but also the end of democracy.

9

The New Left

Largely because its intellectual resources were so slender, Leftist advocacy as we once knew it in the economically successful "Western" democracies clearly suffered a body-blow from the collapse of its great "alternative" and alleged exemplar of equality — The Soviet Union — so most Leftists have had to find new directions for agitation in recent years. Criticizing our unequal capitalist society has become much less plausible now that capitalism seems to be the only show in town.

This has by and large simply meant a redirection of the Leftist's energies into other well-established equality-seeking causes — such as anti-racism, radical feminism and treating criminals as simple unfortunates who can be set on the right path with a bit more "education" (Criminals are equal too, it seems). There has been an attempt, in other words, to move the focus of agitation away from economic reform towards social reform. As well as such old ideas, however, there have also arisen various new foci for Leftist discontent and agitation.

Leftism is in fact Protean. It has no fixed beliefs or principles and what Leftists advocate changes all the time. Its only coherence is psychological. For instance, as I document at some length elsewhere, the contrast between the Leftism of the prewar (WW2) period and the postwar period is quite amazing. There is therefore a need to look at what Leftism is at the time of writing early in the 21st century:

POLITICAL CORRECTNESS

One of the newer leftist causes is the "political correctness" movement. This movement functions in two major ways: It attempts to change the way we think about less fortunate groups in the world by altering the words we use to describe them, and, in good Nazi bookburning fashion, it also attempts simply to suppress knowledge and debate. For example, it suppresses mention of any proposition that offers explanations of why some groups are less fortunate and are likely to remain so regardless of any amount of Leftist agitation — the claim that Negroes have an inherited lower average IQ than whites, for instance. For a relatively recent and striking example of such a suppression effort, witness the pulping of Brand's (1996) very scholarly book on IQ by his own publisher (Wiley of the US) when the political unpalatability (to Leftists) of his inheritance data became obvious. There is obviously no way that Leftists/liberals believe in such "bourgeois" ideals as freedom of speech.

Political correctness has now been entrenched in law in many countries — as was shown in 2002 in Australia: An Australian conservative Senator gave a private interview in which he spoke disparagingly but not unreasonably or abusively of Australian blacks. The outcome? He was eventually found guilty in the Federal Court of breaching the Racial Discrimination Act — at a cost to him of $10,000. There is no doubt that Leftists are deadly enemies of our liberties when even our elected representatives can have their freedom of speech punitively curtailed. See Alex Robson for more details of the case. Excerpt:

The Federal Court ruled that Liberal Senator Ross Lightfoot broke the law when he called Aborigines in their native state the most primitive people on earth: Justice Christopher Carr said the West Australian Senator had breached the Racial Discrimination Act with his comments to a journalist in May 1997. He ordered Senator Lightfoot to pay costs of up to $10,000.

And note this report from Britain of someone (Tyndall) who was JAILED there under "hate speech" laws.

The judge at our trial exhibited the typical do-gooder liberal attitudes in this respect. He could not possibly gainsay, and therefore condemn someone for saying, that blacks perform intellectually at a lower level than whites. At the same time his emotions could not bear the thought that this state of affairs was unchangeable and not capable of remedy by education and social engineering. The first thought was just about acceptable to him; the second was not. It is essential to the liberal's faith in his ability to guide people forward that he have the capacity to lift up the low by civic action, whatever their depressed condition. Offend that faith, and you make the liberal very angry!"

But anti-American hate-speech is OK, of course: A Columbia University professor told an anti-war gathering that he would like to see "a million Mogadishus" — referring to the 1993 ambush in Somalia that killed 18 American servicemen. At Wednesday night's "teach-in" on the Columbia campus, Nicholas De Genova also called for the defeat of U.S. forces in Iraq and said, "The only true heroes are those who find ways that help defeat the U.S. military." And he asserted that Americans who call themselves "patriots" are white supremacists.

Political correctness even has the potential to trump religious freedom. Church schools in the Australian State of Queensland had only a narrow escape from it in 2002. The Labor Party government in Queensland tried to pass a law that would have forbidden them from rejecting homosexuals as teachers in their schools. Excerpt from a report of 27 November:

Religious groups moved closer to resolving an impasse over the Queensland government's new anti-discrimination laws. Church and Islamic leaders today met with Premier Peter Beattie to discuss the bill, which will effectively remove the right of religious schools not to employ people in de facto or gay relationships.

An escape clause for church schools (but not other schools) was built in only at the last moment after some heavy lobbying. I suspect that a lot of conservative Roman Catholic Labor union leaders burnt the Queensland Premier's ear about the issue. Australia has a lot of Roman Catholic schools. I sent my son to one.

How heavily the Leftist obsession with equality (and their consequent procrustean unwillingness to handle the complexities of the real world) influences the PC movement can perhaps be seen most clearly in the actions of a British welfare agency who banned a job advertisement because it discriminated against UNFRIENDLY PEOPLE! A company placed the advertisement looking for a "friendly person" for a catering-related job but the local Job Centre rejected it because they said it "may discriminate against certain applicants". See here (originally from the *Bolton Evening News* of June 7th., 2002 but no longer online at that site).

Less of a laughing matter is the way political correctness can actually endanger lives. Take, for instance, the case of a UK surgeon reported in the UK Daily Telegraph of July 23rd, 2002 who had to stop in the middle of surgery because the immigrant nurses employed by Britain's cash-strapped National Health Service could not understand enough English to follow his instructions. He filed a complaint claiming that patient's lives were being put at risk by nurses who do not understand English. The immediate result? A threat of disciplinary action against the surgeon for racism!

And the logic of political correctness can be unbelievable. Leftist logic always leaves lots out but it is at least usually easy to follow — far too simplistic if anything. But a recent innovation in political correctness — that American Indians should not be allowed to use Indian mascots or use such Indian terms as "Braves" to refer to themselves or name their sporting teams — leaves me crosseyed with the deviousness of its "logic". Apparently it is supposed to be "non-racist" and "inclusive" to ban Indians from referring to their own group names and their own past. I guess that whites who refer to themselves as "Anglo-Saxons", "Germans", "Italians" etc. will be in the firing-line next. And Americans who remember and praise the deeds of George Washington must be a bad lot too by the same logic. David Yeagley (an American Indian) has been fulminating about it for some time. He has good reason to be angry at such oppression in the name of "tolerance" (of all things!). Only George Orwell would not be surprised by it all.

So the supposedly "anti-racist" Left is now not only persecuting Jews again (particularly on U.S. College campuses) but it is now persecuting the poor old American Indians too, because they have the temerity to be proud of their warrior past! With friends like the Left, who needs enemies?

GLOBALIZATION

Censorship is however obviously not a dramatic enough pursuit for many Leftists so they have turned to such unlikely targets as globalization and the World Trade Organization as foci for their ire. That anti-globalization is a psychologically easy step from Leftism is explained in The Economist — which concludes that the anti-globalization protestors of today are the direct intellectual heirs of Karl Marx. Excerpt:

"Anti-globalism has been aptly described as a secular religion. So is Marxism: a creed complete with prophet, sacred texts and the promise of a heaven shrouded in mystery. Marx was not a scientist, as he claimed. He founded a faith. The economic and political systems he inspired are dead or dying. But his religion is a broad church, and lives on."

The sole aim of the World Trade Organization is to increase co-operation and interdependence between nations and thus reduce barriers to the free movement of goods and people between nations, so one might naively have thought that the advocates of "all men are equal" would approve of it. That modern-day Leftists in the economically successful "Western" democracies oppose the WTO and other summit organizations with broadly similar aims (such as the Davos World Economic Forum) is, then, an index of how desperate they have become for something to protest about in the post-Soviet world.

Globalization as a general concept too is a rather surprising target for the Left — given that the United Nations was once a great icon and hope of Leftists in the economically successful "Western" democracies and given that Leftists once prided themselves on being internationalists: "Workers of the world unite", the Comintern (Communist International) and the "international brigades" of Leftist volunteers who fought Generalissimo Franco in the Spain of the 1930s, for instance. And as Fonte (2002) points out at some length, Leftists today are very keen at using transnational organizations to achieve their aims where it suits them — particularly if such organizations give them the prospect of achieving things that cannot be achieved through the ballot box.

And there are some remnants of support for globalization on the Left. Australian philosopher Peter Singer is something of a hero on the loony Left but he seems to have had an attack of good sense recently and come out IN FAVOUR OF globalization — on the undoubtedly true grounds that it will reduce global poverty. This article by Gregg Easterbrook (apparently a moderate Leftist) reviews Singer's book and even makes the point that, as globalization has been progressing, global inequalities in income have been DECLINING. Excerpt:

Singer discusses the work of three Norwegian researchers who have applied buying-power indices to international income statistics, and found that from 1970 to 1997, as globalization was reaching around the world, international inequality steadily declined

It must be so sad for Leftists to hear even from their own that, under wicked old capitalism, the poor are getting richer, not poorer.

Globalization has of course been doing its work of spreading prosperity throughout the world for well over a century (at least since the repeal of the corn laws in 1846 by British Conservative Prime Minister Robert Peel) but only recently do Leftists seem to have discovered its "evils". Prince Albert, 19th century humanitarian and consort of Britain's Queen Victoria, was one of the most prominent early advocates of globalization — precisely because of its effects in reducing poverty. So the Leftist opponents of globalization would appear to have been missing the big game for a long time! If Leftists were sincere in their advocacy of the interests of the poor, they would in fact be urging MORE globalization. The biggest single remaining barrier to globalization in the world today is agricultural protectionism — preventing farm products being imported by way of tariffs, subsidies and other barriers. Such protectionism is practiced principally by rich countries (Japan, the USA and the European Union) and hurts most the poor countries of the world who rely principally on primary production and exports for their livelihood. One of the few ways poor countries could get richer is by producing and selling primary products to us but it is the LACK of globalization in agriculture which prevents them from doing so. But when did we hear Leftists arguing for more globalization? That they do not shows the hypocrisy of their claim to care about the poor.

And even without globalized agricultural trade, the degree of globalization we have had has been highly beneficial to the poorer countries. As it says here:: "Evidence supplied by the World Bank and United Nations strongly suggests that multinational corporations are a key factor in the large improvement in welfare that has occurred in developing countries over the last forty years...." And, as a result the people of the third world are big fans of globalisation. Now why would that be? Simple. Because they know from experience that it makes them better off, not worse off — contrary to what the lying Leftists of the West say.

It also shows something of Leftist motivation that their opposition to free trade generally puts them in league with big business and conservative farmers — groups that they would normally anathematize. Obviously, being protestors matters more to Leftists than whom or what the protest is in aid of.

THE "GREENS"

Opposition to globalization etc is however too readily identified as a lunatic fringe activity to satisfy everyone on the Left so other things needing change have had to be found. And, in fact, even reactionary change has been embraced. "Reactionary" was once almost a swear-word to the Left but, if a reactionary is someone who wants to put social and economic change into reverse gear and return the world to some sort of idealized and simpler past, the major reactionary movement in the world today is undoubtedly the "Green" movement. One sometimes gets the impression that only the entire elimination of the human race would satisfy the Greens in their desire to return the world to a pristine state. Certainly, no concession to their aims ever seems enough to satisfy them.

The wish for nature conservation and reclamation has a long and honourable past — including among its advocates most English-language poets from at least the 18th century onwards (Who can forget William Blake's "dark Satanic mills"?). And no-one has ever set aside a greater area for nature conservation than US Republican President Theodore Roosevelt did — and that was roughly a century ago. And only a little later, Benito Mussolini, the founder of Fascism, also showed great concern for trees and the environment. Mussolini was a Marxist, however (Bosworth, 2002).

And while there are still some environmental causes that represent undramatic, largely uncontroversial and sensible improvements to our quality of life and the prospects for our future (e.g. control of farmland degradation), many others are quite fanciful, extreme and ill-founded (as the statistician Lomborg, 2001, has shown at length). Modern-day "Greenies" go well beyond mere nature conservation in what they seek and are very strong and relentless advocates of change to practically all of our existing arrangements and systems. And that suits change-hungry and drama-hungry Leftists down to the ground. So therefore many "Reds" have in recent times become "Greens" and Red-Green alliances spring up with some frequency

The fact that nature conservation and reclamation has never previously in its long past attracted much Leftist attention does suggest that their recent interest in it lies not in the cause itself but rather in the drama and disruption that modern day Greenies create in pursuit of their goals. Many Green advocacy groups — such as

Greenpeace — provide opportunity for drama and self-advertisement aplenty.

Even mainstream Leftist politicians see environmentalism as something of a life-saver for themselves. As Robin Cook, a senior member of the British Labour party put it in "The Observer" of October 8th, 1989: "The new environmental concerns could put Labour's ideology back in business. The politics of the environment are the politics of intervention — firmer regulation, tighter planning and collective co-operation." No ambiguity there about what a Leftist wants.

THE ORIGINS OF ENVIRONMENTALISM

Many people see environmentalism as a recent phenomenon. It is not. Read the typically Greenie quote following and find the one word I have deleted from it:

"We recognize that separating humanity from nature, from the whole of life, leads to humankind's own destruction and to the death of nations. Only through a re-integration of humanity into the whole of nature can our people be made stronger. That is the fundamental point of the biological tasks of our age. Humankind alone is no longer the focus of thought, but rather life as a whole... This striving toward connectedness with the totality of life, with nature itself, a nature into which we are born, this is the deepest meaning and the true essence of Socialist thought."

How many people would have picked that I missed out the word "National" before "Socialist"? Yes. It was a leading Nazi who wrote that. Environmentalism was a part of Nazism just as it is a part of modern-day Leftism. Like the Greenies of today, the Nazis wanted to take us all back to some imaginary and romanticised rural past. And of course the Communist Pol Pot in Cambodia actually tried it! For more on ecofascism see Peter Staudenmaier. Hitler and Pol Pot reveal how dangerous the Greens could be if ever they got real power. History can be *most* inconvenient! Though you don't need history to tell you that Greenies are people-haters.

PEACENIKS, VIETNAM AND THE FADING OF NATIONALISM

The Vietnam war had a huge influence on the thinking of both the American Left and the American Right but it is something of a detour from current politics so I have decided to treat it as a separate topic in a separate article. See here.

A quote from that article may however be apposite here:

The idea that Leftists favour peace is of course absurd. The hate, anger and envy that drive Leftists make them inherently aggressive and bloodthirsty — as we see whenever they gain absolute power — from the French revolutionaries onward through Trotsky, Stalin, Mao and Pol Pot — not to mention more minor revolutionaries. And the great violence that often characterized "peace" demonstrations of the Vietnam era (see e.g. here) gave the lie to any claim that these Leftists were any different from their predecessors

HATE AND "HATE CRIMES"

This is a rather large topic in its own right so I have given it separate consideration elsewhere. Briefly, however, my argument is that Leftists leap to condemn even the mildest negativity as "hate speech" because they themselves are so hate-filled. It is a classic means of diverting attention from one's own failings to condemn loudly such failings in others. Psychologists call it "projection" and Christ knew of it too — Matthew 7: 4,5. And Leftists even cover themselves against accusations of projection too — how else but by claiming to find lots of projection in conservatives!

MENTAL HEALTH MISREPRESENTATIONS CONTINUE: SUICIDE

So although Leftists undoubtedly hate "the rich", "WASPs" etc, their greatest hatred is for conservatives — and one of their favourite ploys for attacking conservatives is to claim that conservatism is bad for your mental health. Britain's Leftist "*Guardian*" newspaper, for instance, had a good chortle over the claim that the suicide rate in Britain and Australia is higher during periods when

Conservatives are in government. They imply that conservatism is so bad for your mental health that it can make you suicide.

This is, of course reminiscent of that old 1950s Marxist nonsense by Adorno and friends (still popular among psychologists — see here or here) to the effect that conservatives have diseased "authoritarian" personalities! If you cannot beat conservatives in rational debate what could be better than a good old "*ad hominem*" response that says your opponent's arguments are wrong simply because he personally is a bad lot? One might as well argue that all dog-owners are evil because Hitler loved dogs.

The suicide statistics are of course fraudulent. The British study actually RULED OUT the period of the (Conservative) Heath government when suicide was low — on the laughable grounds that Britain got natural gas about then and that made it too hard for many people to commit suicide. And even with that big fudge the pattern was still far from clear. As Katherine Mangu-Ward puts it in the "*Daily Standard*" of 30th September, 2002:

"Though the averages are higher for conservative administrations, when one looks at administrations individually, there are numerous exceptions to the supposed trend. For example, in addition to Heath, the suicide rate under Churchill was likewise low, while during Callaghan's Labour administration it was quite high"

Other standard points could and should be made about the "studies" concerned — such as the old truth that correlation does not prove causation — but the real clincher that was overlooked is the time-period when suicides are usually lowest. Guess when that is? When the nation is at WAR! So that means that low suicides rates are necessarily good??? So we need more wars???

All suicides are truly tragic but like everything else there are swings and roundabouts. Clearly there is NO automatic inference we can draw about people's overall wellbeing from suicide rates. Certainly, any claim that a low suicide rate indicates good times for the nation is laughable. On the other hand, if anybody wants to extend "*Guardian*" type logic to saying that being ruled by a Leftist government is about as good for you as having your country attacked by a foreign power, who am I to argue?

CONSPIRACY THEORIES CONTINUE

There is a history of conspiracy theories here that endeavours to show that they are equally prevalent on the Right and the Left of politics. Hogwash! All the current conspiracy theories ("Bush was forewarned about 9/11" and all the rest) come from the Left.

Contrary to what the article claims, Ann Coulter's defence of Joe McCarthy against widespread condemnation is not a conspiracy theory. McCarthy **IS** still widely and systematically condemned despite being eventually proven justified in the general thrust of his enquiries. And JFK defended McCarthy too. And the idea of a new world order is no fairytale. President Bush senior openly proclaimed such an aim after the first Gulf war. And we have certainly got a new world order now — though not the one envisaged.

The prime example usually given of a "Rightist" conspiracy theory is Hitler's theory about the Jews. But Hitler was a socialist! He himself from the very beginning proclaimed his socialism and love of the worker and put his claims into practice too. See here.

The fact of the matter is that conspiracy theories (in the 60's, "the CIA" was responsible for everything) are part and parcel of the simplistic thinking that is characteristic of the Left. That is not to say that there are NO conservatives who sometimes entertain conspiracy theories but such theories are nonetheless far and away the characteristic mental hidey-hole of the Leftist who cannot afford to face reality lest his entire conceptual house of cards come tumbling down.

David Brooks had an amusing article in the "New York Times" about the "neocon" conspiracy theories that are so popular even among the mainstream Left as an "explanation" of George W. Bush's foreign policy. This "definition" gave me a chuckle: "con is short for "conservative" and neo is short for "Jewish"". Some of the letter-writers to the NYT got very huffy about their antisemitism being described so blithely but you don't have to read many Leftist rants on the subject to know the truth behind what Brooks said.

SINS OF OMISSION AND COMMISSION

Leftists sometimes argue, with their usual illogic, that it is OK for them to do harm with their addled programmes of action because conservatives ALLOW great harm to go on in the world— such as the starving children in Africa. Philosophers Jim Ryan (post of March 3rd. 2003) and Eddie Thomas had a discussion about this.

There are various possible answers to the "argument" — the best of which is probably a *reductio ad absurdem* (e.g. If I neglect my child, does that mean that you are right to murder your child?) — but the one Jim chose and that Eddie was dubious about is that actively doing harm is much worse than allowing harm to go on. As Eddie, says, however, that surely depends a lot on the circumstances of the particular case.

I myself would identify the essential point in any answer as being that the amount of harm and suffering in the world is essentially infinite — the world is full of harm going on all the time. So we HAVE TO allow most of it. Our own positive actions are different however. We have lots of choice about them. And if we do harm through them we should rightly be held culpable. We cannot solve all the world's problems but we can at least do our best to do no harm ourselves. As I recollect, that is part of the Hippocratic oath: "First do no harm".

Buffoons?

One of the classic tactics that Leftists old and new use to attack people they disagree with is to do their best to portray their opponents as dumb buffoons. Almost any US Republican President gets so labelled. President G.W. Bush gained a Master's degree from Harvard but even he gets portrayed as an airhead. So this is really just another variant on the Leftist's reliance on lies.

The people Leftists hate most are not in fact conservatives but rival Leftists. And guess how Leftists have always described Benito Mussolini, the founder of the Fascist variant of Leftism? You guessed it: "Buffoon" is by far the most used word. Yet Mussolini read poetry and philosophy voraciously, including Socrates and Plato. He spoke several foreign languages, was always interested in discussing political and philosophical ideas with almost anyone, had considerable acceptance in his early days as a leading Marxist theoretician, wrote over 40 books, and was a tree-lover and environmentalist 50 years before Greenies were thought of. Dumb buffoon!

Advertising: The Perennial Enemy

A favourite whipping-boy of the Left has long been the advertising industry. If people want various non-essential material goods, that is presented by Leftists not as something legitimate and reasonable but as the result of demand "artificially" created by big business via advertising. All the evidence shows, however, that advertising in fact CANNOT create demand that does not exist. There has to be a pre-existing need or desire there first before the advertising will work. So advertising has to find some real need to work on. Advertising people all know that, of course, and do their best to find a need at which they can target their products. Even then, however, they can come a cropper. The most spectacular example of a failure of advertising to create demand for a product was the stylistically different "Edsel" car produced and promoted by Ford from 1957. Ford spent a record amount of money on advertising and hired top advertising brains to promote the Edsel to absolutely no avail. The model was a complete flop. So next time you hear Leftists complaining about the way advertising can "create" demand (thus making people's own choices somehow illegitimate), ask them to tell that to the guys who tried to sell the Edsel.

Modern Leftists even hate Christmas

If any further proof of the ill-natured motivations of Leftists were needed, the way they try to obstruct the enjoyment that ordinary people derive from Christmas would be a good case in point. The great enemy of the Christmas spirit in literature is of course Dickens' Ebenezer Scrooge.

And Scrooge was not exactly a loved or praised figure. That Dickens was a "social reformer" in his day does therefore make it all the more strange that the Left of today have adopted Scrooge as their own. As Trevor Sykes (a.k.a "Pierpont") reports:

"The kindergartens of Victoria have launched an anti-Santa campaign this Christmas. At last count, about 50 kindergartens had banned Santa and were going to entertain their tots with magicians or clowns instead so as not to offend minority groups.

If the teachers are really conscientious objectors to Santa and Christmas, Pierpont assumes they will not recognise Christmas at all and keep working right through the Yuletide holidays. If they did that, perhaps some Australian offspring might emerge from our education system with an IQ somewhere above single-digit levels."

The "liberals" of Canada carry their "multicultural" objections to Christmas almost to the point of insanity. Take a 2002 initiative of the City of Toronto to call their Christmas tree a "holiday" tree so as not to offend non-Christians and a similar move by the Canadian Mint to change "The Twelve Days of Christmas" in their advertising to "The Twelve Days of Giving" — thus offending a lot of Christians. It seems that far from permitting and celebrating all cultures there (which was the original idea of multiculturalism) they have now got to the point of SUPPRESSING Christian culture!

It is of course a pure Leftist lie that Christmas "offends" non-Christians. Nobody had ever heard of any such thing until Leftists invented it and to this day I have yet to hear one non-Christian claim such offence. In reality the whole anti-Christmas project is nothing more than the usual childish Leftist attempt to draw attention to themselves by attacking worthy institutions that are in fact supports to the good life and comfort of ordinary people. Now that Buddhists, Confucians and Communists in Japan and China are eagerly adopting Christmas and its trappings, it really shows how "offensive" to other religions Christmas is, doesn't it? Even to Muslims, Christ is a great prophet.

The Left's "Third Way"

After the demise of the Soviet Union, the great white hope of the Left became the "Third Way" (exemplified in Britain's Tony Blair). This is in fact an old Roman Catholic idea stemming from the famous pro-labour encyclical *"De rerum novarum"* of Pope Leo XIII in 1891.

Famous though it is, many people will not know what *"De Rerum Novarum"* says. It rejects Marxism but justifies intervention by the State on behalf of the workers and proposes that the best solution for working-class poverty would be some sort of combined action of the Church, the State, the employer and the employed. Such "corporatist" solutions were of course put faithfully into practice by various good Catholic sons — such as Italy's Benito Mussolini, Spain's General Franco and Portugal's Antonio Salazar.

Tony Blair is an Anglican so he is more moderate and democratic than Mussolini or Franco but he too rejects the old Marxist nostrum of having government run industry while at the same time still using the power of the State to redistribute wealth from those who have earned it to those who have not. So the British Left's "Third way" and the current "American way" are now rather similar. Roman Catholicism is, after all, America's biggest religious denomination. And a majority of them probably still vote Democrat.

The "Third Way" in Economics

But does it work? How good or bad is a "third way" for the economy and for national prosperity? The British conversion is fairly recent so any long-term effects have not been seen as yet. Are there better examples of a "third way" that would enable us to judge it by its results?

An old favourite of Leftists — Sweden — would seem to be a good case in point. Sweden never did embark on the dismal road of government ownership of major sectors of the economy. It always followed the philosophy of letting businessmen make the money and then having the State redistribute most of it. So how has that affected Swedish living standards?

In mid-2002, there was a bit of a flurry in conservative circles about a study which showed Sweden in a bad light. It was pointed out that the average Swede was less wealthy than even poor Americans. Even an average citizen of a poor American State like Mississippi was better off than the average Swede. This was taken as some indication that "heartless" American capitalism was in fact kinder to the poor than was the Swedish welfare State.

This was of course a bit of a red rag to those who admire the Swedish welfare State and various refutations of the claim were produced. One of the chief debunkers of the claim was Prof. Mark Kleiman, from the UCLA School of Public Policy and Social Research: Kleiman's claims had a number of apparent peculiarities in them, however, so I emailed him about some of them. It turns out that he conceded that Gross Domestic product (GDP) per capita is considerably higher in the USA than in Sweden but disputed that GDP is a good measure of average welfare.

This might seem surprising considering the very widespread use of GDP as a measure of national economic performance but is in fact an old point in economics. GDP is essentially an accounting measure that just adds up all the money that people earn and spend in a given year. Kleiman rightly pointed out that GDP is not the whole picture. A classical point is that GDP ignores the very valuable work done by housewives because it is not paid for in a way that accountants can measure.

As soon as you start "correcting" GDP to make it a better measure of welfare, however, you rush headlong into political judgments. For instance, Leftists might argue that a country with a highly multicultural population is a lot better for you in various ways so a country with such a population should get an extra mark for that. Conservatives, on the other hand, would probably argue that multiculturalism is a pain and would mark a country down for that. So Kleiman is perfectly right to say that welfare is a matter of opinion but it still remains that on the most objective and most widely used measure of national economic performance, socialized Sweden shows up as considerably poorer than the more capitalistic USA.

I pointed all that out on my blog and Kleiman posted a not totally unreasonable counterblast. It should be noted, however, that all the countries which Kleiman mentions as poorer than Sweden have suffered heavily from even worse socialism than Sweden.

Sweden is a high tax and high "welfare" place but has never had massive nationalized industries — unlike most of the rest of Europe. That is why the comparison between the USA and Sweden is so interesting: Two highly capitalist economies of long standing that differ mainly in the different proportion of the national income that they divert into "welfare" expenditure. No prizes for guessing which one has forged ahead.

Kleiman also glided over the point that once you start trying to measure wellbeing instead of productivity you run into pluses as well as minuses. Swedes, for instance, have more leisure but also have to spend a considerably higher proportion of their income just to keep warm.

All of which goes to show that economists who claim to be able to measure wellbeing simply reveal their politics. They should stick to the dollars and cents.

Some less disputable facts about Sweden, however, are these: "No new net jobs have been produced in the Swedish private sector since 1950. None of top 50 companies on the Stockholm stock exchange has been started since 1970....well over 1 million people out of a work force of around four million did not work in 2003 but lived on various kinds of public welfare programs, such as, pre-pension schemes, unemployment benefits, sick-leave programs, etc. Sweden has dropped from fourth to 14th place in 2002 among the OECD countries (i.e., affluent industrialized countries) in terms of GDP per capita since 1970".

The "Third way" in Canada

The comparison between the US and Canada is always interesting also: Two very similar populations with very different institutional arrangements. The US economy is much more free-market while Canada is much more welfarist and highly regulated. So how have the two been doing? A Bank of Montreal study shows that from 1988 to 1997, the GDP per head grew each year in the USA at more than TWICE the rate of the Canadian figure. Canadian unemployment is also now much higher. The same study also showed that it was not the productivity of the Canadian workforce that was at fault but rather the broader economic setting. Enough said.

Randall is speaking here of the "gaps" I described in August. Enumerated briefly, they include a gap in marginal tax rates, a gap in personal disposable income (and overall GDP per capita), a gap in labour productivity, a gap in unemployment, and a gap in the stability of the currency. Basically, between the U.S. and Canada, there's a "gap" in any indicator of economic health or standard of living you can conceive. Randall adds a new gap to this list—namely, a gap in the regulatory cost of financial services.

But no doubt Mark Kleiman and his ilk would again want to claim that life in Canada is still so much NICER! A safe claim: It all depends on how you define "nice".

Is Happiness Unimportant?

On another tack, Leftists seem to have discovered only recently the academic psychology literature on happiness — and it seems to have given them some inspiration. The research shows, of course, that money does not buy you happiness. "So why are we worrying about the government trying to give everyone higher incomes or a better standard of living if that will not make them any happier?", some are now asking. The simple answer: "Because almost everybody WANTS higher incomes" does not seem to have occurred to all of them yet. They also seem to think that if money will not necessarily make you happy then there is no reason why they should not take it off you in taxes. But, to use the same logic, if money is not going to make you any happier, why bother redistributing it to the poor??

Happiness research is, however, a big subject so I have covered it in a separate article.

THE STRANGE PRIORITIES OF LEFTIST OUTRAGE

The causes that are highlighted by our Left-dominated media and made the target of outraged denunciations and agitation by Leftists generally today are remarkable for their selectivity. There seems at first to be no rhyme or reason in what a Leftist will express outrage about.

For instance, Leftists in most of the developed world constantly agonize about the "harsh" treatment that their governments mete out to illegal immigrants, no matter how lenient such treatment actually is. One gets the impression that only complete abandonment of border controls would satisfy Leftists. The Australian government, for instance, has had great success in deterring illegal immigrants by sending most of them straight to special prisons when they arrive. So Australian Leftists long mounted huge demonstrations against this policy even though the policy had huge support in the Australian community generally, even though the illegals concerned were treated humanely and even though the illegals were probably better housed and fed in their special prisons than they ever were in their homelands. There was also great agony expressed about the "damage" this policy will do to Australia's international reputation and "experts" were wheeled out to condemn the conditions under which the illegals are housed.

One would think, therefore, that if humane imprisonment of lawbreakers evokes such outrage, mass murder of innocents would induce utter paroxysms of Leftist agitation. And there are plenty of examples of mass murder going on all the time in the world: The incessant massacres of Muslims in India by Hindu fundamentalists and the constant massacres of Christians in the Sudan by Muslim fundamentalists, for instance. So what do we hear from Leftists about these really grave examples of human suffering? Nothing. Absolutely nothing.

Why? Why are Leftists so amazingly selective in their outrage? Why the hypocritical concern about minor examples of human suffering while they ignore really major examples of human suffering? The answer is obvious. Leftists are not concerned about human suffering at all. What they seek is to star in a drama where they can play David to someone else's Goliath. As with globalization, they want to oppose the consensus. They want to demonstrate in favour of unpopular causes, not causes that would be greeted by the population at large as worthy but too routine or distant to bother about. They are only "compasssionate" about causes that will give them the maximum ego-boost, causes that they believe will enable them to promote their fantasy view of themselves as as kinder and wiser and more caring than the population at large.

Selective Greenie Outrage

And if the targets that the Left choose for their outrage seem arbitrary and inconsistent, the selectivity of their "Green" allies is even more amazing. In Australia, for instance, Greenpeace has mounted a sustained campaign to shut down Australia's only refinery for producing motor fuel from shale. They run around in their beloved rubber boats doing all sorts of obstructive things and intimidate any company that tries to supply motorists using the refinery's product. Australia's conservative government has had to introduce special concessionary regulations to keep the refinery company afloat, so severe has been the Greenie pressure on it.

Given the constant Greenie scares about how we are likely to run out of petroleum products in double quick time if we do not mend our evil ways, one might naively expect that they would rejoice at a beginning being made on unlocking the vast reserves of hydrocarbons locked up in shale. Shale is ubiquitous and could potentially supply all our needs for petroleum products for at least hundreds of years. That Greenies do exactly the opposite and attack shale usage makes clear how much they really hate ordinary people.

Greenie extremists WANT people to be hurt by resource shortages so they frantically oppose anything that will make more resources available.

They justify their attacks on the shale refinery by claiming that is a heavy polluter — which it apparently was to some degree in its startup stages — but now that its pollution levels have been reduced to levels normal for the oil industry the Greenie extremists are in no way mollified.

And the pollution produced in Australia by this one refinery is of course absolutely minuscule compared to sources of atmospheric pollution elsewhere in the world. The now well-known "Asian brown cloud", for instance, is studiously ignored by Greenies — even though it is a considerable threat to the respiratory health of more than a billion (Yes. Billion, not million) people. This brown haze that constantly lies over India and its neighbours seems mainly to be produced by the Indian practice of using wood fires to cremate their dead and cow dung to fuel cooking fires. It is produced, in fact, by exactly the sort of traditional "sustainable" low-technology village lifestyle that the Greenies are constantly advocating for us all.

The sad fact for Greenies, of course, is that village Indians will only be able to move to less polluting practices as they modernize and move to the more efficient and clean-burning forms of cooking and combustion that are common in the developed world. But spending time advocating that Indians do more to modernize would not at all assuage the hunger for drama and self-advertisement that seems to motivate Greenie activists. They have the same motivations as Leftists so it no wonder that there are so many Red/Green alliances.

THE CHURCHES AS OPPONENTS OF THE LEFT

For many people, one of the great attractions of Communism (and to a lesser degree of the Left generally) in the late 19th century and for most of the 20th Century was its opposition to the churches and their moral codes. Since the Leftist wants to tear down all existing authorities and centres of power, the Leftist had to oppose such strong existing authorities as the churches. This antagonism was of course particularly notable with the Roman Catholic Church — the most powerful of the Churches. And the best weapon with which to defeat the churches was to attack the discomfort inflicted by religious moral codes.

Religions generally use their influence over people to help enforce conventional morality, including sexual morality. They do this because, like conservatives generally, they see moral codes as essential to the function of a civil society. If sexual impulses cannot be controlled, for instance, fathers would be in great doubt about which progeny are theirs and would be less likely to support the progeny concerned economically and in other ways — with disastrous results for future generations. Before the welfare State came along, fathers were virtually essential for the survival of children.

But moral codes are onerous and Communism offered an escape from them. If all men were to become brothers and all resources were to be shared freely, fathers would not be needed for anything more than the act of procreation itself. This vision was of course a great attraction for both men and women and Leftists were always in the vanguard of sexual liberation. Sex sells and it certainly sold Leftism to many.

Thus Leftists were well-prepared when the advent of the contraceptive pill kicked away the practical foundations of conventional sexual morality. They were ready to justify what had just become practical — irresponsible sex. So they seemed to have come into their own at that time (in the 1960s).

The pill soon caused libertinism to spread very widely, however, and sexual permissiveness soon therefore ceased to be characteristically Leftist. The longer term effect of the pill was in fact to deprive Leftists of one of their strongest sources of appeal. They are no longer the only libertines. Effective contraception has in fact changed social mores so much that it is now permissiveness which is conventional.

What human beings are, however, is dictated more by a million years of evolution than by any religious or political doctrine so the inborn needs for stability, fidelity, trust, affection etc that evolution had attached to human procreative activity ensured some survival of family stability and cohesion. This too meant that the churches became less relevant. It became clear that neither religion nor the church were essential to the survival of a civil society. The family survived with or without the church and with or without externally enforced moral codes. Only some churches and some conservatives have as yet adapted to that new reality, however.

Amusingly, the normal Leftist rejection of conventional Western religion does not seem to apply to primitive religions. American Indian beliefs, for instance, are normally treated with great respect and held up as wise by Leftists. Why? Presumably as just another way of attacking the churches. We are asked to believe that the Protestant Christianity which created the modern world is somehow inferior for some unknown reason. Powerful religion has to be attacked but non-threatening religion is OK.

Also at work when Leftists praise primitive religions is of course the normal Leftist hatred of modern Western civilization in general and of the USA in particular. Anything non-Western or non-Christian is therefore welcomed and praised. And the common Red/Green pretence that primitive practices were more "in harmony with nature" is something of a joke. Primitive peoples constantly used fire to clear land and trap game and this constant fire-load on the environment did of course greatly change the landscape and its resident species from what they "naturally" once were. Primitive man probably changed the landscape nearly as much as modern man did, in fact. Only very high rainfall forests would have been unaffected by fire. And the desertification of large areas on the margins of the Sahara is the work of primitive sheep and goat herders in quite recent times.

Nonetheless, from Rousseau onwards, Leftists (and now Greenies) have always loved to romanticize primitive, tribal life. But here is a quote from Matthew Parris — who saw it close-up for many years:

"In particular I noticed how tribalism-really only an anthopologist's term for an extreme form of communitarianism-seemed tohave dinned the individualism out of people, so nobody cared or dared to take a lead or differ notably from the others. Some people will tell you tribe (or village, or community) humanizes, brings comfort and security. I thought it was stifling, and brutal in its way.

Historian Keith Windschuttle has a good review of a book about the "Noble Savage" myth and there is also a post at Marginal Revolution showing that in primitive societies an average of about 30% of all male deaths are caused by warfare! And the Lestists think primitive man is peaceful! The post also shows that deaths from warfare in the US and Europe are the tiniest fraction of that.

And in another article, Windschuttle points out how nonsensical are the Leftist claims about how wonderful primitive people were. Aside from the mythical Tasaday, they were usually extremely brutal and selfish in fact. Windschuttle reports for instance the "frequently murderous level of violence Tasmanian men heaped on their women".

He notes that even Leftist historians who criticize him in fact confirm his account: "How violent, Clendinnen asks, were Aboriginal men toward their women? "Very", she answers. "What the newcomers saw as remarkable —what I would think would be remarkable anywhere —were the blows Australian men publicly, casually, dealt their women for trivial offences, and their ready resort to weapons. Their women were, literally, browbeaten."

LEFTIST INFILTRATION OF THE MAINSTREAM CHURCHES

The modern Leftist acceptance of non-threatening religions might also help to explain how Leftists have come to infiltrate many of the historic Protestant churches of the "Western" world in recent years. The Presbyterian, Anglican and Methodist churches in particular would appear to have suffered considerably from the secularism of the modern world and appear in consequence to have largely lost their way. They have certainly lost much of the power and influence they once had and no longer seem very sure of what they should stand for. So Leftists now see such churches as more of an opportunity than a threat and have in fact in many cases become part of such churches and have replaced the Gospel of Christ with a pseudo-Christian gospel that exploits traditional Christian teachings of love and compassion to promote the usual Leftist amorality and the usual Leftist goals of enforced equality between people.

The churches also provide Leftists with a "bully pulpit" (to use Theodore Roosevelt's famous phrase). As part of their wish to aggrandize themselves, Leftists love to preach to people and urge on them the error of their ways. The churches are of course ready-made for that and also have some prestige and some reputation for good intentions that is useful to the Leftist in getting his/her message listened to. So Leftists have every reason to infiltrate and use the mainstream churches.

The way they have done so is discussed at some length here

The U.S. Democrats HATE Bible-believing Christians. Why?

I look at that question at some length here. But briefly, there are 3 interrelated reasons:

1). Real Christianity (as distinct from the social Christianity that denominations such as the Episcopalians are known for) and Leftism are rival religions. That explains both the historic Soviet Communist opposition to Russia's strong traditional Christianity and the opposition of the U.S. Democrats today to the still strong following for traditional Protestantism in America.

2). Real Christians favour the GOP very strongly in their votes. Although conservatism and evangelical Christianity are far from the same thing (otherwise there would not be — say — Catholic and atheist conservatives), there are two major ways in which evangelical

Protestants and conservatives share a basic philosophy. They both believe that man is "fallen" and imperfectible and they both believe in the importance and supremacy of the individual in finding his own salvation and welfare. With such basic beliefs in common, the wonder is that the alliance between Protestant Christians and conservatives has not historically been stronger.

3). Leftists need to feel superior to someone else in order to boost their own ego. But being "superior" can only be relative. Superior to whom? So the Leftist always needs to feel superior to particular people or groups. There has to be some group that they don't need to pander to and which they are free to put down and hate. But Leftists are not supposed to feel superior to those people they could most easily feel superior to (homosexuals, blacks, poor people etc) so Christians, conservatives and others whom they see as permissible targets "cop the lot". All their hatred is poured out through the openings that their poses do allow. And Christians are one of the permissible targets. Though that old standby — the Jews — also seems to be making a comeback. And the fervour of hatred towards Christians that the Leftists currently pour out reflects both how limited their opportunities for preening themselves now are and how badly in need of propping up their egos are after their many defeats from the fall of the Soviet Union on.

Anyone who doubts that Leftists do see themselves as superior beings should trawl through the archives of my LEFTISTS AS ELITISTS blog for a while. That will set any doubts completely at rest.

Abortion: Only Conservatives Care

Abortion is a difficult issue for conservatives. They seem to be fairly evenly divided about it. But Leftists are not. Leftists almost all seem to favour abortion. Why?

The key to understanding that is simple. When Leftists get into absolute power — as they often did in the 20th Century — we soon see what their "compassion" really adds up to. From Stalin to Pol Pot, Leftists showed that they do not care about human life at all.

They murdered millions. So what are a few unborn babies to them? A mere bagatelle!

Rightists are divided because they are the only ones who genuinely care and it is a situation of conflict between the rights of the child and the rights of the mother. I myself think it is patently obvious that abortion is murder. A baby that would survive if born premature is destroyed by an abortionist and we are told that no crime has been committed! Absurd.

But my libertarian instincts also tell me that coercion is not the way to stop abortion. I leave coercion to the Leftists. Paying mothers to have the baby would work a lot better. Good old capitalism again! A payment of (say) $10,000 to all mothers who produce a healthy baby should do the trick. And with the now catastrophically low birthrates in most of the developed world we probably need such an incentive scheme for all mothers anyway.

So conservatives should be helping to support and encourage reluctant mothers rather than threaten them with the law — perhaps even setting up special, discreet, resort-style homes for them during their pregnancy.

I am pleased to note that President Bush argues for policies similar to what I have outlined above and I am absolutely delighted that Australia's most eminent Catholic, the traditionalist Cardinal Pell, has actually now put such policies into practice. I quote from a January 2005 announcement:

"One of the last announcements Cardinal George Pell made before taking his annual leave this week was to introduce a program, new to Australia and only the third of its kind in the world, to provide support to pregnant women who are contemplating abortion. "We want to respond to the needs of women facing an unexpected or difficult pregnancy by providing them with life-affirming options," he said. "Through the program, expectant mothers and, if required, their families, will be provided with social, emotional and practical support to enable them to continue with their pregnancy to full term. Women need real alternatives to abortion, and this new program is targeted to meet the specific needs of women contemplating abortion."

Racism and the Left

Some allusion has already been made here to the fact that Leftists make much of their "anti-racism". Anti-racism became so central to Leftism in the second half of the 20th century, however, that a much more detailed consideration of the phenomenon seems reasonable at this point. Since my more detailed comments add up to a rather large article in its own right, however, I present them elsewhere. The central points of my separate article are that some form of racism seems to be virtually universal, that Leftists have in the past been fierce racists and that anti-racism was adopted by the Left in the second half of the 20th century as a temporary expedient which was never wholehearted and which is now being steadily abandoned.

FASCISM LIVES: MUSSOLINI AS A LEFTIST PROPHET

The ideas of Benito Mussolini (1883-1945), the founder of Fascism, are remarkably similar to the ideas of modern-day Western Leftists. If Mussolini was not the direct teacher of modern-day Leftists, he was certainly a major predecessor. Modern-day Leftism is largely Fascist. What Leftists advocate today is not, of course, totally identical with what Mussolini was advocating and doing 60 to 80 years ago in Italy but there are nonetheless extensive and surprising parallels. Nonetheless, Mussolini is very much a side-issue in modern-day politics so I will refer people elsewhere to read my discussion of what the historical reality of Fascism was. See here. Although Leftists today often call conservatives "Fascists", the truth is the reverse. If the behaviour of modern-day Leftists seems Fascist, it is because modern day Leftism IS Fascist!

Supporting the socialist Saddam Hussein

Saddam Hussein grew up as a cadre in the highly ideological and dogmatic Ba'ath party structure. His speeches, from the time he entered government in 1968 until his demise, had a consistent ideological, pseudo-intellectual character, even if in the final decade a layer of Islamist rhetoric was added. From his first declarations to his last, he always presented the Arabs as the master race, whose history and accomplishments are glorious. He has always had a mystical belief in self-purification through violence, the notion that the soul is elevated through warfare and killing

And who created Saddam's Ba'ath Party? One Michel Aflaq:

MICHEL AFLAQ was born in Damascus in 1910, a Greek Orthodox Christian. He won a scholarship to study philosophy at the Sorbonne sometime between 1928 and 1930 (biographies differ), and there he studied Marx, Nietzsche, Lenin, Mazzini, and a range of German nationalists and proto-Nazis. Aflaq became active in Arab student politics with his countryman Salah Bitar, a Sunni Muslim. Together, they were thrilled by the rise of Hitler and the Nazi party, but they also came to admire the organizational structure Lenin had created within the Russian Communist party.

For details of Iraqi Fascism under Saddam Hussein and the generally Leftist and Arab support-base for it see here

SUPPORT FOR ISLAMIC EXTREMISM

In this discussion of late 20th century and early 21st century Leftism, I have left until last the most recent and, arguably, the most curious manifestation of Leftist thinking — their support for the most reactionary form of Islam.

The Left of the Western world seem unable to find a bad word to say about, or any will to resist, what has widely come to be known as "Islamofascism" — the revival of Islamic supremacist thinking that became so influential among Muslims in the late 20th century and which graduallly impacted more and more on the Western world as time went by — with the attacks on New York and elsewhere on 9/11/2001 being the most spectacular example of that.

Islamic thinking has always included major themes that Leftists have campaigned against to the point of hysteria in the Western world — the belief in killing homosexuals, subjugating women, extreme sexual puritanism, theocracy, unconditional obedience to a divine being etc.

So how come such beliefs are anathema to Leftists in the Western world but evoke no protest if Muslims are advocating them? The Leftist failure to oppose reactionary Islam certainly puzzles many (including a small group of sincere Leftists and at least one feminist) but in fact it provides a good test of the account given here about what Leftism really is.

And the reason why the Left are friendly to Islam could hardly be simpler: As I pointed out in the beginning above, hatred of the world about them is fundamental to Leftists. They are people who are consumed by and fundamentally motivated by hate. And that is also true of the Islamofascists. Both groups are great haters. And they hate the same thing. They hate everyday Western culture. They hate the "system" of Western capitalism.

So what the Left advocate in the Western world is merely instumental to their desire to attack the prevailing culture. It is not fundamental to Leftism in any way. It is the underlying hate that is fundamental and they recognize as brothers in arms the haters of the Islamic world.

Given the attacks on Hiroshima and Nagasaki by Democrat President Truman, today's Leftists probably figure that, if fundamentalist Islam ever became a serious threat to the West (and hence a threat to their own comfort), it would simply be wiped off the map. That is certainly what they would do if they had their hands on the levers of power. In the meantime, however, they enjoy the disruption and discomfiture that the Islamists visit on their fellow citzens in the West.

10

Leftists in Power

COMMUNISM

Although it seems most unlikely that it will ever happen again, there were many occasions in the 20th century when the most extreme form of Leftism — Communism — did gain great power in certain countries. Does that experience tell us anything about Leftism?

This paper started out with an endeavour fairly characteristic of modern Anglo-American analytical philosophy (Hospers, 1967): An endeavour to analyse and make coherent the way terms like "Leftist", "Liberal", "Socialist", "Communist" etc are commonly used. Once an underlying focus for such terms had been "discovered", the psychology underlying that focus could be considered. And what was "discovered" was that a love of change — particularly mandated change — defined Leftism in its various guises and varieties. The analysis was however principally of what Leftism/liberalism is in the economically advanced countries of the contemporary "Western" world — where Leftists have only ever had partial success in implementing their programmes. So what happens when Leftists get fully into power? Does the same analysis apply?

For a start, it should be obvious that the personality and goals of the Leftist do not change just because he gets into power. He is still the same person. And that this is true is certainly very clear in the case of Lenin — who is surely the example *par excellence* of a Leftist who very clearly did get into power. In his post-revolutionary philippic against his more idealistic revolutionary comrades, Lenin (1952) makes very clear that *"absolute centralization and the strictest discipline of the proletariat"* are still in his view essential features of the new regime. He speaks very much like the authoritarian dictator that he was but is nonetheless being perfectly consistent with the universal Leftist wish for strong government power and control over the population — as long as they are in charge. So Leftists in power certainly do not cause the State to "wither away" — as Marx foresaw in "The Communist Manifesto".

Lenin's conception of the function of the State shows why:

"Essentially the state is the power exercised over the masses by a group of armed men separated from the people." From the *April Theses* See here

"The state is a special organization of force: it is an organization of violence for the suppression of some class" From *The state and revolution.* See here.

That makes the Leftist position pretty clear, I think. The State exists to suppress people. How useful that is! So power-mad people such as Leftists like big government and do all they can to foster it.

After 1917 change did continue for a few years in Russia while the Communists consolidated their power (e.g. by "liquidating" the Kulaks), but after that Russia settled into a tyranny where State-directed industrialization was the only form of change allowed. After the completion of the revolution, change in Russian society was in fact repressed ferociously. Certainly, no challenges to Russia's new power structure were allowed. At its most basic it was power that mattered, not change. Stalin murdered millions without a qualm to ensure his power.

But that very State dominance of Russian life did of course eventually cause advanced social and economic sclerosis and stagnation in Russia and its satellites — leading ultimately to the complete collapse of the Soviet system via Gorbachev's "perestroika" (reconstruction). "Perestroika" implies change so change was in fact the poison that finally destroyed Lenin's legacy. So does that mean that the Soviets were not Leftists? If hunger for change is the defining feature of Leftism, then surely the Bolsheviks ceased to be Leftists in 1917! Surely Lenin and his comrades became conservatives at that point!

Ludicrous though that proposition sounds at first sight, it is precisely the common usage today. Defenders of the old Soviet order and those who wish to return to it in post-Gorbachev Russia are usually referred to in the press as "conservatives". Clearly, the press has adopted the simple (though very unsatisfactory) dichotomy of being for and against change as the definition of Leftism and Conservatism. This does however create the very large problem that precisely the same political policies that are seen in one country (Russia) as being conservative are seen in other countries (e.g. the USA) as wildly Leftist (See also McFarland et al, 1992).

Since change IS in fact obviously somehow involved in the Left/Right dichotomy and since the aims and practice of the Bolsheviks were perfectly concordant with basic Leftist desires everywhere, this is something of a dilemma. Which is basic? Desire for change or desire for power? In earlier papers here and here, I have leant towards the solution of dismissing the role of change altogether and saying that either Leftists or Rightists will oppose or support change depending on whether they are in power or not. I proposed that it is simply the love or suspicion of State power that defines the Leftist or Rightist. And, as a statement about the psychology of Leftists and Rightists, I still adhere to that view. I think it is evident that most Leftists have a strong basic need for power and control and that that flows very simply into the policies that they advocate.

I also think, however, that a DEFINITION of any collectivity should rely primarily on what the collectivity does rather than on a theory about how the group is motivated. One has to define the group before one can study it. And a definition of the "Western" world's Left (but only the Left) in terms of attitude to change both makes sense of common usage and is readily amenable to psychological explanation. Regrettably, however, it seems clear that one cannot define Leftists as being the change-hungry ones of ALL the world and of all times. It is a definition that is fully applicable only to the present economically successful "Western" democracies because it is only there that advocacy of change enables the Leftist to satisfy his/her ego needs.

If a definition of limited applicability is unattractive, however, we can also grasp the other horn of the dilemma and say that Leftists who attain power cease to be Leftists! This jars a little but does make sense psychologically: Once the Leftist's hunger for power and control is satisfied, he no longer seeks change and in fact actively opposes it. He then opposes change for the same reason that he opposes neo-liberalism: It threatens his power and control. He becomes a conservative (opponent of change) in a way that a Rightist generally is not. There can be no doubt that Margaret Thatcher and Ronald Reagan were Rightists but they actively worked to REDUCE the power, influence and control of the governments that they led. The contrast is very clear. Not everyone is as power-mad as the Leftist. And that hunger for power makes the Leftist IN POWER the most ferocious conservative (opponent of change) of all.

But there is an exception to every rule and the exception in this case is a most instructive one: Mao Tse Tung. Mao's "cultural revolution" was a very strange phenomenon unparalleled in other Communist regimes. And it appeared to do nobody any good — including Mao himself. It was a vast but entirely destructive upheaval. But it is just what one would expect of someone in love with change. In the case of Mao, we saw a survival into the post-revolutionary era of the old pre-revolutionary longings. He was so in love with change that he had his revolution all over again. Mao was so thoroughly in charge of China, that he could indulge his natural inclinations without endangering his power and what those inclinations were is precisely what we see in Leftists of the economically successful "Western" democracies to this day: a love of change, preferably revolutionary change. So we can see that power comes first in a Leftist's scale of values but the longing for change *per se* comes a close second.

In the "West"

This conclusion drawn from the grand sweep of history has some counterpart on a much more humble scale in findings from survey research in one of the economically successful "Western" democracies. Ray (1984) found from a large random sample survey of Australians conducted in the Cold War era that Leftists were sensation-seekers even when the sensations concerned were the sensations provided by consumerism. Rather contrary to their usual image, Leftists were found to be materialists who enjoyed buying mass-marketed "quality" consumer goods even more than Rightists did. Their love of new sensations was so great that they even sought out those provided by their ostensible "enemy" — consumer capitalism. Clearly, like Mao, their love of novelty was so deep-seated that it overcame other considerations.

Although Leftists in the economically successful "Western" democracies have never gained power on anything like the scale achieved by Mao and Stalin, there have of course been Leftist governments in the economically successful "Western" democracies on many occasions and these have certainly managed to lay the stifling and impoverishing hand of bureaucracy on many endeavours. The twin disciplines of the ballot box and constitutional constraints have however limited what such governments can do. Their power has always been far from absolute.

In summary, bitter experience has shown that Leftists in power are very dangerous and destructive people. Where their power is effectively unchecked, they generally seems to resort sooner or later to mass murder (as in the case of the French revolutionaries, Lenin, Stalin, Hitler, Mao, Pol Pot, Jim Jones and many Communist regimes and movements worldwide) and where they are partially thwarted by strong democratic traditions and institutions, they at least bring about large-scale impoverishment (as in post-independence **India** and pre-Thatcher Britain). By contrast, conservatives just muddle along with piecemeal reforms that don't require them to murder anybody. So giving any power to Leftists is a most dangerous thing to do and working to prevent that happening is a matter of no small importance.

Leftists in Academe

As a Luntz poll dramatically showed (Horowitz, 2002), and as Fred Singer explains, there is one area in the USA where Leftists have almost achieved a monopoly of power over at least hiring policies: The humanities and social science schools of the universities and colleges. An overt conservative finds it almost impossible to gain employment in such places and the message to the wider community emanating from such places is almost unfailingly "liberal". So Leftists in power are once again seen to be very jealous of their power, intolerant of diversity, opposed to free speech and oppressive and discriminatory in their employment practices: All things that they would normally try to deny but which in fact simply make them typical Leftists.

The widely-read *Chronicle of Higher Education* has at last given coverage to the problem of Leftist bias in academe and what David Horowitz is doing to overcome it. There is also a site here run by students themselves which gives even more information on how huge the problem is. There is an article from here by David Horowitz that makes clear that there is actually what amounts to a blacklist against hiring conservative professors at almost all U.S. universities. The *Chronicle* has an attempted reply by a Leftist (Stanley Fish) to Horowitz which admits that the Left "have won the curricular battle" (meaning that what is taught at U.S. universities is Leftist) but goes on to such absurdities as claiming that political correctness is used by Leftists as "irony". He must be the only one in the world who thinks it is a joke!

Other attempts have been made to downplay the extent of Leftist influences in America's colleges and universities — such as a study published in 2006 by sociologists John F. Zipp and Rudy

Fenwick under the heading "Is the Academy a Liberal Hegemony? The Political Orientations and Educational Values of Professors" but they collapse when looked at closely.

This is what passes for education at the University of Michigan. Read this excerpt from one female student's account of a COMPULSORY "course" she had to do there:

We had to go around and talk about at least one way in which we have been/are oppressed. When my turn came up, and I answered that I have never been oppressed, the instructor corrected me, saying that I must have been, as I'm female. I persisted, saying that being female has never been anything short of a blessing for me. The instructor was relentless, insisting that I was necessarily oppressed at one point in my life. The instructor asked to speak with me after class. He was visibly shaken and angry. He told me that my classroom behavior was disruptive in the least (although I was never voluntarily disagreeing), and that I would be kicked out of class and would thereby lose my job and my housing for the next year unless I learned to be more cooperative."

And note this report. Excerpt: Kahn had required students, to achieve full credit, to write letters to President George W. Bush "demanding" that he not go to war with Iraq. Several students requested that they be allowed to complete the assignment by expressing their own opinions, which would mean, in some cases, writing letters in support of President Bush's foreign policy. Kahn told the students that letters supporting the president would not be acceptable and would not receive credit. Several students refused to turn in the assignment and were penalized.

And America's academics also show their allegiances in the most practical and persuasive way — with their money. They really do put their money where their mouth is. Note this summary of donations to the campaigns of the Presidential candidates in the year 2004:

"The Federal Election Commission could not have foreseen that when it required employment information on political donations of over $200, it would expose scandalous uniformity in a university community that advertises its diversity. The Sacramento Bee reported that the University of California system gave more to the Kerry campaign than any other single employee group, and that Harvard was second, with only 15,000 employees to UC's 160,000. Campus bloggers computed the percentages of Kerry contributions over Bush: Cornell 93%, Dartmouth 97%, Yale 93%, Brown 89%."

Even the old Soviet Union could hardly have done a better job of constructing a lockstep Leftist monoculture. "Diverse" it is not.

And the Leftist domination of higher education has of course long ago trickled down to the High School level. A good example of the deceit that leads to is reported here under the heading: "Race only skin deep": A group of students were shown how to examine one particular genetic marker that was already known to be widespread among different races. When they found that people of all different races in their class had the marker, that was presented as "proof" that there is no such thing as racial differences. Pity about all the OTHER millions of genetic markers that were NOT examined!

The old nonsense about all races sharing more than 99% of their genes was also trotted out as proving that there is no such thing as race biologically. Somehow they forgot to mention that we share nearly as high a percentage of genes with chimpanzees. So by that reasoning humans and chimps are really the same too. Let's reserve more college places for chimps! Down with chimpism! The truth of course is that percentage of shared genes is a total red herring. Differences in just ONE critical gene out of millions of genes can make a huge difference to one's life — as many people with genetic illnesses have sadly found. The students were also apparently told that "scientists know that traditional notions of race no longer hold up". I guess they must have just overlooked what these geneticists found! There are a lot of comments on the matter on the Joanne Jacobs site for anybody who thinks there is anything more worth saying about such nonsense. See also here for more on the genetics research.

The courageous Edward Feser looks at WHY academics are overwhelmingly Left-leaning. He lists a number of explanations which do undoubtedly play a part but he omits what I think is a major factor: From my observations, Leftist academics are basically second-rate thinkers. Originality is the Holy Grail of academe but most academics in fact have nothing new to say at all — so they say silly things just in order to appear different. They use perversity to create a false impression of profundity. Leftism is their substitute for originality. It was precisely because I DID have something different to say that I got so many articles published in the academic journals. Even though my articles generally undermined Leftist views, their having that all-important originality got them published. And how my fellow academics hated me for it! In most years I got more articles published than the rest of my university department put together. That I could do easily what they found so hard to do was real heartburn for them.

And in my own field I was repeatedly able to show how second-rate was the writing being produced. But this article (also here) about Marxist Terry Eagleton makes "second rate" look like a vast overestimate. The guy has gone from being a big defender of postmodernism (also called "Theory" in literary circles) to now saying it is all wrong but still calls himself a Marxist and is still treated worshipfully by other Leftists. How desperate can you get? They've got about as much intellectual rigor as a flea! It's not what you say but whom you hate that counts. But we read: "Nowadays Mr. Eagleton lives the life of an academic superstar" so I think that tells you all you need to know about Leftist intellectuals. They are just con-men but some people are fooled.

Just to emphasize what a dead-end "Theory" is, there is also a scathing review here (by a feminist author) of Eagleton's *After Theory* — excerpt:

"What I hoped to find in *After Theory* was ideas about what type of thinking and writing might flourish in a post-theory world. I soon discovered that Eagleton doesn't seem to be the least interested in thinking, only in potted ideas... Eagleton himself is so bombastic it's hard to read him straight... *After Theory* takes us into a vacuum where bits of past theories collide, supported only by vacuous commentary".

Very Leftist.

Finally, this academic survey of Canadian university professors by Nakhaie & Brym (See also here) gives a good reply to the claim that there are some academic disciplines that tend to the Right. For the survey, professors rated themselves on a scale of 1 to 7 in terms of Right to Left — meaning that a score of 3.5 would mean neither Right nor Left. Table 5 shows that the only subgroups that averaged below 3.5 (i.e. were slightly Rightist) were professors of accounting, finance and mechanical engineeering. But they were all only slightly below the midpoint. They were in other words centrists rather than Rightists. Professors in all other disciplines tended Left, mostly well to the Left. The most far-Left group was, of course, the sociologists—the most meaningless of all the disciplines. I taught in a university school of sociology for 12 years so I have some cause to know the emptiness of most sociology. There is more on the causes of academic Leftism here.

THE "STUPIDITY" ACCUSATION AGAINST CONSERVATIVES

On the rare occasions when they feel pressed to justify their vice-like grip on higher education, the explanations that Leftist academics give are little credit to them. One of the most publicized apologias was by a Duke University philosophy professor — commenting on why he does not hire conservatives to teach philosophy: "We try to hire the best, smartest people available," Brandon said of his philosophy hires. "If, as John Stuart Mill said, stupid people are generally conservative, then there are lots of conservatives we will never hire. Mill's analysis may go some way towards explaining the power of the Republican party in our society and the relative scarcity of Republicans in academia". So he takes an attack by Mill on his political opponents that Mill made in

Victorian-era Britain and treats it as good information about the USA today. And even if that were a reasonable thing to do, note the *non sequitur*. Even if stupid people are generally conservative (and there is no EVIDENCE offered of that; I have met a lot of stupid Left-voters in my time), it does not follow that conservatives generally are stupid. Note the usual Leftist elitism too. Brandon is clearly implying that society generally is stupid. Nice type!

One reason why the accusation that conservatives are dumb gains some weight is the great preponderance of Leftists among professors. That overlooks, however, that the situation was not always thus. Up until the 1960s, the professoriate was in general politically moderate. There were of course exceptions. The elite universities have always tended Left. The best known examples of that are England's two great universities, Oxford and Cambridge. We have all I think heard of the Cambridge spies (Philby et al.), and the Bloomsberries were far Left too. Such leftism can perhaps most economically be described as a "spoilt brat" syndrome. Less well known is the prewar fascination of Harvard with Nazism — which was a popular form of socialism in its day.

The general moderation of the pre-1960s professoriate was however its undoing. Precisely because of its moderation, it came under ferocious attack from the 1960s student radicals and it responded in a typically moderate way — apologetically. Curricula were revised in response to the radical demands and more and more Leftists were hired and promoted. And when in the course of time the radical academics so appointed rose in seniority and power, they behaved in a typically unscrupulous way and used their power to squeeze out as many conservatives from academe as they could. So smart conservatives these days go on to get rich in business while the Leftist academics fume away in their ivory towers!

Perhaps most amusingly, however, it should be noted that the Democrats and the GOP split the college-educated vote about equally in the 2004 Presidential election. In other words, about half of the people *whom the Leftist professors themselves have certified as academically able* in fact vote GOP!

The intellectual poverty of the Left shows itself very clearly in their lack of ideas. The only way that they can ever think of for bringing about their desired utopias is the brutishly simply one of FORCING people to behave in the "right" way, by way of legislation in democatic societies or on pain of death in Communist societies.

We have an excellent example of such brainlessness in a recent article which argues that the U.S. Left needs to become more socialist. The article consists of nothing but one long wail about the injustices of the world and simply ASSERTS that socialism is the answer — with no supportive reasoning at all about HOW socialism might fix things — which is all the more remarkable given the known FAILURES of socialism to fix anything. A few illustrative quotes:

"With corporate capitalism everywhere in command, the outlook is for increased poverty, more environmental degradation, ever more uneven distribution of resources and the undermining of traditional societies and ways of life... Doing battle against the prevailing inequality means invoking the idea that we all belong to a community, as opposed to the illusion, voiced famously by Thatcher, that "there is no society, only individuals."... On the road to shaping an alternative, the left might respond with a time-honored socialist insight, namely that "I" only exists within a "we," and that unless we look out for everyone, no one is secure.

Note the *non sequitur* in the last sentence. It is reasonable enough to say that "I" only exists within a "we" but such a statement is only trivially true. Our socialist friend, however seems to think that the truth concerned also implies that "unless we look out for everyone, no one is secure". But England and early America existed in excellent security long before there was any welfare legislation! It is true that private charity at that time looked after the less fortunate but I don't think that private charity is what our socialist friend is advocating!

And another counterfactual assertion above is that capitalism will increase poverty. Since capitalism is provably the the best and surest way of increasing wealth, the statement is deliberately wrongheaded. And it is of course the advanced capitalist societies that have done most to clean up their environment and prevent further degradation of it. You have to be devoid of all knowledge and understanding of how the world actually works (and has worked) to spout the nonsense that our brainless socialist does.

Just to REALLY ruin the party, however, let it be noted that the ONLY adult general population survey I know of that obtained both IQ scores and a record of political attitudes was Martin's study (which I helped write up for the academic journals). And that study showed that it was LEFTISTS who were most likely to be dumb. The correlation in the general population between anti-authority attitudes (which Leftists pride themselves on) and low IQ was quite substantial as such correlations go. So survey research shows that it is in fact Leftist attitudes that are associated with stupidity!

Fortunately, the best brains in America have always gone into business first rather than into any form of teaching. And the fact that the US has survived as a thriving and generally healthy society is proof that it does not need its nutty "liberal" professors. They have only a message of hate to purvey anyway — mostly hatred of America — and most people are decent so few of them will be long persuaded by such a message.

So this monopolization of academe by Leftists ought perhaps to be of some concern but its main effect is probably that it simply makes our universities boring. The message emanating from them is so predictable that it is hardly worth attending to. And in a pluralistic society there are many alternative sources of information and influences on attitudes. The internet and Right-wing radio commentators such as Rush Limbaugh in the USA and Alan Jones in Australia spring obviously to mind as alternative sources of information and countervailing influences on the public mind.

LEFTISTS IN THE MEDIA

Perhaps because most of them are the product of a university or college education, journalists tend to be Left-leaning to various degrees as well. There is much evidence of that in US sources (see for example the summary in a December 11th., 2002, article by Michael Kelly, an article by Jeff Jacoby and also Cook, 1998) but the Australian case is probably much less well-known. Following are listed three research reports published in the academic journals that demonstrate clearly that Australian journalists are overwhelmingly to the Left of the Australian general population in their attitudes: Henningham (1995, 1996 and 1998). The author of the studies cited is now retired from the Chair of Journalism at the University of Queensland and is Australia's specialist in such matters.

In a way, though, it hardly needs an academic study to show how Leftist Australian journalists, academics and media commentators are. In Australia's 2001 Federal election, the conservative coalition government was returned to power on the back of Prime Minister Howard's strong and effective opposition to illegal immigration from the Middle East. So strong was popular support in the Australian general population for this stance that even the nominally Leftist opposition party (the Australian Labor Party) dared not oppose it publicly for fear of being totally routed at the polls. Yet in mid 2002 the media were still absolutely brimming with denunciations of the Prime Minister and his Minister for Immigration as "heartless", "Fascist" etc. because of their immigration policy. It is of course these media figures who are the real Fascists — opposing as they do a policy that has been given the overwhelming support of Australian voters. What the Australian people want seems to be of absolutely of no interest to these anti-democratic Leftist "commentators". Only if the government were completetely undemocratic and defied the popular will would they be happy.

And British journalists seem to be no better. Speaking at a meeting of British Trade Unions, Jeremy Dear, General Secretary of the National Union of Journalists said of the US and British war on terrorism *"If justice was the motive we would be considering sending troops in now to end Israel's occupation of Palestinian territory"*. (Source)

And the American media still commonly treat former Communists as little short of heroes — as in the case of John

Randolph: "But the tributes to this un-American symbol of Hollywood subversion just don't stop... Let me tell you about the real John Randolph. He was a member of the Communist Party USA during its heyday. This was during the time that Josef Stalin was murdering millions in the name of communism in the Soviet Union. And the Communist Party USA took its orders and received its funding from Moscow".

One of the most unarguable examples of how facts are subjugated to "spin" in what seems like factual reporting in the American media would have to be the contrast below in how two of America's major newspapers described the same speech by George W. Bush:

"As expected in a speech to fellow heads of state and diplomats, President Bush on Tuesday dispensed with the red-meat phrases beloved by his supporters on the campaign trail.... Instead, the president was conciliatory, intent to show that he can play with others. He didn't quite break out in Esperanto, but he spoke admiringly of the principles and values embodied by the United Nations."—editorial, *Los Angeles Times*, Sept. 22, 2004.

And

"Mr. Bush delivered an inexplicably defiant campaign speech.... Even when he talked about issues of common agreement, like the global fight against AIDS and easing the crushing third-world debt, Mr. Bush seemed more interested in praising his own policies than in assuming the leadership of an international effort. The speech would have drawn cheers at an adoring Republican National Convention, but it seemed to fall flat in a room full of stony-faced world leaders. Mr. Bush has never exhibited much respect for the United Nations."—editorial, *New York Times*, Sept. 22, 2004.

So unfactual is the account given that you would never guess that the same speech was being described: A truly Soviet achievement.

It is a tribute to the good sense of ordinary people that the constant Leftist slant that they get through the mass media has not convinced everyone.

SO WHAT ARE RIGHTISTS?

The prime focus in this monograph has been on defining and explaining what Leftism is. It would nonetheless be remiss not to give also some account of what Rightism is. If Leftism and Rightism are NOT mirror-images in what they advocate, as this work asserts, some such account does appear necessary in order to complete the picture. I have written one book and many previous papers for those who wish to study conservatism at length (See Ray, 1972b, 1973, 1974, 1979 & 1981) but I have also put up a comprehensive article on the topic here. The central contention of the article is that attitude to change is as irrelevant to conservatives as it is central to Leftists and that a defence of individual rights and liberties against the encroaching power of the State has always been what defines conservatives. Conservatives are not, of course, as simplistic as anarchists or extreme libertarians. They do believe in SOME role for the State — but they have always seen it as a role that should be minimized and have always believed that the individual should have important rights *versus* the State. And that Rightist desire to *limit* the power of the State crashes right up against the Leftist desire to *extend* the power of the State.

Bibliography

Arendt, Hannah, 1982. *Lectures on Kant's Political Philosophy.* Chicago: Chicago UP.

Beiner, Ronald and William James Booth (eds.), 1993. *Kant and Political Philosophy: The Contemporary Legacy.* New Haven: Yale UP.

Fleischacker, Samuel, 1999. *A Third Concept of Liberty: Judgment and Freedom in Kant and Adam Smith.* Princeton: Princeton UP

Guyer, Paul, 2005. *Kant's System of Nature and Freedom.* Oxford: Oxford UP

Höffe, Otfried, 2006. trans. Alexandra Newton. *Kant's Cosmopolitan Theory of Law and Peace.* New York: Cambridge UP

Kaufman, Alexander, 1999. *Welfare in the Kantian State.* New York: Oxford UP.

Kersting, Wolfgang, 1984. *Wohlgeordnete Freiheit.* Berlin: Walter de Gruyter.

Louden, Robert, 2000. *Kant's Impure Ethics.* New York: Oxford UP.

Mulholland, Leslie, 1990. *Kant's System of Rights.* New York: Columbia UP.

Riley, Patrick, 1983. *Kant's Political Philosophy.* Totowa, N.J.: Rowman and Littlefield.

Rosen, Allen, 1993. *Kant's Theory of Justice.* Ithaca: Cornell UP

Saner, Hans, 1973. trans. E. B. Ashton. *Kant's Political Thought: Its Origins and Development.* Chicago: U of Chicago Press

Timmons, Mark (ed.), 2002. *Kant's Metaphysics of Morals: Interpretive Essays.* Oxford: Oxford UP

Williams, Howard (ed.), 1992. *Essays on Kant's Political Philosophy.* Chicago: U of Chicago Press

Yovel, Yirmiyahu Yovel, 1980. *Kant and the Philosophy of History.* Princeton: Princeton UP.

INDEX

J

L

M

O

P

R

S

T

W

□□□